The Governor's Road

The Governor's Road

Early buildings and families from Mississauga to London

Mary Byers and Margaret McBurney

Photographs by Hugh Robertson

UNIVERSITY OF TORONTO PRESS

Toronto   Buffalo   London

© University of Toronto Press 1982
Toronto Buffalo London
Printed in Canada
Reprinted in 1983
First printing in paperback 1983
ISBN 0-8020-2483-1 (cloth)
ISBN 0-8020-6533-3 (paper)

Canadian Cataloguing in Publication Data

Byers, Mary, 1933–
    The Governor's Road

    Bibliography: p.
    Includes index.

    ISBN 0-8020-2483-1   ISBN 0-8020-6533-3 (pbk)

    1. Governor's Road (Ont.) – History.   2. Historic
    buildings – Ontario.   3. Pioneers – Ontario.
    4. Ontario – History – 1791–1841.* I. McBurney,
    Margaret, 1931–   II. Title.

    FC3062.B93   971.3   C82-095114-5
    F1057.8.B93

The Canada Council
Conseil des Arts du Canada
1957-1982

This book has been published with the assistance of the Canada
Council and the Ontario Arts Council under their block grant
programs.

Frontispiece The William Romain house, 40 First Street, Oakville

CONTENTS

MAPS

On the following pages are six detailed maps of the area covered by this book, followed by a general map of the region.

Throughout the book buildings in urban areas are normally identified by street addresses, and in larger centres local maps may be needed to find them. In rural areas buildings are generally located by concession and lot number. The location of some houses is not given at the owners' request.

The townships of Upper Canada were surveyed in concessions separated by 'concession lines,' usually one and a quarter miles apart. The concessions themselves were divided into lots, each of which had two hundred acres.

In most townships the concessions are simply numbered, with no other designation. In Peel and Halton Counties, however, the geographic description North of Dundas Street or South of Dundas Street is part of the concession names. These titles are commonly abbreviated to NDS or SDS.

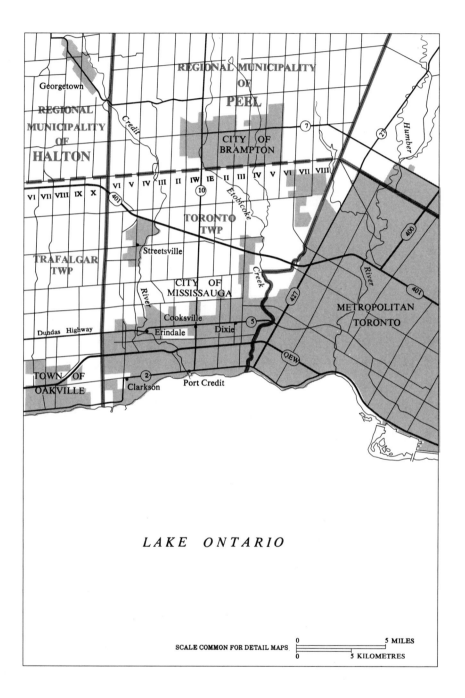

REGIONAL MUNICIPALITY OF PEEL

Georgetown

REGIONAL MUNICIPALITY OF HALTON

CITY OF BRAMPTON

Credit

VI VII VIII IX X

VI V IV III II IW IE II III IV V VI VII VIII

TORONTO TWP

Streetsville

TRAFALGAR TWP

CITY OF MISSISSAUGA

River

Creek

Etobicoke

Cooksville

Dundas Highway

Erindale   Dixie

TOWN OF OAKVILLE

Clarkson   Port Credit

Humber

River

METROPOLITAN TORONTO

QEW

LAKE ONTARIO

SCALE COMMON FOR DETAIL MAPS

0   5 MILES

0   5 KILOMETRES

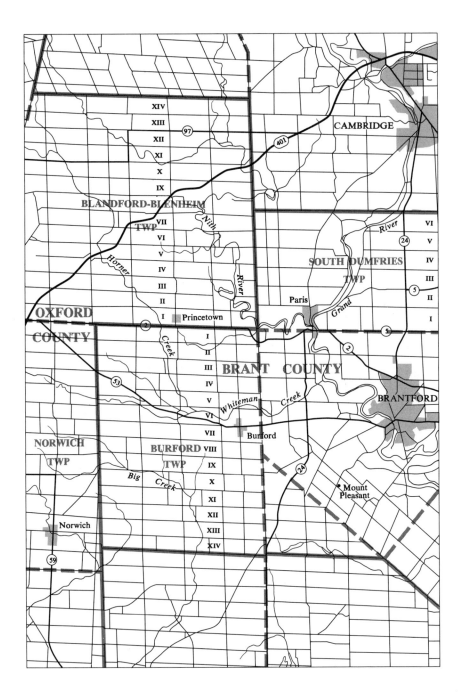

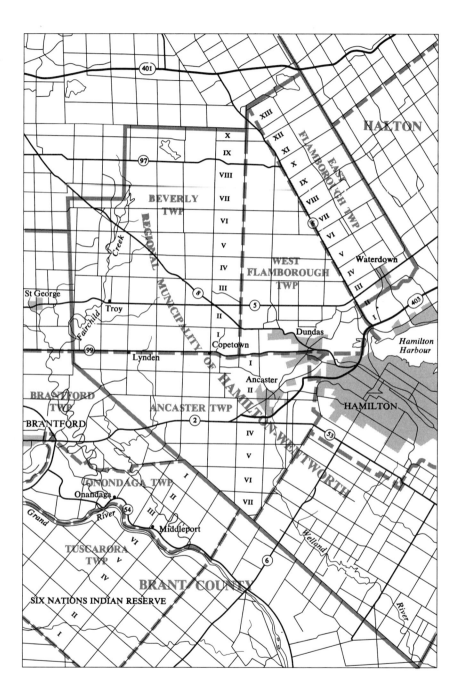

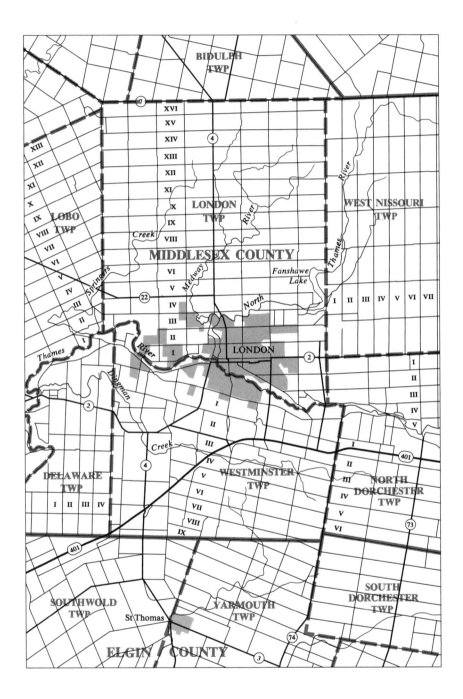

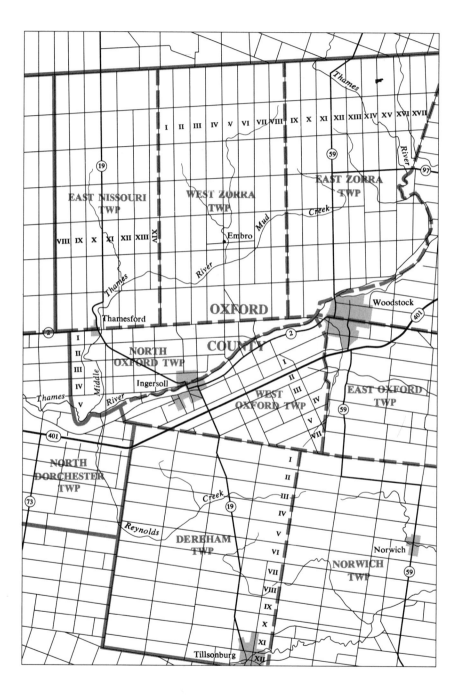

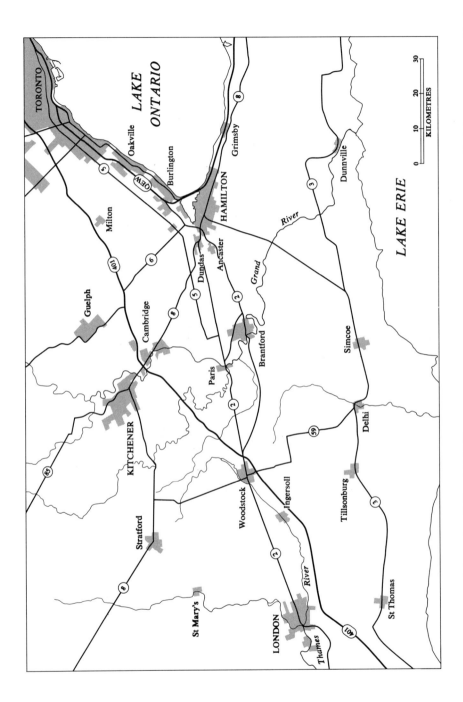

The Governor's Road

I never realized that there was
history too, close at hand, beside
my own home. I did not realize
that the old grave that stood
among the brambles at the foot of
our farm was HISTORY.

STEPHEN LEACOCK

INTRODUCTION

'The Governor's Road' was a name coined in the 1790s for the road proposed by Lieutenant-Governor John Graves Simcoe in 1793 as a military link between Lake Ontario, Lake Erie, Lake St Clair, and Lake Huron, a spur to settlement and a deterrent to expansionist American interest in Upper Canada. In fact, the Governor's Road, although blazed and cut, was barely passable by the time Simcoe left for England in 1796. One wagon's width across at best, its path was set with boulders and stumps and it was sufficiently hazardous to both man and horse that Indian trails were frequently the better route – hence its grand name was a term of derision. Yet, the Governor's Road (officially Dundas Street) would, with its eastern and western extensions, become the spinal cord which supported the settlement of southern Ontario.

John Graves Simcoe arrived in Upper Canada in 1792, the first lieutenant-governor of the province. His prime task was to initiate and supervise settlement. In addition he needed to make plans to meet the fear of invasion from the south. Second only to the prevailing concern for survival in the wilderness, the expectation of attack from land-hungry residents of the New England states dominated the thinking of Upper Canada's pioneers. This concern affected not only settlement patterns but road development in the eighteenth and part of the nineteenth centuries. The choice of sites was frequently prompted by questions of vulnerability to attack or suitability for defence. Simcoe's astute military mind sensed immediately that American control of shipping on the lakes was quite possible and that therefore an inland military route was the only way to ensure the safe transport of troops and supplies.

With this problem in mind Simcoe and his military party travelled in the early months of 1793 through the western part of the province, guided by Indians and following their trails on foot through the woods, proceeding by sleigh where possible, until they reached the border at Windsor. At the conclusion of this journey Simcoe had made certain key decisions. The capital of the province, then at Newark (Niagara-on-the-Lake), would be relocated to a safer site on the Thames River, where London now stands, and it would be linked to Lake Ontario by a road which would run from Burlington Bay to the forks of the Thames. This western route would be called Dundas Street after Henry Dundas, secretary of state in the British government. The trail would provide a link with the network of rivers and branching trails cutting east through York to Kingston and with a north-south axis joining York with Lake Simcoe. In the words of an officer who was with Simcoe when he made these decisions: 'The Governor ... judged it [London's site] to be a situation eminently calculated for the metropolis of all Canada ... [with] ... facility of water communication up and down the Thames into lakes St. Clair, Erie, Huron and Superior.' Indian trails already existed along the lakes as a supplement to water transport, but Simcoe was basing his plan for an inland route on a strategy for the defence of the province. In so doing he was directing settlement inland as well.

Having made these crucial decisions, the lieutenant-governor elected to pick the exact spot at which his surveyor, Augustus Jones, would commence work. Proceeding through the marsh at Burlington Bay with Jean Baptiste Rousseau as guide, Simcoe came to an Indian landing place. Here with due pomp the royal representative proclaimed the name of an old dock at the eastern end of Coote's Paradise (later called Dundas) to be King's Landing.

Shortly after the ceremony at King's Landing Augustus Jones began his survey following Simcoe's instructions. He was to mark a line '70 degrees west' which should, when continued from Coote's Paradise, bring him out at the upper forks of the Thames. The survey, which covered eighty miles, was completed in less than a month. At this point a Captain Smith and one hundred men undertook to cut the road. Mrs Simcoe recorded their progress in her diary:

Sept. 23, 1793. Captain Smith has gone to open a road to be called Dundas Street, from the head of the Lake to the River La Tranche (Thames). He

has 100 men with him ... I hear that they kill rattlesnakes every day, yet not a man has been bitten, altho they have been among them for six weeks. Captain Smith sent two of the snakes in a barrel that I might see them; they were dark and ugly and made a whizzing sound in shaking their rattles when I touched them with a stick.
October, 1873. Captain Smith is returned from cutting the road named Dundas. It is opened for 20 miles. They met with quantities of wild grapes, and put some of the juice in barrels to make vinegar, and Captain Smith told me it turned out very tolerable wine.

By 1794 the Governor's Road was cut through from Dundas to the site of London, the section considered to be the key part of the route. Transport from York to Dundas and from London to Lake St Clair would be available by water. It was six years before the extensions were complete. Augustus Jones made the survey for the section from York to Lake Simcoe (Yonge Street) in 1794 and in 1799 Asa Danforth was at work on the Kingston Road. By the time the transportation network was established, however, Simcoe had left Upper Canada. Before his departure, and in fact while the road was being cut through to the site of London, he had changed his mind and designated Toronto (the city's first name, meaning harbour) the official capital instead of London. The name of the new capital was immediately changed to York at Simcoe's insistence in order to honour George, Duke of York, son of George III. (Joseph Brant once remarked of the governor: 'General Simcoe has done a great deal for this province, he has changed the name of every place in it.')

The Governor's Road had no sooner been cut through than it began to grow over again. Since London was no longer destined to be the 'metropolis of Canada,' it might be thought that at least the westerly portion of the road would quickly revert to forest and that without traffic in that direction the whole might soon return to the wilderness it had previously been. Simcoe had, however, set in motion a chain of events which ensured the survival of his road.

The first move made by the lieutenant-governor after the trail was cut was to grant lots along its path to the military personnel who had opened it. Although these grants were not all taken up as farms, enough traffic was generated to make it worthwhile for the new owners to try to keep their portions of the road open. Settlement duties required that the pioneer keep his frontage clear, but, these duties notwithstanding, the real reason a farmer was prepared to spend time cutting back new growth on the road was that it was his lifeline of transport. Simcoe had made the land grants in the knowledge that it was the only way to ensure the viability of the road. Just as the survival of Dundas Street depended on the settlers, the reverse was also true. The inland route ensured the safe, orderly, and permanent settlement of the province by guaranteeing easy access for troops and supplies. In some cases Simcoe granted a whole township to one individual on the understanding that he would select and supervise other settlers who had the intention of making a home in the area, and not simply hold land as an investment. Such a settler was Thomas Hornor, who received the whole of what would become Blenheim Township.

Hornor used his own grant for the one purpose which, more than any other, would ensure the success of Simcoe's scheme. He built a mill. By 1800 other key settlers had constructed mills at the junction of the Governor's Road and any one of the several rivers which crossed its path. The inevitable traffic followed as communities grew near the mill sites and the road then provided the means of joining these mills with the lake ports, which were built to ship out surplus grain and timber.

As well as the land available from the Simcoe grants, there was another source of farm sites, particularly in the Grand River area. The Six Nations Indians had been deeded six miles of land on either side of the Grand River from its mouth to its source (675,000 acres). Their chief, Joseph Brant, leased much of this land to settlers. Later there were problems concerning the Brant leases, for the government questioned their legality, but they did nevertheless prompt settlement in the vicinity of Brantford and the surrounding area. One of those who received land in this manner was Augustus Jones, Simcoe's surveyor, who rented his land from Brant for one peppercorn annually.

By the 1820s the tenure of the Governor's Road was secure. Traffic was proceeding along it to the lake ports, where timber, grains, and other farm products were being exported. Taverns had opened every six or seven miles along the road to respond to the needs of those who were forced to suffer the jolting experience of using the muddy path which hardly merited the designation of 'street.' Stage lines had been established by the 1820s, and the coaches brought mail delivery with them. Commerce quickly gravitated to the lake ports, such as Oakville and Port Credit, and shipping brought prosperity to all the towns whose access routes linked them to Lake Ontario from Dundas Street.

While the communities oriented to shipping were the first to thrive, there was a second impetus to growth which accounted for the prominence of the communities in the area originally designated as the western end of Simcoe's military route – London, Woodstock, and Brantford. The alternative key to prosperity was to be selected as an administrative centre. The same reasoning which had led Simcoe to propose the site of London as a provincial capital later made it an excellent choice for a district capital. It was safe, located on excellent water routes, and set in the midst of some of the choicest farm land in the province and thus in 1827 London was made capital of the Western District. Immediately a court-house was built, district officials made the town their home, markets increased as the population grew, and artisans gravitated to the source of work. Simcoe had seen London as a military site. Similar thinking located the 32nd regiment there in 1838, a move which brought traffic along the road and business to the town, as well as joy to the hearts of young Londoners. As a garrison town London was a natural military link, as Simcoe had forseen. In a similar way Woodstock and Brantford eventually outstripped the nearby lake ports, for they were also designated as county seats. New roads were built, forming links throughout western Ontario, but the first road, which remained in spite of deviations from the original plans, was the road the lieutenant-governor had built.

The route this book follows is primarily that of the 1793 road, now highway 99. The section from York (later its original name, Toronto, was restored) to Dundas was and still is called Dundas Street (highway 5). Beyond Paris and Woodstock the route is called highway 2. Although we recognize that the Governor's Road is the official name at present of only the Dundas-to-Woodstock portion of the eighteenth-century trail, we feel, nevertheless, that the name encompasses Simcoe's intent and therefore our intent in following in his path. The fact that Hamilton is not included on our route is explained by its position south of the Governor's Road and by virtue of that city's having grown to prominence after the period in which Dundas and Ancaster held sway.

Along that lifeline stand many significant buildings constructed by the men and women who first settled its path. Both the buildings and the people are our subject. We have selected a number of representative structures in each community along the way. These buildings are emphatically only a selection, for many others remain to be studied. The eye quickly becomes accustomed to the construction details which announce a building's relative age. Most of the buildings we have chosen were built before Confederation, for they show most clearly the period of 'home-made' architecture, where the input of the owner/builder is found in the wood, brick, or stone. Our selection primarily includes buildings which are for the most part unaltered, in order to show best the look of an early settlement. Included are a variety of construction materials and some buildings noted chiefly for their historical value.

Having selected the buildings, we then set out on the trail of their original occupants. Through land titles, assessment rolls, census records, wills, diaries, newspapers, and any available original documents we have attempted to bring the people to life. Much of this material was found in the Archives of Ontario, but still more is in the hands of local historical societies, libraries, and museums. The old memoirs and notes in their files and in the attics in the area are our history. We have enjoyed getting to know the men and women whose stories appear in the following pages, and we have concluded that human nature changes little over the years. One difficulty we have encountered is the uneven nature and amount of the surviving documentation regarding our families. Sometimes a diarist would record so much detail of a personal nature that the personality emerged clearly; sometimes little could be gleaned; sometimes the family's accounts of itself were too good to be interesting and every last skeleton was hidden. The atlases of the day provide a perfect example of the latter problem, for a family wrote its own story and paid for it to be included. (This kept many a good Scot out of the pages of the atlases.) In the end the determining factor in our decision regarding which families to include was the buildings with which they were associated. If a building had architectural merit, we included it in our study with as much information about its pioneer occupants as we could find.

It is impossible to ignore local legend. It is colourful and it survives. In fact it often takes on different hues as time passes. We have sometimes included legends, because we feel there is often a basis of truth in them and because they form a type of mythology. We have, however, noted when our remarks are based on legend and not on documented sources.

We hope that the cumulative effect of the stories which follow will be a feeling for the times based on the viewpoint of men and women from a variety of origins and life styles. Although there is a certain homogeneity to their histories, each settlement had its own atmosphere, and it is this flavour we have attempted to convey. It has been impossible to write a complete history of each community, however many excellent publications are available locally. It did not seem advisable to include complete genealogies of the families mentioned. We have confined our remarks to two or three generations in most cases. In any work such as this one of the chief stumbling-blocks is the variety in the spelling of surnames in the early 1800s. It is common to find half a dozen different spellings on old census records and land titles. We have tried to stay with the spelling on a will if such is available or alternatively with the earliest original version of a name. Often the various versions of a name were all acceptable.

The newspapers of the nineteenth century are a unique resource, for nothing equals their ability to immerse the researcher in the milieu of the times. These early newspapers had functions other than simply conveying the news of the world, functions which no longer exist in their counterparts today. They were, for example, the only available records of the proceedings of Parliament prior to Hansard. From Confederation until 1874 the proceedings of the House of Commons and the Senate were covered by and reported in the newspapers of the day. These reports, kept in scrap-books in the library of Parliament, are now called the scrap-book debates. They were eagerly read, for politics elicited a personal and emotional commitment at the time (and could erupt into a physical one on the spur of the moment). The actions of elected members were followed meticulously.

Newspapers also functioned as literary journals, allowing wide scope for the publication of original works of poetry and fiction at a time when it was difficult for Canadian authors to get into print. These works were not concealed beneath an advertisement for the latest miracle remedy or for painless dentistry. They were featured on the front page, often occupying half of that sheet.

Editorial comment, personal invective, and political bias were unrestrained. Not even the popular Prince of Wales escaped criticism. The *Brant Expositor* of 1860 noted: 'He evidently possesses great goodness of heart but no one capable of judging character would, we think, come to the conclusion that he would ever distinguish himself by great strength of intellect.' When the governor-general, Lord Elgin, visited Dundas in 1849, the *Hamilton Spectator* expressed its views of that neighbouring town, calling Dundas 'the most purely and violently radical place of its size in Western Canada ... the somewhat notorious Wm. Lyon Mackenzie here began his career; succeeding we believe the other reptiles for which the place was noted and which procured for it the ... designation of Rattlesnake Den.'

It seemed to be the custom to make a public statement of one's family problems in the local paper. The Pomeroy family was one of many who opened their personal disputes to public scrutiny. In the *Gore Gazette* of 31 March 1827 they told the world their woes:

INGRATITUDE
Three or four and twenty years ago my wife and I adopted an infant about three months old ... We raised him as our own. This child whose initials are TCP was at an early age sent to school and continued until he had a good education ... When he reached the age of twenty-one, retaining a parental fondness for him, we gave him 150 acres, but previous to this he married and we paid the cost and gave him a small outfit of furniture ... Now I lay before the public the returns he has made to our kindness and solicitude. He has contracted the habits of idleness, card playing, deceiving, defrauding, cheating and every species of idle and wicked speculation ... my wife left in charge of TCP cash to the amount of $100 ... she wrote for it but he did not send it ... It matters nothing to me the many idle and false reports that TCP has spread, such as my whipping him as a child till blood from his back trickled down into his shoes ... I here pause and leave the Public to judge for themselves, and guard against this ungrateful fellow accordingly. Timothy Pomeroy.

It is possible that the ungrateful TCP may be the same man who was the victim of the first murder in London to result in a public hanging; see chapter 11.

The study of early newspapers is fascinating and completely unpredictable – an example of serendipity at work. While we were searching for birth notices, the following reports in the *Canadian Champion* of Milton, 18 January 1874, came to light, proving that, in spite of the prevalence of violence, there was one spot in Ontario which was a veritable Eden:

JAIL TO LET. Not a single criminal is now confined in the County Jail at Milton. This speaks volumes for the morality of the County.

TOWN COUNCIL. Next Monday evening will be the regular meeting of the Town Council, but there being no business to transact it is most likely the town fathers will not meet.

Some events ran like a common thread through the fabric of life in nineteenth-century Ontario. Perhaps the most memorable of these was the visit in 1860 of the nineteen-year-old Prince of Wales, later Edward VII. The excitement occasioned by this royal tour touched nearly everyone in the province, resulting at times in near hysteria when the social élite of the day vied to meet, greet, or dance with the young prince. Typical of the effusive reports that appeared in the papers at the time was an item in the *Brant Expositer* on 14 September 1860. It described the prince's visit at some length, going on to state that a stand had been built, upon which 'five hundred lovely fair ones were placed in a position to enjoy a full front and side view of the youthful prince and thus gratify their native love of sightseeing.' Mention of the royal tour appears in the historical records of every community he visited and in the family histories of those fortunate few who actually met the young heir to the British throne. His visit was, undoubtedly, the social event of the century.

Excitement of a less edifying nature was provided throughout most of the 1800s by the occasional public hanging, an event which always brought forth hordes of curious onlookers. They came by the thousands, often bringing with them their children – the spectacle presumably providing a moral lesson for their impressionable off-spring. Those unable to attend the event were not, however, neglected, for the newspapers of the day recounted the entire course of action with obvious relish and in sickening detail. Anyone concerned about the standards of journalism today would do well to examine some of the newspapers that flourished during the last century.

The 1820s saw the beginning of the Underground Railroad, an organization that facilitated the escape of slaves from the southern United States. 'Stations' were set up along concealed routes and the fugitives were spirited to freedom in Canada, where they, along with the descendants of slaves brought to Canada by the United Empire Loyalists, become dedicated settlers. Gradually their numbers grew until by 1861 an estimated fifty thousand blacks had found shelter in this country. The resulting racial tension, plus the arrival from the United States of slave-catchers, caused new hardships for the blacks, although many people were sympathetic and helpful. One such man was London's Elijah Leonard, who witnessed the abduction of a black child who was being taken by train to Detroit. He mentioned the incident to Anderson Diddrick, 'the coloured man who carried the Union Jack in front of our firemen in procession.' Leonard recalled: 'I told [Diddrick] I was afraid that boy was going into slavery and it was too bad to see him dragged off free British soil to work all his life for someone else, and perhaps be badly treated ... This brought tears to Diddrick's eyes. I asked him if he knew anyone in Chatham. "Yes, several" ... I gave him [some money to telegraph] and he immediately wired the state of affairs ... When the train stopped at Chatham, sure enough, there were nearly a hundred colored men and women with clubs and staves who surrounded and boarded the train and demanded the boy ... Mr Kidnapper was very glad to get out with a whole skin from this desparate company.' The following year brought an increase in the number of blacks escaping to Canada. The Dundas *True Banner* on 27 May 1859 carried the following wry comment, reprinted from the Detroit *Advertiser*: '[a large] number of fugitive slaves have recently landed on the free soil of Canada, making 94 in all, worth at the present market price the handsome sum of $94,000! The Underground Railroad was never before doing so flourishing a business. At the rate these ungrateful fellows are stealing themselves, the market must be seriously affected.'

In our study of wills we frequently found the sort of sentiment expressed by one early settler, who decreed that his widow should receive from the son and principal heir 'kind and generous treatment [and] abundant wholesome food and becoming raimant.' These remarks were not merely loving sentiments. They spoke to the fact that a woman who did not come from a wealthy family and have an income of her own settled on her was in an exceedingly precarious position when she became a widow. By law she could rely only on her dower right – the right of a married woman to an interest on one-third of her husband's property. On her husband's death this dower right was transferred to the principal heir, no doubt one of the sons. In return, compensation was required but this often came in kind – food, firewood, a horse to use, a room to sleep in. In the agriculturally based society of the nineteenth century there was rarely enough cash to leave any widow independent. For these reasons the thoughtful husband would specify clearly how his wife was to be looked after by the new head of the family. The heir could well be a younger son, for as each young man of the pioneer family grew and married, he was, if he was fortunate, given a piece of land to farm. This meant that the son who was heir to the homestead inherited, along with the house and the land, the care of his mother, any unmarried sisters, and any young children. An unmarried sister of the heir must now seek his approval of her choice of a husband and he in turn must provide a dowry for her or care for her if she remained unmarried. The new widow, until recently the hub around whom the pioneer farm revolved, was instantly replaced at the head of the table by a daughter-in-law. Thus it was foresight to spell out in the will such seemingly odd matters as which fruit trees a widow could pick from, which side of the stable she could use, which half of which rooms were hers, and what foods she should be given to eat. It was better than the reverse – the pioneer who said merely 'I hope that my children will look after their mother.'

Historian George Sandfield Macdonald once remarked that 'the people of Canada have been left out of Canadian histories.' This may explain why, for many people, our history has seemed something less than exciting. Certainly generations of Canadians have grown up convinced that, for the most part, the people who built our country were unremittingly pompous, long-winded, or just plain dull. No doubt some of them were. Most, however, were strong individualists, often with a very human side to their character, an aspect too long ignored. Imagine, for instance, the powerful and controversial Bishop John Strachan as a lovesick young man of twenty-four. To a certain lady named Laura he poured forth his tormented feelings in a lengthy poem that ended with these heartfelt lines:

As such a wish has long been mine
Perhaps the auspicious pow'rs divine
No longer on our hopes may frown
But grant us soon bright Hymen's Crown.

Poor John Strachan. His poetry, it seems, left Laura unmoved, for within a few months she married another. This unhappy development caused Strachan to pen yet another poetic discourse, a vituperative piece with a title almost as long as the poem itself: 'On finding that a lady deceived her lover after coming under the most solemn engagements and married a man she had formerly despised and who had no qualifications whatsoever to recommend him – but a little and only a little – money.'

Picture, too, the redoubtable Sir Allan Napier MacNab, a bristling individualist if ever there was one. Shortly before his death MacNab was suffering from gout – but he found his own way of coping with the excruciating pain. When his friend Henry Becher came to call, MacNab could be heard long before Becher reached his bedroom, since the great man was singing 'Rule Britannia' at the top of his lungs. 'It was better,' said MacNab 'than groaning or swearing.' He epitomized the age.

Of course, it was not only the famous who contributed significantly to Canada's growth. Ordinary people were the ones who, through hard work and quiet service, laid the foundations for its development. Their stories are equally important. Together they left a rich legacy, a legacy of churches, houses, and public buildings – structures that still stand near the Governor's Road and throughout Ontario. It is a legacy that demands constant vigilance, for if it is neglected, our tangible heritage will most certainly be lost. It can never be replaced.

1

Along Dundas Street through Mississauga

Twenty-two-year-old Joseph Silverthorn of Niagara brought his bride to York in April 1807. Their destination was their land grant in Toronto Township. Gale-force winds, hail, and heavy ice made the crossing of Lake Ontario hazardous. A night spent in a tavern in York, a trip to the Humber in their damaged vessel, another night spent sheltering at the mouth of the Humber, a ten-mile walk through the forest from their landing-place at the Etobicoke River, and finally 'home' – two hundred acres of dense forest, no clearing, no building on the land. The bride, Jane Silverthorn, was sixteen years old. Her fourteen children would be among the first white infants born in Toronto Township, she and Joseph among the first settlers.

Philip Cody, their only neighbour, gave them temporary shelter while they erected a shanty. Within four years the Silverthorns had constructed a sturdy stone house on their partially cleared farm (lot 11, concession 1 North of Dundas Street, Toronto Township), and by 1822 they had completed a large frame home attached to the stone building. They named their homestead Cherry Hill. Sturdily constructed, the buildings are still in use over one hundred and fifty years later, although they have been moved to the corner of Silver Creek Boulevard and Lolita Gardens, near the northwest intersection of Cawthra Road and Dundas Street. This new location is only a short distance north of the original site and still on the early Silverthorn estate. Joseph and Jane lived to celebrate their seventieth wedding anniversary in Cherry Hill.

Joseph Silverthorn had come to Upper Canada in the 1780s, carried, an infant in arms, by his parents, John and Johanna Silverthorn. Their route followed Indian trails from New Jersey to Nia-

Cherry Hill, the Silverthorn home, lot 11, concession 1 NDS, Toronto Township

gara. Once established in Niagara, the elder Silverthorns had nine more children. When Joseph, their eldest, married and left for Toronto Township, they once again relocated and settled near his new home, thereby commencing wilderness farming for the third time. John and Johanna's daughters Rebecca Chisholm and Esther Thomas settled in Oakville and were among the founding families of that community.

Joseph and Jane's Cherry Hill homestead derived its name from the rows of cherry trees which lined the driveway from gate to barn. Known as Silverthorn cherry trees, they recalled Joseph's great-grandfather, Oliver Silverthorn, who, when he left England in 1700, brought cherry shoots to New Jersey. Descendants carried shoots from the original trees to various parts of the continent over the succeeding years.

Extensive family records provide glimpses of life at Cherry Hill. Of the fourteen children born to Joseph and Jane, twelve lived to maturity, nine daughters and three sons. They wrote affectionate letters to their parents expressing strong ties to the active home in which they grew up. Always industrious, the Silverthorns nevertheless created a warm and welcoming atmosphere, and visitors were frequent. Their nine daughters were, it seems, part of that appeal. A letter of January 1855 comments upon the family hospitality and responds to its with an unusual gift.

Dear Madam, Mr Labatt and I have met with such warm and hearty receptions on the two happy occasions when we had the good fortune of visiting you ... We have frequently thought of showing our appreciation of your kindness by presenting you with some mark of our esteem and have come to the conclusion to send you the very last thing that anyone would think of sending to a Lady and that is a half Barrel of London ale manufactured by Mr Labatt's father. Peter and Alex when up here said they never could get such Ale in Hamilton or Toronto. Mr Labatt joins me in kindest respects to Mr Silverthorn and yourself. Robert says you must kiss all the girls for him, to that I say ditto ... Thomas C. Mason

Much of the correspondence seems to centre on Janet, one of the nine daughters. This generous lady was wont to lend money to younger family members, one of whom, who signed his name as 'Boy Willie,' possibly a grandnephew, wrote of Janet: 'That dear, noble woman, I dare hardly think of. I should willingly give my blood drop by drop if I could repay and send her in high triumph the money. But helas! It makes one weep every time I think of it and I grumble against providence for the hard lot I have to take in this world.'

Janet Silverthorn did not marry until she was sixty and then to a twenty-two-year-old artist, Leonard H. Wilder. But it was not for lack of ardent suitors that Janet waited until her sixtieth year to marry. The Silverthorn papers contain the following two letters to Janet (their authors no doubt never expected their words to become part of a collection of historic papers in the Ontario Archives). From John: 'My dearly beloved Jennet. How can I express my deep love for you, how can I tell you how I long to fold you in my embrace. It is impossible!! I shall be out on Saturday and then we shall settle about your residence, where you and I are to spend the remainder of our lives in the midst of all the little Johns and Jennets.' From Barney:... 'How I long to see you and press you to my panting bosom. Why will you not name the happy day ... when it will be out of the power of mortals to put us asunder ... From your adorer and burning-hearted worshiper.'

After the death of Joseph and Jane Silverthorn Cherry Hill passed to their three unmarried daughters. Eventually it became the property of William Stanislaus Romain, their nephew and an actor. After this time it deteriorated to a state of near ruin. It has recently been purchased by a developer who, instead of razing the building, has moved it to its present location near the original site. It is now a restaurant.

Joseph, Jane, and many of their descendants are buried near the simple stone chapel across Cawthra Road from where their home originally stood. Fronting on Dundas Street, this trim building was built in 1838 by the Anglicans, Methodists, and Presbyterians jointly, as their numbers did not warrant a separate church for each denomination. The chapel is built of Credit Valley sandstone. Set in the front gable of the simple, dignified building is a metal clock face. Its hands permanently mark 11:02 o'clock, in order, it is said, to urge latecomers to hurry. Since only the Anglicans held services at eleven, this may have created confusion for members of the other denominations.

The Union Chapel replaced an earlier log structure built in 1816 by the Silverthorns and other settlers in the area. Among them was Absalom Wilcox, in whose home William Lyon Mackenzie sheltered after the mêlée at Montgomery's Tavern, and whose son Allan accompanied Mackenzie on his escape. While clearing the site for the chapel, Absalom broke his leg and, according to the Perkins Bull papers, was carried to York where an army surgeon amputated it. Absalom Wilcox and his wife Barbara are buried in the cemetery which surrounds the church.

Much of the history of the settlement can be read on the tombstones in this old graveyard. A row of six small stones crumbling from age marks the graves of young children in one family, suggesting that an epidemic was ravaging the community in the early or mid-1800s. Other stones provide wry advice, such as that of Philander Horning, who died in 1837 at the age of 34:

> As I am now, so you must be
> Prepare to follow after me.

Much the same advice appears on the stone of Charles W. Cordingly, but it is couched in language less poetical:

Dixie Union Chapel and cemetery, Dundas Street and Cawthra Road

> Children dear, assemble here
> Your parents grave to see
> Not long ago we lived with you
> But shortly you must dwell with us.

Yet another grave is marked with words of faint praise: 'She hath done what she could.'

When the Union Chapel was built, the village it served was called Sydenham. Later it was renamed Dixie to honour a greatly loved doctor who served the district for many years. Beaumont Wilson Bowen Dixie was descended from a distinguished British family. According to family research, his ancestors included a sister of Egbert, a ninth-century Saxon king of England, Sir Walston Dixie, merchant adventurer and lord mayor of London, Elizabeth Hastings (ninth in descent from Henry III) and her husband John Beaumont, master of the rolls, these last two also descended from Louis VIII of France.

Dr Dixie, heir to these illustrious genes, was born in Wales in 1819 and arrived in Canada with his parents in 1831. His father was Captain Richard Thomas Dixie. After schooling at Upper Canada College Beaumont Dixie studied medicine and in 1843 was licensed to practise 'Physic, Surgery and Midwifery.' The licence, issued at Kingston, was signed by the Rt Honourable Sir Charles Bagot 'one of Her Majesty's Privy Council, Governor General of British North America and Captain General and Governor in Chief in and over the Province of Canada, Nova Scotia, New Brunswick and the Island of Prince Edward and Vice Admiral of the same etc' – few documents could look more official. Two years before he became a doctor, Beaumont Dixie married Anna Skynner. He practised first in Oakville and then in Grahamsville, a village north of Malton. In 1846 the Dixies moved to Springfield (later the name of the village was changed to Erindale) and there they remained. Tragedy struck the young family nine years later when their four children died in the diptheria epidemic of 1853–4. Two daughters were subsequently born to them, for the 1861 census lists Margot, aged four, and Christianna, aged one.

In 1854, possibly just after the death of their children, the Dixies purchased property at the end of Dundas Crescent North in Erindale. It is likely that they moved into a house that already stood on the property, for some of the neoclassical details of 1437 Dundas

Crescent suggest that it could have been built in the 1820s. Of particular interest are the Venetian windows that flank the door. Each window consists of a twelve-over-twelve-paned sash surrounded by plain pilasters and flanked by five-paned vertical sidelights. Although now covered with aluminum siding, the building's pleasing proportions and interest of detail are still in evidence.

In 1867 Anna Dixie died. The following year Dr Dixie married Elizabeth Blakely, thus providing a step-mother for his daughters, who were at the time about ten and seven years old. Elizabeth also bore a daughter, Sarah, who lived in the Dixie family home until her death in 1951. Beaumont Dixie provided medical care for the people of Erindale for fifty-two years. He died on his seventy-ninth birthday in 1898.

In recent years the Dixie house has acquired a degree of notoriety, for during the summer of 1973 the body of Christine Demeter was found in the garage which adjoins the house. Her husband was

Dr Dixie's Erindale house, 1437 Dundas Crescent

charged with arranging for her murder and, after a lengthy and widely publicized trial, was found guilty.

The house on Dundas Crescent was not the Dixie's first house in Erindale. When they first moved to the community in 1846, they lived for four years in a remarkably attractive cottage situated a short distance west of Mississauga Road, at 1921 Dundas Street. It is easy to understand why the young couple found the house desirable, for it is an elegant structure, well proportioned, with fine architectural details and large windows which flood the house with light. Obviously it was a house meant for a gentleman and who better than Beaumont Dixie of distinguished lineage.

When Dr Dixie bought the cottage, two years before the family actually moved to Erindale, the building was ten or fifteen years old. The original owner was also a gentleman – Sir John Beverley Robinson, chief justice of Upper Canada. His life has been well documented, yet nowhere is there a mention of his fine cottage at

Erindale cottage of Sir John Beverley Robinson, 1921 Dundas Street

Erindale. Anthony Adamson, long-time resident of Peel County and authority on Upper Canadian architecture, suggests that Robinson may have enjoyed the idea of having a 'playful elegant small house' in the country and speculates that the designer could have been William Chewett, Deputy surveyor-general. Certainly the designer was skilled and creative. Adamson refers to the building as a 'hipped roof cottage with lots of fun on the exterior.' In 1833 Dr Coleman, one of two physicians living in the village at the time, remarked in a letter to his sisters in England that 'A Mr Robinson, who holds the official situation of Chief Justice of the Province, is about to erect a country seat immediately opposite the place fixed for my cottage on the opposite side of the road.' Robinson probably spent little time in Erindale as he was also completing his impressive home, Beverley House, in York at this time and was beset by both financial and political difficulties. As Adamson comments, Robinson was 'building two houses and suffering from very poor cash flow, as the government never seemed to get around to paying him for his services as solicitor general.' Finally he sold the cottage and fifty acres of land. It passed through the hands of several owners until it was purchased by Beaumont Dixie. During his tenure Dr Dixie built a summer kitchen and added outbuildings, but the house was cold and draughty, possibly because of its many windows. According to Anthony Adamson, the Dixies sold the Robinson house four years later and lived in Dr Coleman's home until they purchased the frame house on Dundas Crescent.

Dr Dixie sold the Robinson cottage to John Irvine, who, four years later, sold it to Charles Mitchell. Mitchell's wife was a daughter of Colonel Peter Adamson, one of the township's first settlers. Her uncle, Joseph Adamson, was the first doctor in Toronto Township, a man greatly loved by his patients, both white and Indian. The journals of the Reverend Peter Jones of the Credit Reserve mention Dr Adamson's work there: 'After meeting I called the men together to lay before them the proposition of Dr Joseph Adamson respecting his attendance on the sick of this place. His offer is to attend them one year if every man will engage to give him two days work during the year. After explaining this to them they unanimously agreed to accept the Doctor's offer.'

Dr Adamson's young partner, Dr Coleman, described him as 'an elderly man who has been in practice in this neighbourhood these ten years and is exceedingly beloved and respected.' Dr Adamson, who was forty-seven at the time these remarks were made, might not have thought of himself as 'elderly.' Four years later, during the Rebellion of 1837, he was active enough to serve as surgeon to the First Batallion, Incorporated Militia. Before his death in 1852 he lived with his niece and her family in the Robinson cottage.

In 1867 the house was sold again to yet another distinguished gentleman, the Very Reverend Dean Henry J. Grassett, DD. He was for many years dean of St James Cathedral in Toronto and used the Erindale cottage as a summer home. Subsequently the house changed hands several times until it was purchased in 1911 by Arthur and Henry Adamson, grandsons of Dr Joseph. Because of this link the house is known as the Robinson-Adamson cottage. Today this splendid building is owned by the city of Mississauga. It has been beautifully restored and stands as a significant architectural and historical site. So designated by the Ontario Heritage Act, the house is now used as Boy Scouts' Headquarters.

In the 1820s Erindale was little more than a stopping-point on the Dundas, but there were enough British families in the area to make feasible the building of a church. With the help of the Adamson brothers and other local families the Anglican parish of St Peter's was formed and a small church was erected in 1827. Before the church building was completed, the parishioners met in a local hall. The owner, however, found it bad for business because some were reluctant to rent a hall for 'dancing and other purposes when it was devoted every Sunday to Divine Worship.'

The first rector of St Peter's, an enterprising Irishman by the name of James Magrath, was nearly sixty years of age when he arrived in Upper Canada. He was accompanied by his wife, four sons aged eleven to twenty-three, and a daughter aged eight. As well, Magrath brought seven tons of household goods, said to be the largest shipment ever landed on the wharf at York until that time. One of the Magrath sons, Thomas William, wrote letters from his new home to Dublin, and these highly imaginative accounts of life in the new world were published as *Authentic Letters From Upper Canada* in 1833. In one letter the writer described his pet bear 'of the fair sex. The name to which she answers Mocaunse. Her qualities, mildness and docility.' This docile creature was, according to Magrath, trained to sit at table and eat breakfast, always waiting to be served except upon one occasion after which the writer spanked her. The thrilling Magrath accounts of sporting life in the colonies were eagerly received at home.

The Magraths first built a log house, but before long they started work on a substantial house that they called Erindale. In honour of the Reverend James Magrath, who became the moving force in the development of the community, the village known as Springfield later adopted Erindale as its new name.

The Magraths had left Ireland in order to provide their children with better opportunities than those available to them at home. Through family connections they had introductions to many of the influential people in York who helped them become established. Like them, and like many Anglican ministers, Magrath began to specu-late in real estate in order to augment his income. This was undoubt-edly a necessary measure for, although his mission stretched from Hamilton to York, his parishoners were scattered and money was scarce.

By the time of his death in 1851, twenty-four years after he came to Canada, Magrath had established a respectable estate which he divided as fairly as possible among his children: 'Whereas my son Thomas William has a house of his own and my second son James has a house rented in which he carries on his business as merchant and my third son Charles has chosen a profession which keeps him in Toronto ... I leave the 200 acres on which Erindale ... stands to my son William Melchior who has neither house nor profession.' Mag-rath instructed that his daughter Anna Cordelia and his niece Maria be given bed and board and the running of the house. He also instructed that any of his children who needed it should receive asy-lum at Erindale as long as they paid £30 in rent and were prepared to help 'cheerfully on the lands, conducting themselves peaceably and kindly.' His home was obviously of great importance to the old gentleman for he said: 'It is my earnest wish that Erindale not be sold but that it remain to the family,' adding, to emphasize the point with his children, 'As You Value Your Father's Blessing.' The strong Magrath personality continues to emerge through phrases such as 'Now James cannot complain much. He gets one lot, his own lot which produces £80 per annum ... Charles I think has the box given by Lady Mountland to his grandmother ... so I leave him nothing more.' Meticulous to the last detail, Magrath adds in conclusion 'I forgot to say' ... and then disposes of the money which might be in his pocket at the moment he dies or on his desk or around the house.

The house which Magrath loved did stay in the family for many years until one March morning when a spark from the chimney ignited some papers and Erindale burned to the ground. A new home was immediately set under construction.

Magrath's Erindale had served as the rectory of St Peter's and after his death the church was without both minister and rectory. The two clergymen who followed Magrath probably lived in rented quarters. However, during the tenure of the Reverend Honourable Thomas P. Hodge a new rectory was built. Now called the Old Manse, it is located at 1556 Dundas Street West and is a real estate office. It is a handsome building, described when it was built in 1861 as being 'as nice a parsonage house as is in the Diocese.' Recent restoration by the present owners has given it a new lease on life, and while changes have been made to the interior, the basic character of the building has been retained. Like many fine homes of the day, the rectory is square in plan, its central door surrounded by sidelights and a simple transom. Stone quoins at each corner accentuate the red brick and contribute to its dignity and feeling of permanence. It is a fine example of how imagination and careful planning allow an old but well-built structure to be adapted successfully to commercial use.

Although Hodge was housed in his fine rectory, his years at St Peter's were difficult ones. One of the problems was money, or the lack of it. The churchwardens were unable to pay his full salary; even the churchyard fence could not be mended and there was no 'protection from cattle.' Hodge's main problems, however, seemed to stem from an awkward but intense personality clash with William Magrath, the youngest son of the church's first rector. Magrath left St Peter's to attend the church in Streetsville. Naturally there were different views of the situation. Church records state that Magrath was prone to insist on 'his own importance,' but his daughter Mary Harris spoke of him as a dear and affectionate man who was kind to squatters who lived on his property.

In 1866 the Reverend Charles James Stewart Bethune became rector of St Peter's. His grandfather, John Bethune, was a Loyalist and the first Presbyterian minister in Upper Canada. John Bethune's family became leaders in the religious and educational life of the province. Charles Bethune had grown up in Cobourg, where his father, later Bishop Alexander Neil Bethune, was rector of St Peter's church. A prize student of Bishop John Strachan's, Charles Bethune was educated at the University of Toronto and in England.

The Old Manse, the rectory of St Peter's Church, 1556 Dundas Street West

He recognized the need for a larger church building in Erindale, and so plans were made for the construction of a new St Peter's on the same site. The church was completed in 1887 after Bethune had left for Port Hope. The new St Peter's stands just north of Dundas Street at Mississauga Road, its spire a landmark for the small community which Dr Coleman called 'one of the prettiest villages in Upper Canada.'

Most of the good remaining pre-Confederation buildings in the Erindale area were built by men who were active in the founding of St Peter's. These families were wealthy, at least by the standards of the day, and their homes were built to last. It was not that all Anglicans were rich but certainly most of the rich were Anglicans. For many years, of course, the Anglican Church was, in custom although not in law, the established church in Upper Canada. It had, for example, a huge advantage in the disposition of clergy reserves, receiving one-seventh of the waste land of the Crown. The Methodists and other denominations, while collectively outnumbering their Anglican brethren, took longer to become entrenched and it was many years before they were able to match the political and social strength of the Anglican Church.

In Erindale one of the most prestigious of St Peter's parishioners was Oliver Hammond, merchant, farmer, and for many years a justice of the peace. His imposing brick house at 2625 Hammond Road was built on land which had been owned by his wife since 1838. Early records are inconclusive, but an indenture signed in June of that year suggests that Hammond's wife, Sarah Ann Carpenter, purchased the property from her parents for £800. It could, however, have been a gift to Sarah Ann, for it is clear that her mother was anxious to see that she was financially independent. On her death in 1859 Mary Carpenter's will revealed that she had made the following provision for her daughter: 'I desire that the above money, goods and chattels ... willed to my daughter Sarah Ann Hammond shall be for her own separate use and benefit and not to be controlled or used by her present husband or any future husband and in case her present husband or any future husband should use any power they have in law, I appoint my said executors trustees to take said property heretofor devised to keep the same in trust for my said daughter.'

At some time during the 1860s Sarah Ann and Oliver built their large home. It is pictured in the 1877 *Illustrated Historical Atlas of the County of Peel* and must have been a source of pride to them both. To the north of the house is an orchard. To the south and east broad fields lead to the horizon. A small stream meanders through the property. (The sylvan settings pictured in county atlases were paid for by the subscriber.) It is likely that what now forms the rear portion of the house was once the Hammonds' first home. A verandah originally stretched across the front of the house but, as was so often the case, it failed to withstand the rigours of a harsh climate. In recent years the front door has been recessed to form an umbrage.

Oliver Hammond died in 1874, Sarah Ann six years later. The house was left to their son Thomas, who had been farming the land with his parents for some years.

In the late 1830s, at the same time that Oliver and Sarah Ann Hammond were establishing their first homestead near Erindale, an English gentleman, his wife, and infant daughter arrived in the neighbourhood and settled on land a few miles south of the Ham-

Hammond house, 2625 Hammond Road

monds. He was Captain James Beveridge Harris, formerly of the East India Company's 24th Foot Regiment. Harris had resigned his commission in order to emigrate to Canada so that he could provide a better life for his family in that rapidly growing colony. When at the age of 78 Harris wrote his will, he was able to leave extensive holdings in land and shares in the Royal Canadian Bank and the Merchant's Bank of Canada. The family was educated, industrious, and enterprising, typical in many ways of the half-pay officers and their relatives who came to the province to settle as landed gentry.

Harris may have been lured to the area by an advertisement which appeared in the *Upper Canada Land, Mercantile and General Advertiser* on 12 August 1835. It told of an attractive property for sale 'between the Lakeshore Road and Dundas Street, 18 miles from the City of Toronto.' An 'elegant stone house, built in the first style and well adapted for any gentleman's family' was part of the property. One of the men acting as agent for the sale was James Magrath, the rector of St Peter's. The 'elegant stone house' was the work of the previous owner, Edgar Neave. It was completed except for the fact that it had no doors or windows, which meant that it was not subject to taxation.

Not long after the advertisement appeared, Harris purchased the house and the nearly two hundred acres surrounding it. He named his estate Benares, after the city in India in which he had served. By this time Harris was thirty-eight years old and his Irish wife, Elizabeth Molone, twenty-five. Their first child, Bess, had been born on board ship when the couple emigrated. Their family grew to include eight children, four boys and four girls. During these years Harris managed the farm and enjoyed the country pastimes of a gentleman farmer, such as hunting and salmon-fishing. Once a week, according to family tradition, he would walk the eighteen miles to Toronto to pick up his mail, returning home the following day. The entire family, of course, attended St Peter's.

In 1851 the Harris's oldest son died. Not long afterwards, while they and their other children were in church, their fine stone house was gutted by fire. Arson was suspected, since two of the servants and the family silver vanished at the same time. A second house was built, but six years later it too was burned to the ground. Once again arson was suspected. Captain Harris had been serving as a magistrate at the time and he believed that the fire had been set by a disreputable character to whom he had given a severe sentence.

Footprints were found around the site in the snow.

When spring came, construction began on a third house. This time it was to be of brick and built on the foundations of the first stone structure. Specifications stated that only the 'best hard-burned bricks' were to be used, 'the whole laid in Flemish bond excepting the rear wall which will be laid in English bond.' Flemish bond, a popular method of laying bricks in the early to mid-1800s, alternated headers (bricks laid at right angles to the wall, thereby exposing their ends) and stretchers (bricks laid lengthwise); English bond laid bricks in alternate rows of headers and stretchers, each header centred over a stretcher or a join.

The new Benares was completed before Christmas of 1857, but the family's pleasure in their home was destroyed by the death of their second son, James, who died after being gored by a bull. Two years after the Harris's moved into their new home their third son, Charles, also died. His death was the last in the series of blows which struck the family in the 1850s. Their daughters lived to maturity and their fourth son, Arthur, stayed on to manage the farm. In 1881 he married Mary Magrath, daughter of William and grandaughter of the first rector of St Peter's. After nearly half a century at Benares Captain Harris died in 1884 at the age of eighty-seven. His wife died one month later.

The Whiteoak family of Jalna in Mazo de la Roche's novels was modelled after the Harris family. One of the Harrises explained that 'Mazo de la Roche became a friend of the family through Mr. Livesay of the Canadian Press. She became interested in the family history and used their background for her Whiteoak family. When writing her first book of the series she also used the house as it is until her editor ... pointed out to her that she'd have to add another storey to the house to accommodate all the characters ... That's why Jalna was three storeys instead of Benares' two.'

The Harris house is now owned by the Ontario Heritage Foundation. It stands at 1503 Clarkson Road North, partially screened by trees and surrounded by a broad expanse of lawn. At the rear of the lot are two outbuildings that were part of the estate when James Harris bought it in 1835.

The trail that led south from the Harris property to the lake was a 'given' road as opposed to a road laid out on township land. It was composed of portions of the holdings of Captain Harris and his neighbour to the south, Warren Clarkson. In 1845 both Harris and

Clarkson gave land for the road and in time the trail became known as Clarkson Road.

The man for whom the road was named arrived in Upper Canada in 1808 as a lad of fifteen. He came from Albany, New York, with his father Richard and his brother Joshua and family. After a year or two in York the members of the family went their separate ways. Warren had made contacts which led him to Toronto Township, where there was the prospect of work and the chance to get his own land. Thomas Merigold, a Loyalist from New Brunswick, and his son-in-law, Benjamin Monger, were moving to settle in Toronto Township and they needed skilled help in establishing farms and business ventures. Warren Clarkson worked for Benjamin Monger and gained the business acumen that was to serve him well in later life, for this hardy pioneer produced a family whose financial demands were never-ending.

Clarkson's early years in Toronto Township were interrupted by

Benares, the inspiration for Mazo de la Roche's Jalna, 1503 Clarkson Road North

The verandah at Benares

service in the War of 1812. By 1814, however, he had managed to pick up enough business experience between battles to establish himself on a farm and marry. His bride was Susan Shook, the daughter of the family who had settled across the road from the Mongers. Warren and Susan Clarkson made their home on one hundred acres of land just north of Lakeshore Road. The first of their children, George, was born in 1818. One year after George was born Warren and Susan completed construction of their first small house. The birth of a daughter, Charlotte, in 1822 prompted the completion of a larger house where in due course two more sons were born, William Warren in 1828 and Henry Shook in 1834.

Warren Clarkson did not confine his energies to working the farm. He operated a general store on his property. It stood beside the trail that led from Erindale past the Harris farm to the Lakeshore Road. A few miles to the east, where the Credit River flows into Lake Ontario, a promising village had begun to grow, and there Clarkson built another store in order to take advantage of what seemed to be the assured prosperity of the place. The prosperous port at the mouth of the Credit was one of the largest on the Great Lakes, and for many years it had been serving farmers in the area, as vessels made regular stops to load grain. It was here that Warren Clarkson had first stayed on his arrival in Toronto Township, at the government inn run by Thomas Ingersoll. The innkeeper was well enough known in his time but history was to dictate that his real fame would arise from the fact that he was the father of Laura Secord.

Through the first half of the nineteenth century Warren Clarkson prospered. At the same time, however, his family was growing and, in direct relation, so were his problems. In the 1930s a bundle of letters was found in the Clarkson homestead which testified to the fact that even a century ago young people were not always industrious, mannerly, or respectful of their parents.

The Clarkson letters were written by the three older children, George, William, and Charlotte, to their younger brother, Henry. Henry was the solace of his father in that he held a job and stayed out of debt and jail. George farmed in Milton with limited success and William accumulated debts. Charlotte, since her brothers administered some property which was hers, depended on them for

Clarkson house, just north of Lakeshore Road

pocket-money and was always short of it.

From Milton George wrote to Henry, usually asking for money. One letter, however, dated November 1855, seems to indicate that George was marrying without his father's knowledge or consent: 'Sir – I want you and Charlotte to come up on Monday night for I am going to get married on Tuesday ... I wish you would come to Milton ... and don't goe any where else for wee want to keep it as sly as Possible ... Try and go through Palermo after Dark so no one will see you at all.' A letter written two years later suggests that things were not going well, for George asked his brother to 'Tell father to sell the plase iff possible so that I can get out of truble.' In the spring of 1858 a baby was born to George's wife and shortly thereafter George fell ill. By December the family was in dire straits and he wrote to Henry: 'If you could lend me $100 I shuld be very glad to get it ... Debrah and Baby is well ... It is as mischevious a child as you ever saw. I wish you could come and see her for she looks jest like you.'

Henry was unable to send any money to his brother, and in March 1859 George and his family moved back to his father's farm. Warren Clarkson paid his son's debts but it was not surprising that, as Charlotte remarked, 'George's trouble frets him [Warren] all but to death.' By June the situation seemed no better, according to Charlotte: 'the old folks cannot bare George here another summer. He nearly killed one of father's horses he worked it so hard ... do not write anything to George that you dont want told again for he tells every thing he knows and more too.'

Warren Clarkson's wife, Susan, died in 1858 and the widower married again two years later. His new wife was Mary Ann Kirkus, a widow from Richmond Hill. She is frequently referred to in the letters which George, William, and Charlotte wrote to Henry as 'the old woman.' Mary Ann shared with Warren his concern about his grown children as problems accumulated with the years.

While George was back on the family farm causing trouble, William was now deeply in debt. In 1857 his wife, Lorenda, was pregnant. This news was relayed to Henry, who was in Minnesota training to be a surveyor and working as a foreman for a railway construction firm, by both Charlotte and George, each in his or her own style. Charlotte wrote: 'you are in a fair way for being an uncle.' George wrote: 'Lorenda is Nock up as high as Gilderoyes Kite.' William, because of his debts, was constantly on the move in an effort to keep out of jail. He went to Ohio, returned to the homestead, was committed to jail, jumped bail, and left with Lorenda for New York State. Warren, in spite of his exasperation, was nevertheless sorry to see his son depart. Charlotte summed it up: 'Father felt very bad to see William go off for he said perhaps he would never see him again for if he got sick William could not come and see him.'

Charlotte was continually without funds. She wrote to steady Henry for ten dollars or so, adding on one occasion that 'I might as well get a fart from a dead man as to get any money from father.' Charlotte married in 1859. Prior to the wedding George wrote to Henry, speculating on what he would do 'iff she does marry that ass. She shant never darking my door.'

Poor industrious Warren Clarkson deserved better. His worries, however, did nothing to affect his longevity, for he lived until the age of 89.

Clarkson barn

Of the three Clarkson sons, only Henry measured up to his father's expectations. After about three years in Minnesota he returned to Canada in 1860, working as a produce merchant in Toronto and Port Credit and helping his father to manage the farm. When Warren Clarkson died in 1882, Henry inherited the bulk of the estate, including the house and outbuildings.

For many years the Clarkson house remained in the family but by the 1930s it had fallen into a state of near ruin. Fortunately it was purchased in 1936 by Major John Barnett, a man whose passionate interest in history led him to undertake the gradual restoration of the house and the surrounding property. Where indiscriminate logging had denuded the nearby woodlands, the Barnetts planted over five thousand trees. Today some thirty-eight distinct species survive. The house that Warren Clarkson completed in 1825 still stands at the end of a long driveway. His first house, built six years earlier, is joined to the main block by a spinning-room that Clarkson added in 1857.

Hidden in the trees behind the house is a splendid barn that dates from the mid-1820s. One of the many legends surrounding the escape of William Lyon Mackenzie after the rebellion suggests that he hid in this barn for a time, although there is no mention of this area in Mackenzie's own account of his flight. If, however, the barn did shelter one of the fleeing rebels, in all probability that man would have been Joseph Clarkson, a nephew of Warren's and one of Mackenzie's loyal followers. Joseph Clarkson too was charged with high treason and fled to the United States, but no further account of his escape has been found.

In the 1790s there were possibly 600 Mississauga Indians in the Credit River area. Basically a nomadic people, they moved about in pursuit of game or fish, establishing villages and then moving on. For them the advent of increasing numbers of Europeans brought some benefits primarily from the fur trade, but there were also liabilities in the form of new diseases which began to decimate their ranks. In 1805 the chiefs of the Mississaugas signed a purchase agreement with the Crown in which the Indians surrendered 84,000 acres of land along Lake Ontario for £1000. By this agreement they retained the lands on either side of the Credit River, a mile in extent altogether, for their exclusive use, with hunting and fishing rights throughout the territory. In 1818, however, the chiefs surrendered the Credit lands and by 1820 they had given up all but two hundred acres as well as their fishing rights. The government then made plans to establish a permanent village for the Mississauga and in 1826 constructed thirty log houses on a site near the present Mississauga Golf Club. By 1837 there were in the Mississauga village some fifty log houses each of which would hold two families.

Peter Jones, a young Methodist missionary and a Mississauga himself, came to help his people become established in the new village. Jones was described in his formal attire as a chief: 'a coat of deer skin, dressed in the Indian method without the hair, of a golden colour, and as soft as glove leather ... The head-dress – a valuable silk, or fine cotton handkerchief, in turban form, worn by some tribes with feathers. Leggins, – reaching to the hip, and ornamented on the sides, serve as trowsers. Mocassins – curiously ornamented with porcupine quills, complete the drawing room habit.'

Jones had the assistance of his brother John, and shortly thereafter the remarkable influence of another Methodist missionary,

James Wilcox's inn, 32 Front Street, Port Credit

Egerton Ryerson, was felt. Ryerson, who established the Ontario educational system, was instrumental in arranging for the construction of a schoolhouse and a Methodist chapel in the village. He considered it essential to erect the chapel quickly, for the Anglicans had ideas in the same direction. Both groups were actively competing for the souls of the native people, who had recently been converted to Christianity. The chapel, built after the settlement was established, is located today at Peter and Lake Streets. It is important more for its history than for its architecture, for it has been altered and moved from its original site, but beneath the present stucco exterior is frame and possibly log construction. For many years it has been the Masonic Hall.

James Wilcox was an Englishman whose fortunes were tied to those of Port Credit and so prospered and declined with the village. In 1850, in the period of the lake port's prosperity, he built a fine two-storey inn overlooking the harbour, and here for the following six years came sailors, travellers, and farmers bringing their grain to be shipped. Upstairs the ballroom could double as sleeping accommodation when other rooms were full. In 1855, however, the Great Western Railway was opened through Port Credit. The shipment of goods by rail was much easier, and the decline of the port set in. This spelled disaster for Wilcox. The number of people visiting the harbour diminished and Wilcox converted his inn to a two-family dwelling. Conflicting local histories suggest that the hotel at one point served as a temperance inn for sailors, a contradiction in terms that provides another possible explanation of its commercial failure. For many years after his inn went out of business Wilcox earned his living as a sailor. The census of 1871 shows that he was still following that occupation at that time. Today his inn stands, beautifully restored, at 32 Front Street. It is now used as an office. In the latter part of the nineteenth century some of the schooners which had formerly been used for shipping became involved in stone-hooking, carrying stone from the bottom of the lake to be used in construction in Toronto.

In 1808, the year in which Warren Clarkson had come to Upper Canada from Albany, his neighbour, Lewis Bradley, arrived in Toronto Township from New Brunswick. Bradley received a Crown grant of more than two hundred acres and promptly set about meeting the settlement requirements. Less than three years later, Samuel Smith, a justice of the peace, spoke on Bradley's behalf: 'the settling duty has been done on lot 28 in the 3rd concession South Side Dundas Street ... a house twenty feet by sixteen has been erected and five acres cleared and under fence ... as also the road cleared in front of said lot.' Bradley's land stretched south from the Lakeshore Road to Lake Ontario on the lot immediately to the east of the farm purchased a few years later by Clarkson.

Bradley was a Loyalist. The years of the American Revolution had meant turmoil and disruption for him and his family. His father, Richard Bradley, was a commissary at Savannah, Georgia, a civilian who served the needs of the military in that area. He died, possibly when the revolutionary forces successfully attacked Savannah in 1777. He left a widow and two sons, William and Lewis. In time Mrs Bradley remarried, her new husband John Jenkins, a lieutenant and deputy muster master in the Loyalist forces in South Carolina. When the war came to an end, the family fled to New York City and then to New Brunswick with other Loyalists. When Fredericton became the capital of New Brunswick, the land adjacent to it was greatly in demand. With requests from government officials and from other Loyalist families the best sites were being taken up, and thus Lewis Bradley and Thomas Merigold, with three other families, decided to relocate in Upper Canada. At this time Bradley was thirty-seven years old.

Bradley and Merigold, the leader of the small group from New Brunswick, received adjacent land grants in Toronto Township. This proved a convenient arrangement because Bradley's wife, Elizabeth, was a daughter of Merigold. The Bradleys may not have married until after Lewis had settled on his farm. Their first child, William F. Brown Bradley, was born circa 1815 when his father was forty-four. In time three more sons and two daughters were born to the Bradleys. About 1830 the Bradleys replaced the original house referred to in the statement of settlement with the trim frame building on the property today.

Little is known of Lewis and Elizabeth Bradley during their life in Toronto Township. They were devout Wesleyan Methodists and must have welcomed the itinerant ministers who travelled through the countryside. When Lewis Bradley died in 1843, his obituary in the *Christian Guardian* of 26 April stated that he 'raised a numerous and respectable family ... He was a very affectionate father and kind and attentive husband – charitable and liberal – always cheerful and lively and was highly esteemed by all who had the pleasure of his aquaintance.'

A few years after Lewis's death Elizabeth married Major John Button, after whom the village of Buttonville in York Region was named. In 1846 the Bradley house was sold to Bartholomew C. Beardsley, whose wife, Mary Jenkins, was a half sister of Bradley. Today the Bradley house is a historic-house museum under the supervision of the Mississauga Heritage Foundation and city of Mississauga and is open to the public from April through November. Before its restoration it was moved a short distance from its original location by the lake to a site near the intersection of Meadowwood and Orr Roads in Clarkson.

Beside the Bradley house and awaiting restoration is the Anchorage, probably built by James Taylor but given its nautical name by John Skynner, whose naval career began in 1795 and took him throughout the Mediterranean for forty-three years until he retired

Bradley house, near Meadowwood and Orr Roads in Clarkson

as a commander. Like the Bradley house the Anchorage has been moved. The original location of the Skynner land was at the foot of Southdown Road. This land was deeded from the Crown to Stephen Jarvis, who came from New Brunswick, as did the Bradleys and Merigolds. Jarvis related that he came to York in 1808 to obtain land. After receiving twelve hundred acres he returned to Fredericton for his family. For part of the journey he used the same log canoe which Thomas Merigold had used to reach York. Although the Jarvises are mainly associated with Toronto, they also had long family ties with Toronto Township. Frederick Starr Jarvis, Stephen's son, raised his twelve children there, and the Jarvis family did not move to Toronto until after his death in 1852.

It was Frederick Starr Jarvis who in 1832 sold the land on which the Anchorage was built to James Taylor. Taylor held it for six years before he sold it to Skynner. The building was built either by Taylor during those six years or by Skynner, who like so many military men would have had a strong preference for the Regency style in which the Anchorage was built. The house is now standing empty until funds permit its restoration.

The city of Mississauga today encompasses many former villages, each of which had a distinct identity, history, and unique atmosphere. Even in the mid-1800s, however, there were connections between these disparate communities brought about by marriages and ties of family. A contemporary account of a wedding which took place in 1851 brings vividly to life many of the men and women whose houses are mentioned in the preceeding pages. This description of the marriage of Henry Skynner and Mary Adamson, which took place in the Jarvis home, Brunswick Farm, was written by Frederick Starr Jarvis. He includes comments upon all who attended – and even some who were absent, such as the lady who 'had no servant and could not leave her brat.' Among those present were Mrs Dixie, the former Anna Skynner, and her daughter, 'Dixie being called to a patient,' and Captain Harris and his daughter.

Jarvis writes: 'The bride came downstairs and took my arm, Louisa Jarvis and Fred Forster, Miss Adamson and John Skynner, Julia and Charles Adamson as bridesmaid and groomsman and formed in the middle of the drawing room. Parson and self in front ... Henry said "I will" before the first question of "will thou take this woman etc." and of course had to say it at the finish which made quite a laugh and revived Mary's thoughts and her colour ... I

shed a few tears and Mrs Dixie had a nice cry.' The wedding table
was laden with 'Tea, coffee, two turkeys, two geese, two ducks, six
chickens, two hams, tarts, jellies, blamonges ... whipped cream,
Italian salad, raisins and almonds, apples, peaches and grapes, Port,
sherry, toddy, whiskey and cold water.' The evening ended with
'Hurrahs, hip, hip and health to all good lasses,' but not before dancing and 'supper' had followed the wedding feast. Jarvis concludes
with an account of his coup: 'Miss Adamson had a nice tete-a-tete
with John Skynner as I locked them up in the parlour together.'

2

Oakville

'The Lakes on one side of you, Railways on the other; a great country in your rear; Mills, Foundries, Shipbuilding, Cabinet-Making etc. in your midst; what in the world is to prevent this place growing to be an important city. It must, there is no preventing it!' This ecstatic endorsement of Oakville's future was written in 1855 to the Oakville *Semi-Weekly Sentinel* by a visitor who called himself 'Friend Shea.' In the two years since Friend Shea had last seen the village he estimated that real estate had jumped by 400 percent. Having passed up the chance to buy a farm less than a mile from the centre of the village for $20 to $50 an acre, he would now be forced to pay up to $200 per acre. The writer attributed this astonishing progress to the presence of 'a good sprinkling of Yankees,' whom he saw as an omen for what he called the 'go-a-headitiveness' of the place. In fact, the early settlers who established the village at the Sixteen Mile Creek in the 1830s and 1840s were immigrants from the British Isles – the Irish heading the list numerically, followed by those from England and Scotland (according to the 1841 census). The latter were particularly in evidence as they were seen about town in their plaids and 'grey stove pipe hats.'

The impetus for Oakville's rapid growth was the shipbuilding and shipping industry which was well established by the early 1830s. The *Canada Directory* for 1857 listed fifteen ships captains whose residence was Oakville, plus others described as shipbuilders, shipowners, ship's carpenters, ship's caulkers, wharfingers, and a wide variety of artisans whose work was tied to the shipping of grain.

The man who is called the founding father of Oakville, Colonel William Chisholm, was born in Nova Scotia, the son of George

Chisholm, a native of Inverness, Scotland. After William's birth George moved to Upper Canada, where he lived until his death in 1842 at the age of ninety-eight. William, who was eulogized later as the 'father, friend and protector of our settlement [Oakville],' fought in the War of 1812 at Detroit and Queenston Heights. After the war he took up land in Nelson Township, Halton County. The following notice in the *Gore Gazette*, 26 May 1827, shows the extent of Chisholm's success even before he established his port in Oakville: 'Notice – The subscriber takes this opportunity of informing his friends and the Public in General in Upper and Lower Canada that he now has four schooners on Lake Ontario viz. the Mohawk Chief ... the Rebecca and Eliza ... the General Brock ... and the Telegraph ... that he has taken every precaution in the selection of sober and industrious men to be Masters and Crew of said Vessels ... [The ships] ... were all built since the year 1822 and they now ply between the head of Lake Ontario, to Kingston and Prescott regularly.'

By August of the following year Chisholm had purchased the land which was to form the town site of Oakville and he issued a warning in the *Gore Gazette*, 18 August 1827: 'Caution – All persons are strictly cautioned not to cut or carry away any timber, or trespass in any manner Whatever, on that tract of land lately purchased by the subscriber from Government lying on the lake shore at the mouth of Sixteen Mile Creek ... Any person or persons who may be found trespassing on said land after this notice will be prosecuted to the utmost extent of the law. Wm. Chisholm.'

Chisholm was responsible for building the Oakville harbour. He built and owned several more sailing vessels, established a farm on his 960 acres, ran a merchant business, represented Halton in Parliament for sixteen years, and was collector of customs at Oakville from 1834 until his death in 1842. His wife was Rebecca Silverthorn, a daughter of the Silverthorns of Cherry Hill in Toronto Township. The Chisholms had seven sons and four daughters. Such was the influence of Colonel William Chisholm that, on his death in 1842, a resident of the town wrote that the colonel 'died a week ago to the day with a fit of the apoplexy in a very few hours sickness let the inhabitants go in mourning from Arthur to Owen Sound ... my hopes are blited and I must wait for fortunes wheel to take another turn.'

When Chisholm purchased the land on which Oakville would be laid out, he was still in residence in Nelson Township. He therefore entrusted the initial planning of the new community to his young

Verandah of the Thomas house, with steps leading to the sleeping loft

Thomas house, Lakeside Park, Navy and Front Streets

and industrious assistant, Merrick Thomas. The house which Thomas built is probably the oldest surviving structure in its original condition in the area.

Thomas was only twenty-five when he undertook the task of supervising the orderly development of Oakville. Since the age of ten he had been forced to make his way alone and as a result had learned a variety of trades in the ensuing years. Merrick's father, Seneca Thomas, was born in Massachusetts in 1774, one of a family whose pioneering ancestors first settled in the American colonies in the 1600s. The outbreak of the War of 1812 found Seneca in Queenston, Upper Canada, employed as a mason at the English fortifications. He immediately fled to join the American forces but was captured and imprisoned on 12 October 1812. That same day his wife died. The younger three of their four children were taken in by relatives in the United States, but Merrick, the eldest at age ten, was left on his own. He made his way to Saltfleet Township in Wentworth County, where he found work with a ship-owner, William Kent, who took young Merrick into his home and trained him in all aspects of his marine business. With this extensive experience in shipping Merrick Thomas was ideally suited to serve as manager for William Chisholm and to draw up plans for the harbour and clear the forested area on which Oakville would be built. Thomas organized the allotment of land and did the initial work on some of the first homes on the site. He married Esther Silverthorn, the sister of Chisholm's wife, Rebecca.

Because her husband's multitude of responsibilities kept him fully occupied, Esther Thomas had to supervise the work on their two-hundred-acre farm. Merrick and Esther had seven children. The Thomas's first home, a simple frame building, has been preserved and moved to a location in Lakeside Park at Navy and Front Streets. It stands beside the original post office, built in 1835, and also moved from its first site. Both buildings, which are under the supervision of the Oakville Historical Society, are open to the public in the summer months.

The house in which Merrick and Esther Thomas lived for the first years of their married life was built in 1829. It was heated only by a fireplace. The children (several died in their youth) slept in the upper loft in the summer months but no doubt all huddled in the small living area in winter. The building contained only two rooms (with loft) – the parents' bedroom and the living-sleeping-cooking-working room.

Thomas's mentor, Colonel William Chisholm, whose interests spread in so many directions, nevertheless died a bankrupt according to family records. After his death, the responsibility for Chisholm's affairs passed to the fourth of William and Rebecca's eleven children, their third surviving son, Robert Kerr Chisholm.

Born in Nelson Township in 1819, Robert was educated in Hamilton. He had been living in Oakville for eight years at the time of his father's death in 1842. Since he had already been serving as deputy customs officer, he was soon confirmed as his father's successor in the customs post. He also replaced the colonel in the management of the post office. In addition, he operated and expanded the family's private interests. The Oakville *Sentinel* of December 1855 contained a notice which detailed an unusual combination of functions: 'R.K. Chisholm / Agent for Provincial Insurance Co / Fire and Marine Risks / Issuer of Marriage licenses.' Another notice announced the completion of the 'Chisholm Brothers New Mill at Oakville' and solicited the 'patronage of the people of this section of the country which it will be their study to deserve.' Robert was also active in community affairs, serving as mayor and reeve of Oakville and of Trafalgar.

In 1856 Robert constructed a new customs-house by the lake at 8 Navy Street, adjacent to Lakeside Park. It replaced a frame building which had previously served that purpose. A red brick building, classical revival in design, the new customs office housed its official operations in the front while the rear portion served as a bank. Almost one-third of the floor space was taken up by two large brick vaults fitted with double iron doors. These vaults were used for the customs and banking operations but they contained as well a more important treasure. During the last century many people in Oakville, aware of the ever-present danger of fire, stored valuable documents and family records in these vaults for safe-keeping. Many of these papers, now of great historical value, were discovered by a Chisholm descendant, Hazel Mathews, when she purchased the building many years later. This find marked the beginning of Mrs Mathews's lifelong study of Oakville and resulted in the publication of her book, *Oakville and the Sixteen*. This work, one of the most comprehensive and well-documented local histories in the province, is a lasting gift to the residents of Oakville.

When, at the age of twenty-three, Robert assumed his father's business responsibilities, he also became the titular head of the family, a position which carried with it the responsibility for his mother and seven younger brothers and sisters. All the Chisholms came to Robert when they had problems (chiefly financial), and nearly all the Chisholms had problems. In 1852 William McKenzie Chisholm, two years Robert's junior, wrote from New York, apologizing for the trouble he had caused his elder brother: 'You I have deeply and grievously offended. For I ask myself where could a parent be found who could treat his or her child with more kindness and generosity than you have done me ... To return to you again is impossible. I shall wait here until I hear from you when I shall leave for England and thence for Australia ... And to my beloved Mother, Brothers and Sisters I would say farewell. And believe – be my life long or short Love for you all shall be the first feeling of my heart. W.M.C.' Six months later William McKenzie Chisholm died in Quebec at the age of thirty-one.

The Chisholm house, Erchless, on the left and the customs-house on the right, 4 and 8 Navy Street

In a letter to Robert his sister Barbara Amanda Chisholm, the wife of Robert Wilson of Whitby, expressed the warm ties all the members of the family felt to their home and to Robert. Barbara, herself a recent bride, spoke of his forthcoming marriage to Flora Matilda Lewis: 'I was very much disappointed at not seeing you last evening, we thought you would surely be down. Why did you not come! Perhaps you intend waiting until you can bring your wife with you. I suppose you are to be married soon ... nothing would give me greater pleasure than to have you and Tilly come and see me ... oh! do. I should like it so much ... Tom says you are very gay in Oakville. I am glad to hear it as it will make it so pleasant for Tilly. Do you still think of having an assembly or have they given it ... dear Robert good night. Write or come soon and believe in your fond sister, Barbara.'

Robert was thirty-eight at the time of the wedding. His bride, to whom Barbara referred in her letter, was nineteen. According to family records, Tilly was 'tiny and favoured elaborate toilettes.' She 'was likened to a little French doll by those who knew her as a young matron.' Prior to their wedding Robert enlarged the small family home and called the new house Erchless. The name was taken from the seat of clan Chisholm in Inverness-shire, Scotland. The stately Georgian building was designed by a master carpenter from Scotland. It is located at 4 Navy Street.

In 1868 two more young members of the Chisholm family died – Robert's brother James Bell Forsyth Chisholm and his sister Barbara Wilson, the author of the loving letter. Barbara was twenty-nine at the time of her death. Her grief-stricken husband wrote poems of mourning in true Victorian style:

I think of thee my darling,
I think of thee at even,
When I see the first and fairest star
Steal peaceful out of heaven

And memories old and tender
Come fresh and fast to me
I mourn for thee my Angel wife
And shall ever mourn for thee.

Robert Wilson never recovered from his wife's death. He was

unable to continue his legal practice, nor was he able to look after Edward and Rebecca, his son and daughter. They therefore became wards of Robert Chisholm. Wilson died eight years to the day after Barbara's death.

Five years later, in 1873, another of the younger Chisholm men, Thomas Charles Chisholm, disappeared while on a trip to New York. He had been faced with bankruptcy as a result of losses in his grain business and was trying to raise money to pay his debts. The family offered a $500 reward for word of his whereabouts. They described Thomas as having a 'sandy complexion, side whiskers and moustache, clean shaven chin.' Finally Robert received a terse telegram from New York City: 'Your brother's remains found in river now in Jersey City Morgue personal effects on body.' Thomas was probably the victim of an assault since a sum of money which he had been carrying was missing from his personal effects. His body was returned to Oakville for burial in the family plot.

29 Thomas Street, the MacDougald home

In 1854 Mary Jane Chisholm, the seventh of the family of Colonel William, became engaged to a young Oakville businessman who had just entered into partnership in a grain-buying business. His name was Peter A. MacDougald. Born of Scottish parents at Port Glasgow in Elgin County, Peter was educated by his father and a Presbyterian minister who was his tutor, and was consequently fluent in Gaelic. Peter started in the dry goods business in St Thomas and moved to Oakville in 1844. By 1854 he had ten years of experience in the mercantile business, and a wide knowledge of the lumber and grain trades. This background served to ensure his survival as a merchant even when his partner, William Romain, went bankrupt.

When he became engaged to Mary Jane Chisholm, MacDougald purchased a small house at 29 Thomas Street. Of frame construction, the house was about fifteen years old when the young couple took possession. As the MacDougald fortunes improved, so did the house. As well as building a one-storey addition that stretched across the rear of their house, the MacDougalds added a verandah and French doors to the original structure. The treillage or trelliswork from that first verandah now forms a grape arbour on the property. In later years a second storey was added, first over the original house and later over the addition at the rear.

MacDougald was active in local politics. He was reeve, warden, and, for many years from 1874 on, mayor of Oakville. Early council records suggest that MacDougald was an ebullient and outspoken man, possibly as a result of an overindulgence in one of the by-products of his grain business. (His death in 1884 was reportedly due to 'congestion of the liver caused by exposure and whiskey.')

On 24 February 1876 the Oakville *Express* reported that at the last council meeting Mayor MacDougald told another council member, Mr Young, that 'Arrogance, Incapacity and Presumption are the leading features of your character. You are an ignorant, arrogant upstart.' The newspaper's editor remarked that this 'frenzy of passion' on Mr MacDougald's part was 'unbecoming any person who claims to be a gentleman.' Obviously Oakville council meetings were rarely dull, for on that same day Mayor MacDougald announced that all of the town's auditors had resigned as a group because council members had gone about making remarks 'derogatory to their characters as private citizens.'

In 1883 MacDougald's store was destroyed in a fire that ravaged most of Oakville's business section. In April 1884 Peter MacDougald disappeared. The tragic event is described in the diary of George Sumner, a member of one of the town's old families and a police constable: 'April 17. The town is in a state of Excitement over the disappearance of P.A. MacDougald. We have had a big search for him. And was found near Mrs. G.K. Chisholm's hanging by the feet head down fast and nearly dead.'

During his business life MacDougald acquired another fine building which, as a commercial structure, enhances the architectural landscape of Oakville today. Known as the Granary, it was first leased by the partners MacDougald and Romain, and then purchased by MacDougald after the break-up of the partnership. Built of Kingston limestone and lake stone brought out by the stone-hookers, the Granary exemplifies the credo that beauty results when 'form follows function.' Its unadorned classical lines produce an aesthetically pleasing building, well suited for its original purpose. It still stands, overlooking the creek, at 103 Robinson Street.

The partners, William F. Romain and Peter MacDougald, married sisters. Romain's wife was Esther Chisholm, the older sister of MacDougald's wife, Mary Jane. In the mid-1850s William and Esther built a pleasant brick house at 40 First Street. It was in this simple, well-proportioned building that they raised the first of their family of six children. Today, however, the original part of the present structure pales in comparison to the elaborate central portion which they added in the 1860s. It has heavy trim under the eaves and above its central window a carved coat-of-arms. In its design a fleur-de-lis represents Romain's French ancestry while a cross of St Andrew represents his union with the Scottish Chisholms. French doors once opened onto a covered verandah which sheltered the front of the house. The slump in the grain market, combined perhaps with the expense of constructing the grandiose addition to the house, caused Romain to declare bankruptcy in 1869, and he was forced to sell the house and its contents. At this point Esther's brother, Thomas Chisholm, came to the rescue by purchasing all the furnishings. This was only four years before he too encountered financial difficulties and disappeared, to be found later in the river at New York.

The cycle of Romain's fortunes turned upward again and he was once more able to establish a business in Oakville. This time he was strictly a merchant. The Oakville *Argus* of 28 April 1876 carried his ad:

Romain house, 40 First Street

Hep Goods
at
W.F. Romain and Cos.
Just received and to be sold at
Half Price
Ready Made Clothing – Buffalo Robes
Cornwall blankets, Grey Ditto, Horse Ditto
Mens and boys caps – Ladies Dress Goods
Groceries
The Cheapest Store in Halton!

Robert Chisholm continued as the benevolent head of the wandering Chisholm family. Not only did he assist his brothers and sisters when the need arose but he seemed to be the one to whom cousins, nephews, and various in-laws turned. The Silverthorn papers contain a letter from Zamer Romain, whose connection was that he was the husband of Robert's cousin Elizabeth Rebecca Silverthorn. He told of his lack of funds: 'Fortunately Robert Chisholm, being advised of my sad position sent me one hundred dollars which I agreed to pay him in January but God only knows how I am to do it.' Robert sent money to his nephew Ted Wilson, son of his sister Barbara. Ted had been wandering in Mexico and Arizona and wrote in thanks 'my Heart is not in the right place, I got it dislocated sleeping under the shadow of fences.'

Although the Chisholm family founded the port of Oakville, it was the shipbuilders and ship's captains who made it a vital centre and magnet for the produce of the area. One of the shipbuilders was Irish-born David Patterson, a skilled artisan with the eye of an artist. Patterson had served an apprenticeship in carpentry before he emigrated to Upper Canada as a qualified craftsman. He was still in his teens when he left his native Ireland. Work in the Chisholm shipyard was readily available for skilled men, and Patterson spent several years there while establishing a home. By 1834 he had purchased land by the lake at Front and Navy Streets. It is probable that the small building which now forms the east wing of his substantial brick dwelling was the first simple structure which David built for his bride, Polly. In 1858, when she was nine, their daughter worked a sampler which is now in the possession of the Oakville Historical Society. It depicts a small building practically identical to the east wing of the Patterson house – the portion which faces the lake. She was no doubt recreating her parents' first home.

Patterson had a good business building houses in response to the increasing demand in his growing community. With his own labour he was able to complete his two-storey house by the late 1830s. This aesthetically pleasing building stands today at 19 Navy Street. It appears on the 1840 and 1841 assessment and census records, which are among the earliest available. It is listed under the category 'frame, brick or stone over two stories.' Although the exterior is brick at present, the building is frame beneath and would have been so at the time of the assessment; the brick veneer was added by the second owner in the latter part of the nineteenth century. Other alterations which have been made to the Patterson homestead over the years (the addition of balconies and dormers) have done nothing to disturb the essential beauty of the building, one of the finest in the area.

The Pattersons' neighbour to the east was Peter McCorquodale, mariner, who was captain and part-owner of the Royal Tar. When David Patterson built his first small house, the McCorquodale family, Peter, his wife, Elizabeth, and their young son, were living in a similar small frame house which in later years was enlarged and stuccoed over. The McCorquodale house, at 143 Front Street, has three dormers which were a later addition. Peter died in 1850 at the age of forty-three of 'inflamation of the lungs.' In his will McCorquodale had made provision for such an untimely event, leaving all his estate to his wife, Elizabeth, unless she should remarry, in which case the three oldest boys were to take charge and make sure the younger children had 'a good english education.' His obituary in the Oakville Sun, 7 September 1850, noted that McCorquodale 'died as he lived beloved and esteemed by all ... and after sailing through this tempestuous world with ardour and integrity has now cast anchor in that haven from whence no traveller returneth.'

After the passing of the United States fugitive slave law in 1850, many slaves escaped to Canada where they could be free. Their escape was no simple matter, sometimes taking the form of concealment in a packing case. The slaves were assisted by a wide circle of men devoted to their cause and the term 'Underground Railroad' described this ubiquitous group. In many cases slaves were assisted by the lake captains, who smuggled them to safety hidden in their cargo. Oakville became a temporary haven for these black Americans because of sympathetic men among its numerous ship's cap-

The early portion of the Patterson house, 19 Navy Street
The later addition

tains and also because of the presence in Oakville of James Wesley Hill, himself an escaped slave. Hill, who found employment and support when he reached Oakville, stayed to settle on the ninth line (457 Maplegrove). His house became a way-station for the fugitives.

Captain Robert Wilson of Oakville was another who earned the gratitude of many American blacks for his part in the Underground Railroad. Robert and his brother William were both lake captains, listed in the 1857 *Canada Directory* as among the fifteen mariners operating out of the thriving port at the time. Robert and William settled in Oakville in the 1830s. Robert's home, at the corner of King and Navy Streets, has been much altered. Originally a single-storey building, it was converted into a two-storey structure at some point after 1847, for in that year the assessment rolls show Robert Wilson to be living in a single-storey frame house and owning 'one milch cow.' William Wilson lived next door, a happy arrangement since the two Wilson wives were sisters. When they reached middle age, however, both families moved to more spacious homes. Robert called his new dwelling at 311 Trafalgar Road Mariners Home. William built the handsome brick house at 390 Lakeshore Road East. The William Wilson house has a side-hall entry and hip roof. The fine interior detailing is in perfect scale with the size of the house. David and Suzanne Peacock in *Old Oakville* have noted that the Wilson brothers probably employed the same builder for their homes, as the hardware which was installed in William's house was actually intended for Mariners Home. Captain Robert was away at the time and discovered only at the end of his voyage that the mistake had been made.

When the American Civil War came to an end, blacks from all over western Ontario assembled in Oakville each year to celebrate Emancipation Day. It is reported that after a picnic in George's Square on Trafalgar Road many of those who had been assisted by Captain Robert walked the short distance to his home to pay their respects. Here at Mariners Home Wilson housed sick and homeless sailors. A man who adhered strictly to his principles (he would never sail on the Sabbath), Wilson was well loved. On the occasion of his fiftieth wedding anniversary he was presented with a gold-headed cane inscribed 'presented by his sailor friends, 1881.'

Melancthon Simpson and his brother John were responsible for

390 Lakeshore Road East, the William Wilson house

building some of the finest and most colourful vessels launched from the port at Oakville – bright trim and exquisitely carved figure-heads were a mark of their work. Tradition held that all vessels launched at the port must comply with the practice of having that ceremony take place at twelve o'clock noon. Excitement always reigned as the hour approached and, according to the diary of John Aikman Williams, a local resident and shopkeeper, 'quite a bit of whiskey was launched down the necks of those who came to town for amusement.' The era of shipbuilding in which the Simpson brothers prospered lasted for more than half a century. At that time, again according to Williams, 'Navy Street was expected to be the business street as steam boats were loaded constantly with freight and passengers. 'Grain which had been brought down in wagons filled the storehouses at Oakville, awaiting shipment to other ports on the lake and on down the St Lawrence in fleets of vessels built and owned at Oakville.

Regency cottage of Melancthon Simpson, 235 Trafalgar Road

At the height of the shipbuilding boom Melancthon Simpson and his wife lived in a graceful Regency cottage at 235 Trafalgar Road. It is uncertain whether Simpson built or bought this house, but it does bear indications of his occupation. Certain techniques used in its construction are common to those employed in shipbuilding. Simpson acquired the property in 1846, two years before his marriage to Esther Louisa Terry. In 1858 the house was sold. Melancthon and Esther left Oakville when the days of the shipping era were over.

The Simpson brothers were caught in the crash which occurred as a result of the construction of the railroads. Because it was easier to ship by rail, shipowners, builders, and captains found that their livelihood had disappeared. Williams, commenting on the many bankruptcies, states: 'Captains who had put their all in ships, mortgaging them for large balances expecting to pay all off in two or three seasons (freight being high and no end of grain pouring down ... from Owen Sound),' were the victims along with the owners. 'Suddenly

George King Chisholm's house, 85 Navy Street

the railroad from Toronto to Sarnia through Georgetown and other feeders of lake Ontario traffic' left the Oakville warehouses half empty. Today the maritime tradition of Oakville continues: it is now one of the leading yacht-building centres on the continent.

A short distance north of Erchless and the Customs House at 85 Navy Street is the home of Robert Chisholm's older brother, George King Chisholm, one of the family who seemingly needed no help, financial or otherwise. George, born in 1814, was educated at Upper Canada College. Much of his life was spent in politics. He was reeve of Trafalgar Township and mayor of Oakville, and in 1854 he was elected a member of Parliament. As was usual at the time, the heat of elections prompted many letters and much name-calling in the local papers. It is obvious that George Chisholm had been subjected to his full share of abuse during the recent campaign, for the following letter appeared over his signature in the *Hamilton Spectator* of 13 January 1855: 'To all who were cognizant of the policy adopted towards me during the late election in Halton by Mr. White and his friends; to those who witnessed his wailing and gnashing of teeth towards me and all my connexions; to those who have since heard his threat that he would follow me and mine to the day of my death for revenge; to all such it will be a matter of surprise that his open attacks have been so long deferred.'

George and his wife, Isabella Land, grandaughter of the founder of Hamilton, built their Regency-style cottage on Navy Street in the late 1840s. They lived there until 1857 when they moved to a larger home on a farm just west of Oakville. Like his brother Robert, George raised a family of four sons and a daughter. He died in April 1874, only a month after the discovery of his brother Tom's body in New York.

Meanwhile the head of the Chisholm family was still coping with the plights of errant family members. Probably one of the most imaginative of the requests for money Robert received came from his cousin William McKenzie King, the son of Robert's aunt Barbara. William's devious letter, written in 1845 when he was thirty-four years old, gives some insight into his character. Writing from New York he said:

Dear Robert,
I am ruined not worth a rap in debt for my board. Send me some money [details of selling some property]. Bad off as I am I would not come to you

only that you may as well profit by weakness or follies as any body else and I am sure that you can make a hundred dollars or so ... lot No. 4 in block 53 is yours make the deed and record it. In all this I mean what I say, act accordingly. You have seen me for the last time in life perchance you may hear of my death, but I am going very distant to spend the remnant of my days. It is a misfortune to have weak friends whom we cannot help loving even in their follies, I am weak foolish mad always have been to all the things that pertain to life and usefulness personally ... If not the world at least to me death will make clear the mystery, I wait for it. What you do, do quickly, for I am in a strait ... My brain is on fire to give way to the rush of feelings that oppress me but it cannot be, twould only make you weep when strength is needed. Don't spare me in your answer. Speak your mind plainly I desire. Yours truly, W.M. King.

Perhaps Robert did speak his mind. Certainly, in spite of King's assurance that 'you have seen me for the last time in life,' this was not the case. He lived on for another thirty-four years after penning this sorrowful missive. His wanderings took him to California in seach of gold and on whaling expeditions. In all, this intrepid traveller is said to have circled the globe three times, after which he turned up again in Oakville, where he established a newspaper, the *Oakville Advertiser*.

In 1858 William King purchased land (south half of lot 16, concession 2 South of Dundas Street, Trafalgar) from his cousin Robert Chisholm. Here he built a picturesque and striking neo-Gothic villa which was immediately dubbed 'King's Castle.' The house, with steep-pitched roof and high pointed gables, was patterned after the country houses and cottage residences found in architectural pattern books of the time. These villas were considered suitable for gentlemen of refinement and taste, which is no doubt exactly how King saw himself. Misfortune, however, stayed with him. He was forced to sell the house in the following year to none other than his cousin Robert, who, in turn, sold it to his brother Thomas. In 1871 the property was purchased by Richard Postans who established vineyards there. The King house at 21 Regency Court is a striking building, its steep gables the dominating feature. It has been named a historic building under the Ontario Heritage Act. King would have been proud.

William King's turbulent life was mentioned by shopkeeper Williams, who summed up the latter part of King's career succinctly.

He 'built a castle intending to marry rich young lady – failed, married housekeeper. He edited newspaper for awhile, failed, his aunt Mrs. Barnett Griggs left him hotel on Navy Street, got through it by gambling and becoming destitute, no credit, no money, no hope and died refusing help R.K.C. [Robert] offered but his wife accepted with thanks.'

A notice published by King after a celebration of the Queen's birthday one year shows that he was not unwilling to take a stand on a matter of principle. Protesting the expense of the celebration, he stated:

There are many in this Town, County and Province who respect Her Majesty in common with other women, as the mother of a family and for her domestic virtues, but for nothing else, because she has earned no title to further distinction.

There are many English women whose claims to have their birthday's

'King's Castle,' 21 Regency Court

celebrated because of the good they have done to their fellow-creatures, are infinitely greater than Her Majesty's.

... Many of us desire to enter our public protest against the action of Town Council – the same Council which not long since refused to grant $20 towards the sustenance of a helpless bed-ridden old woman – in granting $40 to defray the expense of a useless demonstration beginning and ending in smoke.

The road which led from Oakville past King's Castle was considered to be a great boon to the district when it was built in mid-century by George King Chisholm and other local entrepreneurs. Known as the 'plank road,' it was built as a result of increased demand for a road by farmers anxious to get their grain to market, some from as far away as Owen Sound. Although primitive by today's standards, plank roads were an improvement over the bone-jarring corduroy roads which preceeded them. Constructed of three-inch boards placed across the road bed, the ends on sleepers imbedded in the earth, plank roads were built without the use of nails. The weight of the planks was sufficient to keep them in place. Then, as now, roads cost money. To help pay for the construction of the plank road and its maintenance toll-gates were built every few miles along the route from Oakville to Fergus.

The toll-gate situated at the junction of the plank road and the Dundas (Trafalgar) Road was operated by a Scotsman, Donald Campbell. His house stands nearby at 293 MacDonald Road. A member of the Argyll and Sutherland Highlanders, Campbell was sent on duty to Upper Canada during the period before the Mackenzie rebellion. He stayed to settle in Oakville and spent most of his life working as a tailor as well as serving as a toll-gate operator.

Campbell built his house about 1857, only a year or so before William King erected his Castle, but the two buildings differ radically. Campbell's home is a simple brick structure, not built to impress but managing nevertheless to do so by virtue of its dignity. Stone was used for the sides and rear of the first storey but the remainder of the house is faced with brick. So that it would have its best face foreward, the front façade of the house has brick laid in Flemish bond.

Campbell lived in his house until his death in 1882. He and his wife, Jane Laing, raised three daughters, and their descendants occupied the Campbell house for more than one hundred years. The

Campbells' oldest daughter, Jane Ann, taught school in Oakville for many years. On 16 March 1876 the *Oakville Express* carried on its front page the February results from Miss Campbell's classroom. Only the highest and lowest marks were mentioned:

Arithmetic Sr.	M. Patterson, highest	– 100
	W. King, lowest	– 19
Geography Sr.	M. Patterson, highest	– 99
	W. King, lowest	– 11

In similar fashion the triumphs and failures in every subject were published for the whole town to read. Whether young W. King was the son of ill-fated William McKenzie King is not known – somehow it seems likely.

The events of the late 1830s which were the cause of Donald Campbell's coming to Upper Canada were felt in Oakville as else-

Home of toll-gate keeper Donald Campbell, 293 MacDonald Road

where. Williams recorded in his diary what the rebellion meant to a child: 'Us boys used to see the soldiers riding and marching thro town and going thro the drill down on the lake ... We had our drill too and rode on stiles for horses and got sharp pieces of tin on the end of sticks for lances. A blind man lived in the log house ... at the creek bank ... who could whittle axe handles to make a living. He contracted to whittle wooden muskets for toys for 7½ pence – the rebels might have taken the town had it depended on our company.' The times were hard when Campbell arrived in Oakville. 'Money was scarce,' noted Williams, 'and debts were uncollectable, even the brass coppers were scarce and change very limited indeed. To remedy this want the business men issued shin plasters from 12½ cents to 50 cents ... they passed all right in the immediate neighbourhood.'

Another of the many Scots who settled in the village was John Gallie, who with his wife, Catherine McKay, lived in the small frame

Gallie house, 307 William Street

cottage at 307 William Street. The workmanship on the building is particularly fine, with interesting detail, the result, no doubt, of the fact that its owner, Gallie, was also the builder. Gallie was a contractor who purchased the property in 1854 and began work on the building shortly thereafter. The census of 1861 shows that the Gallie family consisted of John and Catherine, three young children, and one horse and a cow. Their taxes for the year amounted to four dollars. Gallie may not have completed all the work on his house by that point, since time-consuming hand-work was involved.

John Gallie possessed a rich baritone voice. For many years he led the singing in the Presbyterian church, using a tuning fork in the days before organs were common. He and his wife lived to celebrate their golden wedding anniversary. One of their grandsons, William Edward Gallie, became a world-renowned surgeon, one of the most honoured doctors in Canadian history. His students, who revered him, met annually for many years to express their gratitude. They

75 Reynolds Street, home of carpenter James Connor

called themselves 'the Gallie slaves.' Today at the University of Toronto the Gallie course in surgery commemmorates his name.

Although the names of Oakville's Scottish pioneers seem to dominate the shipbuilding industry, the town had more settlers from Ireland than from any other country. James Connor, a carpenter, was one of the Irishmen who arrived before the middle of the nineteenth century. Early in the 1850s Connor designed and built his own gracious home at 75 Reynolds Street. As in the case of the Gallie house, it is evident that particular care was taken in finishing it. The interior trim is of a calibre usually found in larger, more elaborate buildings. The finely carved front door, transom, and exterior trim are evidence of Connor's skill.

Connor and his wife Catherine raised a family of seven children in the house, and their descendants lived there until the 1960s. Two of the Connor sons became carpenters and went into business with their father. It was fortunate that the house contained so many resident carpenters for, according to family legend, it was necessary at one point to remove part of the south wall when one of the sons built a boat in the large upper room and was unable to get it out.

The Connor family attended St Andrew's Roman Catholic Church, a handsome frame building which stands at 47 Reynolds Street, a short distance south of their house. Built in 1840, it is the oldest church building in Oakville, its construction made possible by donations of time, talent, and money by the many Catholics in the area. The land on which St Andrew's stands was donated to the parish by Colonel Chisholm, and it is believed that other Scottish Presbyterians assisted their Catholic brethren as well. The church, it is said, was named after Scotland's patron saint as a gesture of thanks for their generosity.

Before their church was built, Catholic families were served by itinerant priests whose visits were, at best, sporadic. Dean Harris in *The Catholic Church in the Niagara Peninsula* has described how a typical mass was conducted: 'A priest carrying vestments, altar stone, wine and altar breads on horseback arrived in the clearing the night before. The following morning he arose early, placed a table on four chairs, put the altar stone theron, covering it with three linen altar cloths. He then nailed the crucifix to the wall ... and after hearing the confessions of the people blessed the house ... Many times the ceilings were so low that the priest was obliged to offer up the Holy Sacrifice in a bending position ... During this time dinner was being prepared on the hearth (houses generally one room). The priest announced another station some fourteen miles further west and thus, from week to week, in pelting rain, over swollen streams, across fallen timber, he pursued his journey for months.'

While St Andrew's was still being built in the 1840s, Williams in his diary records his mental picture of the first Catholic priest 'conversing in front of Michael O'Loughlin's Tailor Shop' while 'passing snuff box to two or three people.' A sight of a far more startling sort concerned the construction of St Andrew's belfry, described in an undated note in the Oakville Museum: 'When building St. Andrew's belfry John Cavin, father of Martin Cavin, a carpenter, gave freely of his time and labour to help erect the church and was engaged high up when the rope that went through the ... pulley was let loose by some incompetent workman at noon hour and the wind blew it over to where Mr. Wm. Davis now lives. With quick thought and presence of mind he took off his stocking, unravelled it, let it down and the ground men tied the rope to it. John was soon down for dinner.'

When the church was built, it had seating capacity for two hundred people. A growing congregation during the next thirty years necessitated an extension to the nave in 1870. It was probably at this time that the original frame siding was covered with roughcast stucco and the ornately carved altars added – these the work of carpenter James Connor.

In 1832 Matthew Barclay brought his family from Paisley, Scotland, to settle on a farm near Oakville. Twenty-five years later the Barclays moved into town. Matthew, then seventy-four years old, purchased land and built his two-storey frame house at 215 William Street. He enjoyed his new home for ten years, as he lived until the age of eighty-four. Although early Presbyterian church records mention that the Barclays had ten children, Matthew's will mentions only seven, so it seems likely that three of his family predeceased him. To his daughter Mary Jane he left only one dollar, and the remainder of the estate was divided among his wife and the other six children.

After his mother's death in 1881 John Barclay, his wife, and their six children moved into the family home. Like his parents, John was a Presbyterian. He was also active in civic affairs, serving as councillor for fifteen years, then as reeve, and later as mayor. In 1875,

St Andrew's Roman Catholic Church, 47 Reynolds Street

when Peter MacDougald occupied the mayor's chair, Councillor Barclay took part in one of the stormy sessions for which the Oakville town council was renowned.

True to his Presbyterian beliefs, Barclay introduced a motion aimed at curtailing billiards. This was seconded by Mr McCraney. Both gentlemen declared that billiards, 'however harmless in themselves, when in juxtaposition with liquor selling ... were exceedingly baneful.' Added McCraney: 'billiards as existing in the town exert a most demoralizing effect upon the youth of our country upon whom its future prosperity entirely depended.' These sentiments proved too much for a Mr Boon, who remarked that he had seen both Barclay and McCraney drinking beer and even liquor at dinner, and he challenged McCraney's claim that 'one billiard saloon promoted more drinking than many hotels.' Warming to his topic, Boon continued the attack, saying to McCraney: 'You drank whiskey. You said you could not do without it.' McCraney adroitly sidestepped the issue by retorting: 'I never drank a glass of liquor with you in my life.' In its report of the proceedings, the *Oakville Express* stated that 'Mr. Barclay moved the third reading of the by-law, ignoring Mr Boon's allegations that he [Barclay] had drunk beer within the last two months.' It is not surprising that John Barclay served for so many years on the council – It was undoubtedly the best entertainment in town!

3

Trafalgar Village
to Waterdown

'How we escaped here, is to me almost a miracle. I had resided long in the district, and was known by everybody.' With these words, written in his journal from the safety of the American shore, William Lyon Mackenzie described his five-day flight from Toronto to Niagara in December 1837. With Montgomery's tavern in flames, the rebels and the militia in disarray, Mackenzie began a hazardous journey which took him through five townships. And his escape was indeed a 'miracle,' achieved mainly through the support that he received from friends along the way. They hid him, disguised him, fed him, and provided him with horses, all at great personal risk. Mackenzie escaped because he knew precisely who was with him and who was not. Some who aided him were captured and imprisoned. Some died as a result of their efforts on his behalf. Of these loyal supporters Mackenzie remarked: 'I had risked much for Canadians, and served them long, and as faithfully as I could – and now, when a fugitive, I found them ready to risk life and property to aid me – far more ready to risk the dungeon, by harbouring me, than to accept Sir Francis Head's thousand pounds [the reward for his capture].'

Details of Mackenzie's escape from Toronto are contained in a biography written by his son-in-law, Charles Lindsey, an account which uses the rebel leader's own journal entries in describing those five perilous days. The difficulty which Lindsey encountered (and one which has frustrated historians ever since) was that Mackenzie did not name those who helped him for fear of incriminating them. Lindsey did add in an editor's note the names that he felt it was safe to reveal when the book was published in 1862. The difficulty which arises almost one hundred and fifty years after the rebellion is that, in the interim, legend has grown and flourished. Had Mackenzie sought refuge at every place where legend claims he did, his journey would have taken five weeks instead of five days. It is possible, however, to confirm some of these stories and to accept others with a fair degree of certainty. As for the rest, it can be assumed that some, but definitely not all, have a degree of truth in them. There remain today three buildings near Dundas Street that have either definite or tenuous connections with the story of Mackenzie's escape. In any event, all are worthy of mention. As Winston Churchill once said in reference to an apocryphal story: 'If it didn't happen; it should have.'

On the night of Thursday, 7 December 1837, with the rebellion an obvious failure, some of the rebels were anxious to fight on. Mackenzie assured one of the men that 'it was too late to retrieve our loss in that way, and bade him to tell them to scatter ... At the Golden Line, ten miles above the city, I overtook Colonel Anthony Van Egmond, a Dutch officer, of many years experience under Napoleon. He agreed with me that we should at once make for the Niagara frontier, but was taken almost immediately after.' The colonel died in jail. Proceeding with the plan to head for Niagara, Mackenzie travelled through Vaughan Township, where he was given supper by a local farmer, and then set off in a southerly direction. By two o'clock the next morning Mackenzie, with sixteen of his men, reached 'the hospitable mansion of a worthy settler on Dundas Street, utterly exhausted with cold and fatigue.' According to Lindsey's note, this was the home (no longer standing) in Peel County of Absalom Wilcox, whose son Allan accompanied Mackenzie for most of the journey to Niagara. Here some rest was possible: 'Blankets were hung over the windows to avoid suspicion, food and beds prepared, and while the Tories were carefully searching for us, we were sleeping soundly.'

Mackenzie and his men then decided to separate and proceed to Niagara in pairs. From the Wilcox house Mackenzie and young Allan headed west towards Streetsville, where they received help at Comfort's Mills. After seeing the two men fed, Mr Comfort left with them to assist their departure. He helped them in every way that he could, although he had not taken part in the rebellion prior to this time and knew 'nothing of the intended revolt.' His parting words were: 'Good-bye wife, perhaps I may never see you again' – words that proved prophetic, for Comfort was captured after leaving Mackenzie and jailed in Toronto. Government troops later raided the

Comfort's home. Lindsey's note elaborates. Mrs Comfort, then pregnant, had fainted at the sight of the raiding party and been carried to bed. 'One brute cocked a pistol, and placing it at her breast, threatened to shoot her through, if she did not tell all she knew ... They then threw pails of cold water on her in bed. This revolting treatment led to premature confinement, resulting in her death.' Comfort's Mills, now the McCarthy Milling Company, still operates as a flour mill at Barbertown, near Streetsville.

Proceeding down the Streetsville Road, Mackenzie and Wilcox escaped notice although, as they turned west on Dundas Street, 'it was broad daylight [and there were] bills duly posted for my apprehension.' It was not until they approached the Sixteen Mile Creek – so named for its distance from the western end of Lake Ontario – that they encountered trouble and were forced to leave the road with the militia in hot pursuit. 'There was but one chance for escape,' Mackenzie recalled, 'surrounded as we were ... and that was to stem the stream and cross the swollen creek. We accordingly stripped ourselves naked, and with the surface ice beating against us, and holding our garments over our heads, in a bitter cold December night, buffeted the current and were soon up to our necks ... The cold in that stream caused me the most cruel and intense sensation of pain I ever endured.' Continuing westward, the pair found sanctuary an hour and a half later 'under the hospitable roof of one of the innumerable agricultural friends I could then count in the country.'

A well-known legend in Halton County relates that this 'agricultural friend' was Philip Triller, an early resident in the area, who owned a mill at Proudfoot Hollow, a hamlet that grew up by the Sixteen Mile Creek at Dundas Street. Today nothing remains of the mill or the houses that once stood there but the legend lives on. Questions arise, however, when land titles are searched, for Triller owned two lots east of the river, whereas Mackenzie's benefactor lived to the west. However, since the Triller family intermarried with the Howells and the Bucks, both of whom owned land west of the river, there could well be a grain of truth in the story. As the legend tells it, the short and stocky Mackenzie disguised himself in women's clothes and escaped from a second-floor window.

While variations of this legend are recounted at many places along Mackenzie's escape route, his journal makes no mention of any such event. Instead, it suggests that the next stop after fording the creek was at the home of a Nelson Township farmer, and that his 'agricultural friend' lived there and not at Proudfoot Hollow. Today two houses that stand near Dundas Street have become part of the Mackenzie legend, for either one could well have been the home of the Nelson farmer to whom the rebel leader expressed such gratitude.

The first of these houses, on lot 10, concession 1 North of Dundas Street (NDS), was the home of Thomas Alton, his wife, Charlotte Cleaver, and their sixteen children. Through her aunt, Philadelphia Hughes Lount, Charlotte was connected to the Lount family of Aurora and to Samuel Lount, who, with Peter Mathews, was hanged for the part he played in the rebellion. This relationship may explain why Mackenzie is thought to have received help at the Alton's home. According to family lore, the Alton and Cleaver men met a party of Tories in search of Mackenzie and, with their guns at the ready, ordered the militia off the property.

The Alton house stands on land purchased by Thomas and Charlotte in 1830, part of the holdings of her father, John Cleaver. The

Alton house, lot 10, concession 1 NDS, Nelson

foundations for a small log house have been found in front of the present building, suggesting that they first lived there and then, as the family grew and grew, the red brick house was built to provide accommodation for all of them. A kitchen wing projected to the rear of the brick house, and it and the front of the house were protected by verandahs. Fortunately these original verandahs survive to this day, their ornate treillage intact. So does the bell tower which summoned the family from the surrounding fields. Because the farm has always been owned by descendants of the Altons, many records remain, among them an early photograph which shows the Alton women hard at work milking the cows while the Alton men look on. No doubt they were making sure that the job was done properly.

When he died at the age of seventy-seven, Thomas Alton left Charlotte $100, all the furniture, and also certain rooms in the homestead that had been designated in a prior document. Then, after bequests to his children and grandchildren, Alton directed that any beneficiary who disputed the will should automatically forfeit his share, thereby ensuring that dissension would be stopped before it started.

Another candidate for the role of Mackenzie's 'agricultural friend' was David Reynolds Springer, the Alton's neighbour to the west (lot 17, concession 1 NDS, Nelson). Well-known as a Reformer, Springer arrived in Nelson Township two years before the rebellion and purchased land near the village of Nelson, although when he arrived the village was known as Hannahsville. Here he built a home for his bride, Susannah Thomson, and his four children from a previous marriage. Springer's first wife, Sarah Horning, had died the year before.

For a few years David and Susannah probably lived in a small stone house on the property before they built the imposing dressed-stone house that stands today on the north side of the Dundas. It is probably the first home that forms the rear wing of the present building, a spacious and well-proportioned structure where they lived until David's death in 1889.

The history of the Springer family can be traced back to David's grandfather, a Methodist minister and circuit-rider from New York State. His name was also David Springer. He was killed during the Revolutionary War, after which his widow, with their three sons and five daughters, came to Canada, settling near Hamilton. One of the sons, Richard Springer, married Sarah Boyce (or Brice) and, according to The *Historical Atlas of Halton County* of 1877, they produced ten children, 'all of whom are representatives of large families to bless and honor our loved Dominion of Canada.' Loyalist records differ in several respects from the Springer history outlined in the atlas, but both agree that David Reynolds Springer was one of Richard and Sarah's sons.

For thirty-five years David Springer served as a justice of the peace, a position which might well have kept him from offering refuge to the fugitive Mackenzie, in spite of his Reformer sympathies. The Springer family often welcomed travelling Methodist preachers, for David, like his father and grandfather, was a devout member of that faith and was instrumental in founding the little Methodist church just east of his home.

According to the atlas, Springer was the father of three sons and three daughters, two of these children presumably from his second

Springer house, lot 17, concession 1 NDS, Nelson

marriage. In his will, however, only the daughters are mentioned. Possibly his sons had already received their inheritance. To his wife Susannah he left a house in Waterdown, as well as a horse, buggy, sleigh and harness, and, in a codicil, the sum of $300 so that she might erect a monument to herself and to him.

Mackenzie's connection with the Springer and Alton families is tenuous for his journal suggests that he and his friends turned south before they ever reached the village of Hannahsville. However, Mackenzie may have been trying to protect his friends. After a few hours of needed sleep at the home of his Nelson Township friend, Mackenzie stated that they crossed the Twelve Mile Creek at about midnight on Friday, 8 December, and headed south towards Burlington, a village then called Wellington Square. If such was the case, Mackenzie may well have hidden for a time in a cave by that creek, a story that is heard repeatedly, both in this area and in other districts.

An unusual incident occurred in 1928 that gave credence to the cave legend. In that year George Atkins, the owner of a farm known as Woodlands (lot 31, concession 2 South of Dundas Street [SDS], Trafalgar), was visited by an elderly woman who claimed that her father-in-law had hidden with Mackenzie in a cave on that property. At the time of the rebellion this land was owned by the William Bates family. Although frail, the visitor insisted on going to the cave and crawling into it on her hands and knees. Upon her return to the house, she wrote an affidavit stating that:

The undersigned, Mary Davidson, nee McDonnell or McDonald was born on Calumet Island, Que. Feby.7, 1845, and am now residing at 100 Westminster Avenue, Toronto, Ont. My father, Alexander Bain McDonnell was the son of Duncan McDonnell of Clan John of Johns of Inverness, Scotland. My husband, Jacob Davidson was the son of John Davidson of the Middle Road, Fishers Corners, Nelson Township, Halton County, Ont. John Davidson, aforesaid, was Commisary officer in the Rebellion of 1837 under William Lyon MacKenzie and accompanied MacKenzie on his flight through Trafalgar and Nelson Townships and during his stay in the cave now existing on the bank of the Twelve Mile Creek on the Woodlands, former house of John White, M P at Merton, Trafalgar Township.

Mary McDonald

Merton, June 10, 1928
Witness: George Chew Atkins

The cave story is a good one, and may be true, but, unfortunately Mackenzie in his journal made no mention whatsoever of a cave. If indeed he and his companion did take refuge in such a place, even for a short time, it is surprising that he failed to say so since it is not an event that would easily be forgotten. The legend, however, lives on. Even Mackenzie's grandson, W.L. Mackenzie King, knew it, and on 18 July 1936 he wrote of the cave to Atkins, the owner of Woodlands. The prime minister adroitly managed to avoid involving himself in any possible controversy, stating that 'it [is] inadvisable for me to appear to either suggest or endorse anything which is so immediately related to the life of my own grandfather ... I have often heard of the cave in the vicinity of Dundas, and, some day, I hope I may have the pleasure of viewing it in company with yourself.'

It was early Saturday morning when a cold and weary Mackenzie reached Burlington. Proceeding from the home of one trusted friend

Woodlands, lot 31, concession 2 SDS, Trafalgar

to another, he arrived at the town of Dundas that night and then went on to Hamilton, hoping to find his friend Lewis Horning. As Horning was away (a fact which tallies with the Horning family records), Mackenzie left for Ancaster, where he obtained a fresh horse from another supporter, Jacob Rymal. By Monday, 11 December, Mackenzie had reached safety in the United States, and there he remained for more than eleven years, returning under the Act of Amnesty in 1849.

In later years Mackenzie came to regret the hardships that he had caused his supporters and with the wisdom of hindsight he remarked: 'I have long been sensible of the error committed during that period ... No punishment that power could inflict, or nature sustain, would have equalled the regrets I have felt on account of much that I did, said, wrote and published.' Yet he had fought for justice and done so courageously. While his methods were sometimes questionable, his sincerity was not. Egerton Ryerson, with whom Mackenzie often disagreed, later spoke of him with insight and compassion, observing of him: 'Every evil which he discerned was in his estimation truly an evil and all evils were of equal magnitude ... He felt a longing desire to right wrongs which he saw everywhere around him. This therefore, constituted, as he believed, his mission as a public man in Canada.'

In spite of these flaws in his character, Mackenzie obviously had qualities which engendered fierce loyalty in his followers. Undoubtedly his determination and commitment were leavened with a sense of humour, a quality that Allan Wilcox discovered after that first night on the flight from Toronto, when the rebel leader took refuge in the Wilcox home. Before they left for Streetsville and Comfort's Mills, Wilcox brought Mackenzie a bowl of warm water for shaving. The younger man later recalled: 'He stood before the mirror, his bare neck ready for the lather. Looking in the glass, he turned his head from side to side, projecting his chin and said to me: "Allan, I am told they are offering a thousand dollars reward for that neck. I don't think it's worth it, do you?"'

Mackenzie's escape route across Halton County had taken him through the townships of Trafalgar and Nelson, both of which were named in honour of Horatio Nelson, Britain's most famous admiral and hero of the Battle of Trafalgar in 1805. He was also commemorated in the villages of Bronte (Nelson was the Duke of Bronté), Nelson, Palermo (after his Mediterranean headquarters in Sicily), and Trafalgar. Bronte, on the shore of Lake Ontario, still exists, but of the other three places little remains, only a few scattered buildings marking the crossroads that were once the hub of these small but bustling communities.

The village of Trafalgar, on Dundas Street north of Oakville, was for many years the home of an Irishman, James Appelbe, owner of a store and the local post office. Behind the store was his house, a pleasant stucco dwelling that can still be seen on the north side of the Dundas (lot 13, concession 1 NDS, Trafalgar). Appelbe, who owned most of the land in the village, built his house during the 1850s. His life was seemingly uneventful except for a brief foray into the world of politics, a career that lasted for all of four days.

Squire Appelbe began and ended his political life when he was in his late sixties. Becoming a candidate in a provincial election required that Appelbe resign as postmaster at Trafalgar, and this he did in a letter to Sir Alexander Campbell, postmaster-general, on 11 March

Appelbe house, lot 13, concession 1 NDS, Trafalgar

1871, requesting at the same time that his son John be appointed to the position. For some reason Appelbe changed his mind about running for office almost immediately, and thus four days later, in both a letter and a telegram to Campbell, he withdrew his resignation. This was not easily done, however, for there were political ramifications which became evident when Campbell received a letter, dated 10 April, from John Sandfield Macdonald, first premier of Ontario and a man who believed in 'supporting his supporters.' In his letter he said: 'My dear Campbell ... It would be a most dangerous practice to allow a party to go back to an office which he had vacated for the purpose of furthering himself in antagonism to the government.' The unfortunate Appelbe's position as postmaster was eventually restored to him when fifty-eight local citizens submitted a petition on his behalf and the authorities decided that, although he had planned to run as an independent, Appelbe had not actually worked against the government. He lived for another seven years,

Lot 20, concession 1 SDS, Trafalgar

presumably serving his community loyally as postmaster during this time.

Just west of the Appelbe house, at 502 Dundas Street, is a white frame house that was undoubtedly standing there when William Lyon Mackenzie passed by during his flight to Niagara. The property (lot 20, concession 1 SDS, Trafalgar) was owned successively by three of the early families who settled near the vanished village of Proudfoot Hollow. Amos Biggar, who purchased the lot in 1815, is probably the man who built the central portion of the house, for its narrow clapboard suggests an early date. The house was later enlarged, possibly by its next owner, Philip L. Box, who bought the farm in 1843 and sold it ten years later to Jonathan Pettit. While its history is somewhat obscure, this attractive house is undoubtedly one of the oldest buildings in the area and it remains in remarkably good condition.

The village of Palermo, to the west of Proudfoot Hollow, was initially named Hagerstown after its first settler, Lawrence Hager. It later achieved recognition as the location of a foundry established in the early 1840s by Jacob Lawrence and later enlarged by his son, W.A. Lawrence. The business flourished and was described in the 1877 *Historical Atlas of Halton County* as 'an extensive foundry and agricultural business' producing 'reaping machines and other farm implements' which were widely known. Perhaps the firm's success was in part the result of the younger Lawrence's promotional efforts, which were outlined in a local newspaper: 'Mr W.A. Lawrence of Palermo Agricultural Works is preparing BIG GUNS in the way of various agricultural implements for the coming season. His gentlemanly and somewhat ponderous agent, Mr Jos. Long, is giving his chin a rest so that he will be prepared to explain the many excellent qualities of the PALERMO HARVESTER when the proper time arrives.'

On the north side of Dundas Street (lot 29, concession 1 NDS, Trafalgar) stands a frame house that was owned by Jacob Lawrence for the ten years before his death. The house, which is notable for its fine door framed by sidelights and a fan transom, attracts notice from present-day travellers along the Dundas. It is possible that the house was built by William Proud, who purchased the property in 1830, or by his descendants, from whom Lawrence bought it in 1865.

In his will, Lawrence left his wife Eliza all his effects, mentioning that she must always have a portion of the house for her use, even if either of their two younger sons found it necessary to move into the house himself. These same sons were required to provide their mother with a horse 'when she may require it,' a fortunate inclusion since the will left her only a buggy.

As one of his executors Lawrence named his wife's brother, Dr Anson Buck, grandson of a Loyalist who settled in the district in the early years of the nineteenth century. The doctor's grandfather, Philip Buck, had fought with Butler's Rangers and, while he was imprisoned in Philadelphia, his wife along with three other women and their children fled to Canada. They arrived in Niagara in 1783, Philip later joined them there and the family eventually settled in Trafalgar Township. The home of their grandson, Anson Buck, still stands near the southeast corner of Dundas Street and Bronte Road. It was built in 1875.

St Luke's Anglican Church in Palermo is a simple white frame

Palermo house of Jacob Lawrence, lot 29, concession 1 NDS, Trafalgar

structure which was serving a large congregation when Archdeacon A.N. Bethune of York made a visit to Palermo in 1848. In a letter to Bishop Strachan he described the building as extremely spacious, containing forty pews. The reverend gentleman went on to say: 'It is a neat frame building with a good exterior but not yet entirely furnished and as it is comparitively a fresh undertaking they are as might be expected without most of the usual appointments required in a church. To these however I called their attention.' It would be interesting to know if the parishioners at St Luke's took kindly to his remarks, for they were undoubtedly aware themselves of what appointments were lacking. Certainly they were proud of the church bell, made at the Lawrences' Palermo Foundry. Considering that there were at the time fewer than two hundred people living in the village, the local Anglicans had done well just to get their church built. Bethune was undoubtedly correct when he commented on the

St Luke's Anglican Church, Palermo

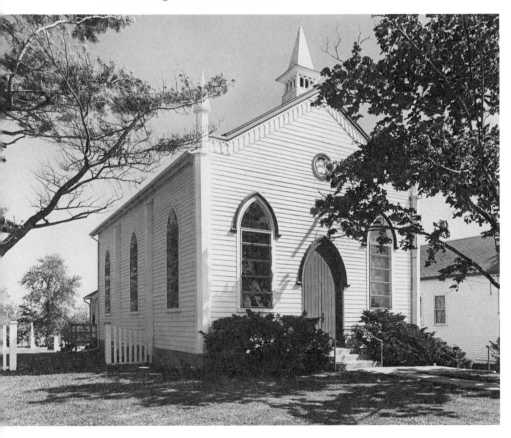

spirit and energy of the people and of their rector, Mr Payne.

Two other churches, one brick and the other frame, still stand along Dundas Street as tangible reminders of the important part that religion played in the lives of the settlers. Not only did their faith help to sustain them in a harsh and unforgiving new land but the church was often the centre of their social life as well. The Presbyterians in Nelson Township formed a congregation as early as 1816, when the area was still sparsely settled, holding services in a house just east of where their present church now stands (lot 12, concession 1 SDS, Nelson). Their first minister, the Reverend William King, arrived in 1819, and within three years he and his hardworking parishioners had constructed their first small church, St Paul's. King had to farm as well, since wages for the clergy were minimal at best. While breaking land for the farm he still found time to travel and conduct baptisms, marriages, and burials, a labour of love that he performed for the next thirty years. By 1867 the first church could no longer accommodate the growing congregation and a new St Paul's was built, much of the work done by the parishioners themselves. It was completed in February of the following year.

The congregation which built St John's Anglican Church in the village of Nelson (lot 16, concession 1 SDS, Nelson) was formed in 1835. Their first church, completed seven years later, is still standing and still in use. It is fortunate that it did not succumb to fire as did so many frame buildings when overheated stoves proved disastrous. Before St John's was built, the local Anglicans had travelled to Wellington Square (Burlington) each Sunday, but, after petitioning the bishop of Quebec, they acquired the necessary funds and built their simple little church at a cost of £378.

In 1848 the congregation of St John's received a visit from Bethune, shortly after he had left St Luke's, Palermo. This congregation too may have welcomed the distinguished gentleman with mixed emotions, for in his report to Bishop Strachan he stated: 'The church is laid out in pews, six of which are free; and I did not omit pressing a higher rent upon those that were conveyed to proprietors, than the very small impost of five shillings per annum. The collections here are only made on occasions on which the Sacrament is administered but I strongly advised the adoption of the ancient and scriptural rule of having them made weekly ... I endeavoured to show them that many improvements might be effected by increasing pew rents and rendering the collections more frequent.' In assessing the response to these suggestions Bethune found that 'there existed some repugnance' to his ideas.

In the cemetery that surrounds St John's are stones marking the graves of many Nelson Township pioneers, among them that of Joseph Ireland, who owned a farm a short distance south of the church, just west of the Guelph Line. His house, which he built in the mid-1830s, remains virtually unchanged except for an addition on the west end made a few years after the house was completed. The property, like Thomas Alton's nearby, has remained in the family ever since, which explains in part the timeless atmosphere of this remarkable building. Obviously succeeding generations of Irelands have treasured the house, for little has been altered either inside or on the exterior, thus providing the visitor with a unique insight into life in a nineteenth-century farmhouse. In the parlour the mantelpiece is marbled, a favourite method of finishing wood trim by paint-

St John's Anglican Church and cemetery in the village of Nelson

ing over a ground coat with a series of wavy lines. According to family lore, the artisan who painted the mantelpiece was so anxious to keep his methods secret that he locked himself in the room while the work was in progress.

Ireland was born in Yorkshire in 1792 and arrived in Canada at the age of nineteen. He fought in the War of 1812 and was for a time in charge of the supply line along Dundas Street. In 1820 he purchased the land for his farm and homestead, and three years later he married Ruth Best. They produced a family of six children, five of whom lived to maturity. Their home was called Oakridge Farm.

Joseph died in 1869. In his will he took great care to ensure Ruth's tenure in their house. She was to have 'free and uninterupted use and enjoyment of the two easterly rooms on the ground floor of the dwelling house in which I now reside; and also of a bedroom upstairs to be selected by herself until a convenient and comfortable kitchen shall be put up and finished for her exclusive use to open off one of

Ireland homestead, Nelson Township

the said rooms on the ground floor.' Along with all the furniture she should need, Ruth was to have half of the beds and bedding and 'all the fruit ... that she may require from the orchard and also the use of one half of the garden [and] firewood to be cut and piled up in the woodhouse by son John.' This son, their youngest, received the remainder of the house and the large homestead farm.

Captain Duncan McGregor, 42nd Highlanders, was left for dead on the battlefield at the Battle of Brandywine in 1777 during the American Revolution. Living to tell the tale, he returned to his native Scotland with his wife, Judith, and son, Peter, the latter born while the captain was stationed in Pennsylvania during the war. In 1812 Peter McGregor, then aged forty-nine and like his father a captain in the 42nd Highlanders, returned to North America, and also like his father he came back to fight for Great Britain. He was stationed in Quebec in charge of transport. Now one year away from discharge, McGregor had attained fame while serving with the Black Watch Regiment during the Peninsular Wars. He saved the life of the prince regent, later King William IV.

After the War of 1812 McGregor returned to Scotland for his discharge and then came back to Upper Canada, this time to settle and farm. In recognition of his service to the prince regent he was granted 500 acres, a larger than usual amount. He took up land in Nelson Township, Halton County. Peter was accompanied by his second wife, Anne Urquhart (his first wife, Jane Maclean, had died in Scotland in 1806). The family located on lot 8, concession 4, Nelson (Walker's Line). The farm was prosperous and at his death in 1827 McGregor was able to leave Anne and his four sons, who had the fine Scottish names of Lachlan, John, Duncan, and Donald, about 100 acres of good land each. Peter was buried at St Paul's Presbyterian Church on Dundas Street. In his will he left instructions for his funeral, which was 'not to be extravagant but decent and becoming my rank.'

It was Peter's second son, John Charles James McGregor, who was responsible for the construction of Limestone Hall (lot 8, concession 5, Nelson). John had received the patent for the land in 1846 but it was not until 1853 that the outstanding dressed-stone house was completed. By that time the McGregors needed the spacious residence. They had ten children when the 1851 census was taken (aged 17, 16, 15, 13, 12, 10, 8, 6, 3, and 1), and another child was born in 1854. At the census-taking the family of twelve was living in very close quarters in the building which forms the rear portion of the present Limestone Hall. John was an eminently successful farmer, for the agricultural census lists a wide range of grains and livestock on his 307 acres of land. Perhaps because of the size of the family farm the children tended to remain at home for many years. In 1871 John, then aged sixty, and his wife Phoebe Zimmerman, fifty-nine, were still surrounded by eight of their offspring (ranging in age from seventeen to thirty-four). One of the McGregors' six sons, John, became a doctor, practising first in Dundas and then in Waterdown, where, according to his obituary, he was for more than fifty years 'a much loved physician of the old school.'

When John McGregor died in 1879, he and Phoebe had been living for some time in Hamilton. Phoebe was left their house in that city and Limestone Hall was sold, with the proceeds divided among the widow and eight of their surviving children as well as their niece. Sons Peter and James, who had previously received financial assis-

Limestone Hall, lot 8, concession 5, Nelson

tance, were left with their father's 'blessing only.'

Another Nelson farmer who produced a sizeable family was Charles Tuck, who, like McGregor, built a handsome stone house in the early 1850s for his wife and their ten children. Situated on the north side of Dundas Street (lot 23, concession 1 NDS, Nelson) and built of dressed stone, the new house was built onto the Tuck's original home, a fieldstone structure that now forms the rear wing of the present building.

Charles Tuck may not have received as much help with the heavier labour in the fields as the number of his children would indicate. Their names were Elizabeth, Martha, Mary, Susan, Charlotte, Sarah, Ann, Emily, Harriet, and William. In his will Charles conscientiously provided for each of his nine daughters, instructing that part of the farm be sold, with the proceeds divided among them; each girl was also to receive upon her marriage 'two good milch cows, one heifer and ten ewe lambs.' Son William was left with part

Stoneacres, lot 23, concession 1 NDS, Nelson

of lot 21 across the road and was also given a detailed set of instructions. He was to furnish his sisters yet at home with necessary firewood but he was not to cut down the trees on the property for any other purpose. When the present owners purchased Stoneacres thirty years ago, there were few trees left on the site. Somehow, Tuck's instructions were bypassed, or possibly his daughters had a goodly number of fires. William was also instructed to pay his mother any rent she deemed equitable, and he was left a bequest of ten dollars.

The executors of Tuck's will were his 'beloved wife Mary Ann' and his 'trusty friends' Alexander Gerrie and Abner Everett. The latter was Charles and Mary Ann's son-in-law. He lived west of the Tucks, not far from Waterdown (lot 2, concession 3, Flamborough East).

The story of Everett's early married life is found on two tombstones in Burlington's Union Cemetery; they record the deaths of

Abner Everett house, lot 2, concession 3, Flamborough East

his first two wives, young women who died nine months and eleven days apart. The circumstances, sadly, were not unusual for the time. Everett married first when he was nineteen, but by the time he reached his twentieth birthday he was a widower and a father; his wife, Lilly Malloy, had died giving premature birth to a son. Married again almost immediately to Mary Ann Sovereign, young Everett was soon once more a widower, for Mary Ann, who was ill when they married, died of consumption shortly thereafter. Two years later, in 1857, Abner was at the altar again, this time with happier results. He and his third wife, Mary Tuck, lived to celebrate their fiftieth wedding anniversary. The couple was photographed on that day, Mary wearing in the picture the same gown that she wore for her wedding. Their fine frame home, which they built in 1876, stands on the north side of Dundas Street on land purchased by Everett in the year before their marriage.

Closer to Waterdown is a sturdy brick house that was built in

Avonsyde, lot 3, concession 3, Flamborough East

1857 by James Forbes, a successful farmer and a native of Scotland. The Forbes homestead (lot 3, concession 3, Flamborough East) is now called 'Avonsyde,' after a book read in later years by Forbes's grandchildren. With his wife, Jane, and their five children, James Forbes lived in his house on Dundas Street until his death in 1870. Like so many of his countrymen, he worked hard and he prospered. He was typical of those Scottish immigrants who were, as Sir William Osler once observed, 'the backbone of Canada. They are all right in their three vital parts – heads, hearts and haggis.'

4

Waterdown

Life in Upper Canada was a subject of intense interest in Great Britain during the 1800s, and thus, when a wealthy and educated traveller from Scotland wrote first-hand accounts of his impressions of the young country and its people, his books were eagerly received. For the most part accounts such as these were the only ones available, as the settlers themselves had little time for journalism. For example, pioneer farmer Benjamin Smith of Ancaster found only a few minutes to note tersely the day's events: 'Was my birthday 27 years. Split stakes.'

The Honourable Adam Fergusson's writings were published after an 1831 visit to Upper Canada, the first work entitled *On the Agricultural State of Canada and Part of the United States of America* and the later *Practical Notes from a Tour in Canada*. Born in 1783, Fergusson was a lawyer, a magistrate, and a director of an agricultural society in Scotland. His interest in promoting effective farming methods led him to pursue this study in Upper Canada and to form in later years an annual agricultural exhibition in the province, the forerunner of the Canadian National Exhibition. In his writings Fergusson described with sensitivity the difficulties of pioneer life, the agricultural possibilities of the land, and the captivating beauty of the country. As well, he touched on the three subjects that evoked comment from all British travellers: the condition of the 'roads,' the native people, and, of course, the Yankees.

With a degree of objectivity not always found in his countrymen Fergusson remarked that the Yankee's

inquisitive disposition has been a frequent theme of abuse against Americans; and that it exists as a national trait, I think no man can deny. I have met with it everywhere and have endeavoured to analyze it fairly and with candour. The conclusion to which I very soon came, and to which I still adhere, aquits the Americans of the most remote intention to be at all uncivil. They must be viewed nationally in some degree as children; it must be remembered that they live much in retired rural circles; that they are intelligent, well educated and ever anxious to acquire information, all of which render them, when a foreigner falls into their hands, rather apt to overstep the European bounds of propriety.

After visiting the Mohawk village near Brantford, Fergusson commented:

After service, I was introduced to two of the chief men, who gave me their hands in a stately and somewhat condescending manner, saying at the same time 'Welcome, Scotsman.' They were all well clothed though the fashions were certainly somewhat grotesque. The head gear of many, especially the boys, exhibited a close affinity to oriental costume. It is impossible not to feel a deep interest in the Aborigines of this vast continent. As yet, (comparatively speaking), nothing has been done, nor any equivalent return made, for what we have acquired from them. Probably this is not the fair criterion to assume, but unquestionably we are called upon to make strenuous efforts towards instructing and ameliorating the condition of this race. Many a noble quality do they possess and too many of their vices, I am afraid, must, in candour, be placed to our account.

On the subject of stagecoach travel in Upper Canada Fergusson remarked on the

awkward provision made in our vehicle for ingress and egress, a provision by the way, devised for the purpose of excluding water in passing through rivers and brooks. Frequent were the requests of our coachman 'just to get out a bit,' calls which however prudent and reasonable ... proved no joke for a man of my caliber to be bolting out and scrambling in at the window every few miles. Besides this harlequinade, our ears were occasionally saluted in more critical circumstances with a shrill cry of 'gentlemen, please a little to the left or right' as the case might require, when, our own sensations readily seconding the call, there was an instantaneous and amusing scramble to restore equilibrium. Broken heads on such occasions are by no means rare.

Two years after his initial visit Fergusson returned to settle in

Canada. His first wife, Jemima Johnston, had died a few years earlier, as had their only daughter. By the time he emigrated, Fergusson had remarried, and he came to Upper Canada with his new wife, Jessie Tower, and six of the seven sons from his first marriage. Accompanying the family were a servant and a tutor for the boys. The Fergussons settled first at Niagara but shortly thereafter bought land near Waterdown. They began construction of a fine house, which was built according to plans drawn up by architect Charles Allan, a friend from Scotland who had also arrived in Upper Canada in 1833. The Fergussons called their new home Woodhill.

Sheltered by an embankment behind it, Woodhill (120 Mountain Brow Road East) overlooks gently rolling hills and the plain below. The verandah that once stretched across the front of the house has disappeared, but otherwise the building has changed little over the years. Isolated as it is from the modern dwellings nearby, the Fergusson farm gives the impression that its owner has only stepped

Adam Fergusson's Woodhill, 120 Mountain Brow Road East

out for a while, perhaps to attend a Reform meeting. The original outbuildings also contribute to the feeling that time in this idyllic place has stood still. Woodhill is built of stone covered with stucco, its unpretentious design and fine proportions reflecting the typically straightforward approach of its Scottish builder. It is now being restored by the present owner.

In 1834 Woodhill was visited by A.D. Ferrier, who recounted the story in *The Early Days of Fergus*: 'After a pleasant ride through a very pretty country ... I found Mr. Fergusson and his family at Waterdown and astonished him not a little at my arrival. The house at Waterdown was just being built by our old friend Mr. Charles Allan. On our way to see it, Mr. Fergusson told me to look over a fence, and there lay a big black snake, which I think he had killed that morning, and he told me there were rattlesnakes on the bank behind his new house.' By 1841 the census for Flamborough East recorded that the Honourable Adam Fergusson was living on concession 2, lot 4, with 35 acres cultivated and 85 acres uncultivated. His house was 'under two storeys with five additional fireplaces,' that is, six in all.

Fergusson's Canadian accomplishments were exceptional in their diversity and long-lasting in their influence on politics and agriculture. He helped to found the Agriculture Association of Upper Canada, whose first exhibition in 1847 was the forerunner of the Canadian National Exhibition. Fergusson was one of the founders of the Canada Life Assurance Company. Shortly after arriving in the country he and James Webster bought over seven thousand acres of land in Nichol Township and together founded the village of Fergus. In politics Fergusson's unquestioned loyalty and prestige brought a measure of respectability to the Reform cause, and it is believed that many of the prominent men of the time were visitors at Woodhill. Fergusson sympathized with the goals of his countryman William Lyon Mackenzie but, it is said, he attempted to instil moderation in the rebel leader – an attempt that met with a distinct lack of success.

In spite of his reform leanings Fergusson commanded a militia regiment at the time of the rebellion. Four years later, in a letter to W.H. Merritt, he expressed his views of the militia and the demands it made on the average farmer: 'I observe that you have been directing your attention to that clumsy machine, our militia system. It strikes me that the best plan would be to abolish not only the fines but the muster as well. It is a dead loss to the Province of at least one day labour of all prime hands in the country. What is it worth? It also leads to drunkeness ... and it is a perfect humbug as regards any benefit or use. I would propose as a substitute to maintain the requirements as they are, guard the officers and have them muster once a year and go over all regimental matters.'

For the rest of his life Fergusson supported the Reformers. In November 1860 he wrote to the Reform Association of Nichol Township, expressing regret at declining their invitation to a dinner: 'The cause of Reform becomes every day of more and more vital importance. It is about time to say that my health alone must prevent me from being with you.'

Two years later Adam Fergusson died, predeceased by his wife Jessie. His estate was left to his surviving sons, with a special bequest to his son Adam Johnston, who, like his father, was prominent and successful in politics. To this son was given 'the furniture, plate, linen, pictures, books and heirlooms, carriages, sleighs ... in and about my residence of Woodhill ... for his sole use ... failing him his issue.' To the oldest son, Neil James Fergusson-Blair, who had remained in Scotland after inheriting his mother's estate and family name, was left 'the sum of £100 sterling clear of legacy duty to purchase some memorial of a father who loved him well.'

When the Fergusson family first arrived at Waterdown in 1833, they found a young but thriving community with several mills operating on nearby Grindstone Creek. The village had been surveyed only a few years earlier by an enterprising man who, at the age of twenty-three, had purchased 360 acres on which he later laid out the town site. His name was Ebenezer Culver Griffin. This land and an adjacent two hundred acres he purchased in 1823, and within a few years he had built a sawmill and then a flour mill. Various other business enterprises were soon begun by the energetic Griffin so it is not surprising that he came to be known as the founder of Waterdown.

The son of Smith Griffin, a Loyalist from New York State, Ebenezer grew up in Smithsville, Lincoln County, a village named for his father. The family milling business eventually expanded to Hamilton and included the younger Griffin's Waterdown enterprises. In 1828 an advertisement in the *Gore Gazette* of 16 February stated: 'TAKE NOTICE. The subscribers beg respectively to inform their friends and the Public that they are paying the highest Market

Price for good Merchantable Wheat delivered either at their New Mills in Flamborough East or at the New Cash Store in this town. (Hamilton). Smith Griffin / Ebenezer C. Griffin.'

Although he was a successful merchant, Smith Griffin was also an ordained minister of the Methodist church whose weekday business activities were replaced on Sundays by preaching. He was called 'one of the old style local preachers who preached with liberty and power.' His son was also a devout Methodist. It is somewhat surprising therefore to find in the same paper on 18 May 1828 an advertisement by Smith Griffin and Company offering for sale: '50 Kegs of Tobacco – Just received ... by the subscribers at their stores in Hamilton and the 40 Mile Creek, 50 Kegs of 12 and 16 hand tobacco, warranted a superior quality ... Also their summer supply of Liquors, Sugars, Teas etc. of the best description.' The Griffins, however, were evidently abstainers themselves. Ebenezer's son George recalled that, when the family firm built a sawmill in 1832, it was constructed in one day, employing 'thirty-eight hands without whiskey.' In comparison, George noted that Colonel Brown's mill took two days to build, with the same number of men and the addition of whiskey.

At the age of twenty-one Ebenezer Griffin married Eliza Kent of Stoney Creek, and by the time he purchased the Waterdown site in 1823 the first of their family of eight sons and three daughters had arrived. Although it is not certain where Ebenezer and Eliza first made their home, it is believed locally that the house was on the street which now bears the Griffin name. The assessment rolls for 1841 showed that Ebenezer Griffin owned in that year two frame houses of 'under two storeys.' Although the small house at 24 Griffin Street is covered in stone, a descendant speculates that the beautiful fieldstone could cover frame siding which, in turn, covers log construction. If this is so, this house could be the original Griffin dwelling, for its two-foot-thick walls and other structural details indicate a very early date. By the time of the 1841 census, however, Ebenezer and Eliza had a family of nine children. Two of the children died that same year. Ebenezer Griffin died in 1847 and that year the stone house was sold to Thomas Dyke, who paid £50.5.0 for the small lot; thus it seems certain that the house must have been on the property at that date at least. After two years Dyke sold it to Matthew Burnes and in 1852 it became the property of wagon-maker Thomas Fretwell.

On 16 October 1847 the *Hamilton Spectator* announced the death at Waterdown of 'E.C. Griffin aged 47 years 8 months. Friends and aquaintances are requested to attend the funeral from his late residence Sunday next at 2 o'clock p.m. without further notice.' His will, dated two days before his death, left to his 'beloved wife Eliza' his house, all the furnishings, and the timber plot on the northeast side of Grindstone Creek, excepting the woollen factory, raceway, and blacksmith shop. To his sons James Kent and George Douglas Griffin bequeathed the sum of £5; they were, presumably, already established. The other children were to receive their share of the remaining estate when they reached the age of twenty-one.

Miller, merchant, landowner, and town-planner, Ebenezer Griffin was also the only magistrate in the district for many years. A staunch Methodist all his life, he named one of his sons Egerton Ryerson Griffin. It was perhaps as a result of that connection that Waterdown was considered as a site for the Methodist's Upper Can-

24 Griffin Street

ada Academy. Although the academy was in fact built in Cobourg, Griffin managed a contribution to higher learning in a different way – the stone from his quarries was used in the construction of some of the buildings at the University of Toronto.

James Kent Griffin, Ebenezer's eldest son, was born in 1823. His maternal grandfather, William Kent, was a brother-in-law of Comte de Puisaye, who led a group of ill-fated French emigrés to Upper Canada in 1797 under the auspices of the British government. Kent is credited with naming Waterdown, the name no doubt derived from the waterfalls on Grindstone Creek. Another, but less likely, story holds that, when construction was completed on a new build-ing, custom demanded that the carpenter hold high a bottle of whiskey and call for a name for the structure; he would then smash the bottle against the wall. In the naming of one of his mills Ebe-nezer Griffin, an abstainer, substituted water for whiskey. A by-stander, noticing the substitution, called out 'Throw that water down!' and the carpenter, catching only the last of the remark, duly named the structure Waterdown. This highly imaginative account claims that subsequently the village took its name from that given to Griffin's mill.

James Kent Griffin's substantial stone house stands at 201 Main Street South. As was often the case, his house appears to have been built in stages, the diningroom of the present building seemingly the oldest section. The 1844 assessment rolls show that James, who was twenty-one years old, was then living in a one-storey frame house, perhaps a very early building on the property, which was altered and enlarged until the structure was complete in the early 1870s. In later years author W.O. Mitchell lived in the house, and at some point a ghost is reported to have taken up residence, a ghost seem-ingly able to move heavy pieces of furniture about when no one was in the room.

As a young man James Kent Griffin studied for the Methodist ministry at Cobourg's Victoria College (previously the Upper Canada Academy), but, like his family before him, he went on to combine his strong religious leanings with more prosaic business pursuits. In 1845 James married Almira Dyke, a daughter of the man who had purchased the Griffin Street cottage. For most of his life James worked as a contractor, building both houses and roads, including a toll road from Hamilton to Carlisle. Like most of the Griffins, James produced a large family, he and Almira becoming parents of eleven children. In 1910 James Kent Griffin died in Seattle, Washington, predeceased by his wife and at least three of his children.

An imposing stone house at 63 Mill Street ranks as one of the finest early buildings in Waterdown, but details of its history are sketchy and, as a result, finding its construction date proves to be a challenge. Called Maple Lane, the house contains architectural details suggesting that it could well have been built in 1830 or earlier. The interior hardware and wood trim and the slender spindles used in the balustrade for the staircase all point to that period. However, the land on which the house was built belonged to Ebenezer Griffin until 1837, when he sold it to a tanner named Henry Ferguson Graham. According to the assessment rolls, Graham lived in a one-storey frame house until 1847, when he was first listed as occupying a 'two-storey house of brick, frame or stone.' These records suggest, therefore, that the house was built in that

James Kent Griffin house, 201 Main Street South

year, although an earlier house on the property may well have been incoporated in the new structure. Adding credence to this latter theory is the former kitchen, which contains the only fireplace in the house and the original pine dado, both of which appear to date well before mid-century.

Beside Maple Lane a narrow road called Leather Street leads to the rear of the property where Graham established his tannery. His business prospered and he later became part-owner of one of the Griffin mills. By 1850 he was tax collector for the township. Three years later Graham and his wife Agnes sold their property to Andrew and Elizabeth Davis, who remained owners for the next twenty-two years.

The history of Maple Lane sheds some light on the enterprising Ebenezer Griffin and the control that he exerted over 'his' village. For example, the small industries operating along Grindstone Creek could utilize the water power from the dam only on days specified by

Maple Lane, 63 Mill Street

Griffin. Levi Hawke, owner of a turning factory, could use the water 'to drive and turn two lathes either for wood or iron except for three days, Monday, Wednesday and Friday.' On the alternate days Henry Graham could use it to operate his tannery. Dayton Reeves, a shoemaker, got 'all surplus water coming over the dam not needed by Levi Hawk[e] or Graham and the use of the water in the Creek.' Margaret Kathleen Donkin notes in her MA thesis: 'The influence of Mr. Griffin was enormous. His restrictions concerning roads, water rights and even public watering places remain in the deeds in some cases today.'

Griffin's influence was equally pervasive among the Methodists in Waterdown and he approached his religious obligations with the same zeal as was accorded to his business concerns. In the early 1830s he founded a temperance society whose members pledged to refrain from drinking liquor, although the consumption of wine was considered permissible. One man, however, protested, claiming that 'It is all very well for you rich men ... to abstain from whiskey and drink wine, which we can not afford to buy; if you will make a pledge against all intoxicating drinks, we'll join you.' His suggestion was adopted. Those members who failed to keep the pledge were sentenced to dig out a stump from either of the two streets that ran through the village.

In 1838 the Wesleyan Methodists built a simple frame church on Mill Street. It served the settlers who, for more than forty years, had been part of the Ancaster circuit, which encompassed an area at the head of Lake Ontario known as 'Methodist Mountain.' Among the many committed 'saddlebag preachers' who travelled the circuit was William Case, a man whose powers of oratory were augmented by striking good looks, charm, fine manners, and a superb voice. One of his converts was Peter Jones, whose story is told in the chapter on Brantford. In 1832 the Nelson circuit was formed, and its first minister was an Irishman, the Reverend Samuel Belton. He was another of that resolute group of itinerant preachers, devoted and courageous men who travelled through the wilderness on horseback so that they could spread the gospel to the farthest reaches of the newly settled country.

An 1865 directory described the Methodist church as built of 'hand-hewn plank' and 'capable of seating 400 persons.' That same year the building was covered in stone and, except for the addition of a Sunday School and minor interior alterations, it has changed little since that time.

Next door to the church stands the original Town Hall, and it too adds much to Waterdown's architectural heritage. Construction of the hall began in 1856 after the town council agreed on 28 June to appoint 'Messrs. Stewart, Foster and Morden [as] a committee to ascertain where a suitable site for a town hall can be obtained.' Three months later, the council purchased a lot for £50 and authorized as well £3.1.3 for the building committee's travelling expenses. (At the same meeting a by-law was introduced limiting the number of taverns in East Flamborough Township to fifteen). By December 1857 the building was finished and council minutes stated that 'L.A. Cummer and James McMonies, Reeve, certify that the Town Hall has been examined and ... the building is satisfactory.' The following month the town council felt it neccessary to establish a few rules regarding the uses to which the new building could be put: 'The Public shall have the use of the Town Hall for any public lecture that

Wesleyan Methodist Church, Mill Street

East Flamborough Township Hall, Mill Street

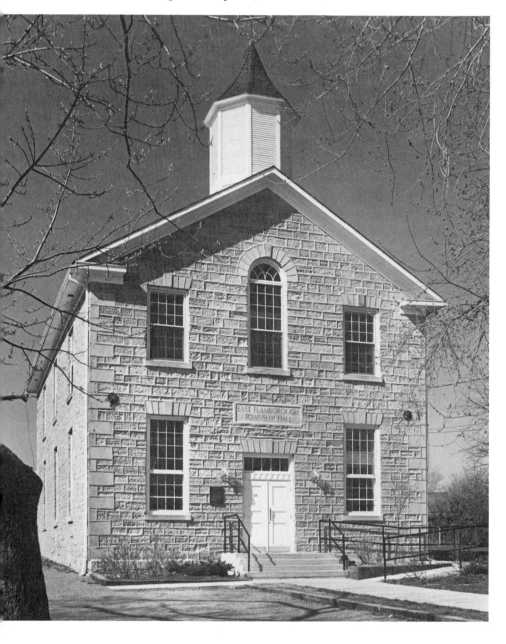

is calculated to benefit Society in general – to the exclusion of all Tea Meetings, Bazaars and Shows, and Religious Worship.' Apparently members of council later decided that religious worship was of some benefit to society, for in March 1858 they agreed 'that the Episcopalian Church have the use of the Gallery of the Town Hall each Sabbath for Divine Service for one year – for the use of which the said members agree to pay thirty dollars.' In recent years the interior of this handsome building has been renovated, a project that commemorated the one hundredth anniversary of Waterdown's incorporation. The old hall now serves as the Waterdown library.

Across the street and to the north of the Town Hall is a trim stone house at 50 Mill Street North. Built during the 1860s, it is among the best of the numerous stone buildings that remain in Waterdown, all of which suggest that there were superior stonemasons at work there throughout the nineteenth century. A search of the title to the

Miller John Creen's house, 50 Mill Street North

Mill Street property indicates that the house standing there today was built for miller John Creen shortly after he purchased the land in 1864. His nearby flour mill had been built nineteen years before by Absalom Griffin, a brother of Ebenezer and the owner of various business concerns in Waterdown.

According to the 1861 census, John Creen was living in a one-storey frame house that year with his wife Eliza and their daughter Catherine, aged two. Creen was then thirty-four years old, a Wesleyan Methodist and a farmer. Three years later he purchased the mill on Grindstone Creek and his house was probably built at about that time. In 1871 the property was sold to George Washington Rymal, who continued in the milling business for many years.

The name of Hugh Creen appears in the 1865–6 *City of Hamilton and County of Wentworth Directory*, his occupation listed as 'gentleman.' Hugh was the father of John Creen, and of Peter Creen, who in 1875 purchased the Henry Graham house on Mill Street South. Obviously all three men appreciated fine houses. Hugh Creen owned, and probably built, the attractive stone house at 173 Main Street, a building which once stood alone at the end of a long lane that led north from Dundas Street.

The 1840 census indicates that Hugh Creen and his wife were the parents of three daughters as well as sons John and Peter. In 1861, when Hugh was sixty-nine years old and his wife sixty-two, their daughters were still living at home. By the time of Hugh's death sixteen years later two of the daughters had married. In his will Creen left to his oldest daughter, Elizabeth McNabb of Hamilton, the sum of $1500; to his second daughter, Mary Patton, he left his house, the 'property known as the Magill property and upon her marriage or death I devise the property to her daughter Catherine Patton ... and if (she) should die before coming of age ... lot to go to her sisters Mary Margaret Patton and Georgina Patton, share and share alike.' To his third daughter, Flora, Creen left $1000.

In referring to his own house and land as 'the Magill property' Creen was undoubtedly conforming to local custom. Because a previous owner, William Magill, had lived there in the 1840s, the residents of Waterdown spoke of the house as though it still belonged to him. Names from the past cling to houses today in the same way.

Mary Patton, Creen's middle daughter, was apparently a widow, for in his will Creen mentions the possibility of her marrying. It seems probable, therefore, that she and her daughters were living on the 'Magill property' at the time of her father's death. Lending credence to this theory is the fact that, according to the 1875 *Illustrated Historical Atlas of the County of Wentworth*, Hugh Creen was living in a spacious house just north of James Kent Griffin's residence on Main Street South, the fourth house in Waterdown that still serves as a reminder of the Creen family.

Frederick Fielde was a neighbour of Hugh Creen's when the latter was still living on the 'Magill property.' It was Fielde and his wife, Elizabeth, who donated two acres of land to the Anglican Church in 1847 as the site for a church building, rectory, and cemetery. Funds to build the church were not immediately available, however, so the Anglicans continued to hold services in the Town Hall until 1860, when they were able to erect a modest structure on Mill Street North. Called Grace Church, it was enlarged five years later when the Reverend H. Stringfellow became rector and his eloquent sermons attracted a growing number of parishioners. The

173 Main Street, home of Hugh Creen

new minister had fled from the southern states during the Civil War, a circumstance which alone would have made him of interest to the people of Waterdown.

As one of the leading parishioners at Grace Church, Fielde was typical of the many half-pay officers who settled in Canada during the 1830s, bringing with them the courage and the convictions inherent in their upper-class backgrounds. They intended to become the aristocracy in their new country and indeed many did. Fielde had served in the Napoleonic wars with his father, Captain James Fielde, and his brother Fulford Fielde, who was deputy commissary general in the British army.

Not long after Frederick and his wife settled in Waterdown, his mother, Jeanne Fielde, arrived to spend the winter with them. The year was 1841 and this doughty lady, at the age of eighty-one, came to Canada from her home in France to take charge of Fulford Fielde's four children. Their mother had died and they were in the

'Foot-a-day' construction at 32 John Street

care of servants. After visiting England to say goodbye to friends there, Mrs Fielde, accompanied by her daughter Sophia and a maid, embarked for New York. With her she brought family jewellery, her candlesticks, some miniatures, and her sewing case. In New York the women were met by Frederick and they proceeded to Waterdown by stage. Since Frederick and Elizabeth were living at the time in a one-storey log house, the accommodation may have proved somewhat cramped, but the visitors stayed until the following year and then, when the weather permitted, proceeded by boat and stage to Prescott, where Fulford and his children were living. Jeanne Fielde died there six years later.

A short distance south of Grace Church, at 32 John Street, is a stucco-covered frame house with a pointed gable and symmetrical façade. Its counterpart is found in every Ontario community but in Waterdown, where stone construction predominated, it is somewhat uncommon. Behind the stucco and the board-and-batten siding is brick fill, employed in a building method known as 'colombage.' Locally this process was called 'foot-a-day,' presumably because the work proceeded at about that rate. In the John Street house the studs are braced with timbers placed diagonally between them and the remaining space was filled with brick and plaster, providing the house with insulation.

The date when this warm and pleasant house was built cannot be determined, but the hardware on the front door is identical to that found on two houses near Waterdown on Dundas Street, both of which were built in the late 1850s. Although the builder is also unknown, the John Street house belonged in the 1870s to the Gilmer family, owners of a wagon shop and foundry on Mill Street North. According to one local account, Gilmer's was known for more than making wagons, since cock fights also took place inside the firm's large workshop.

Waterdown boasts a fine early commercial building, also of frame construction. It stands at 31 Main Street South and, except for the verandah that once sheltered its front windows, it looks much as it did a century ago. For many years this building housed the Waterdown post office when it was owned by Hugh and James Thompson. The 1861 census lists James as a native of Scotland, thirty years old 'at next birthday' and unmarried. His father, Hugh, is recorded as a saddle- and harnessmaker. In an 1869 directory James is described as postmaster, general merchant, and express agent.

William Marnell has described some of New England's early buildings as 'built by carpenters with the instincts of artists.' The same could be said of many nineteenth century Ontario houses – satisfying structures erected by painstaking builders with an unerring eye for proportion and a respect for the materials with which they worked. Typical of these buildings is Evergreen Lodge, which stands at the end of Mountain Brow Road West overlooking Lake Ontario. For nearly one hundred years it was the home of the Horning family, descendants of Loyalist Peter Horning from Pennsylvania.

Research into his family's history by the late Dr William Clark Horning reveals that Peter came to Canada in 1788, a year or so after two of his sons, Abraham and Isaac, had settled on land near where the city of Hamilton later grew. Naturally Peter, his wife, Isabella, and their children were anxious to locate Abraham and Isaac when they arrived in the area. According to family legend, the

The Hornings' Evergreen Lodge, Mountain Brow Road West

Hornings came upon a log house and, although no one was there, knew that it belonged to one of their sons because the flowers growing near the door were from seeds given them by Isabella before they left Pennsylvania. Although Peter was fifty years old when he started life anew in a new country, he lived for another thirty-five years and he prospered. At his death in 1823 he was able to leave 600 acres to each of his seven surviving children and to the children of two daughters who had predeceased him.

Peter's youngest son was Lewis Horning, who eventually settled in Dufferin County, where he founded the village of Horning's Mills. Lewis's younger days, however, were spent near Hamilton, where he farmed and became successful as a miller and merchant. When his wife, Mary Gage, died in December 1817, Lewis was left with eight motherless children. This no doubt explains why only three months later he married again, his bride Eleanor Blaare Bates. With eight children in need of a mother a leisurely courtship was not in order. Eleanor eventually produced seven more children. One of them, Lewis Jr, was one of four children stolen by Indians two years after the family moved to Dufferin County in 1830. One of the children who was kidnapped turned up nearly two years later in Oakville, but nine-year-old Lewis and the two other children were never seen again. Depressed by this loss and his wife's failing health, Lewis sold his Dufferin County land and returned to Hamilton.

It seems likely that upon their return in 1838 Lewis and Eleanor moved into the small frame cottage that stands a short distance south of Evergreen Lodge, at the end of Horning's Lane. The family believes that the house was built by Lewis some time in the 1820s, before the ill-fated move to Dufferin County. William Lyon Mackenzie mentioned in his journal that when he was fleeing after the rebellion he called upon his old friend Lewis Horning but was unable to find him. The cottage has been radically altered in the ensuing years.

William Gage Horning, Lewis's son by his first marriage, inherited the cottage and the rest of his father's farm. It was he who, in 1852, purchased the picturesque Evergreen Lodge which, from its vantage-point on the brow of the hill, commands a view over the Horning farm and the surrounding countryside. It is thought that the house was built by a previous owner, possibly William L. Billings, who owned the land for three years prior to Horning's purchase. When he died in 1879, William Horning left the house to his wife,

Mary Ann Bates, with the farm and outbuildings going to their old-est son, George, providing that 'he cut in proper stove lengths, split and pile the same in the wood house adjoining his mother's residence a sufficient quantity of good wood in each and every year of her natural life.' To his other eight children William left bequests of land (to the sons) and money (to the daughters).

Not far from the Hornings, at 265 Mill Street South, is the home of a man who became a Father of Confederation. Although altera-tions have completely changed the appearance of his house, no dis-cussion of Waterdown would be complete without mention of Sir William Pierce Howland. Mitchell's 1865 directory notes that 'the Waterdown flouring mills are owned by the Hon. W.P. Howland and were erected in 1860 of stone, four stories high with a large stone grain warehouse convenient, the whole costing about thirteen thou-sand dollars.' Howland's illustrious career included posts as minister of finance, receiver-general, postmaster-general, and after Confed-eration lieutenant-governor of Ontario. His son, William Holmes Howland, became mayor of Toronto in 1886 and is credited with changing that city from a filthy, squalid, and politically corrupt place into the city that became known as Toronto the Good. Donald Jones, writing in the *Toronto Star*, commented that, before How-land became mayor, 'The filth and drunkenness in the streets shocked even the most seasoned travellers and you could literally die from drinking the tap water.' Howland set up a morality squad, exposed corruption in the waterworks department, and devoted his life to the people of his city. He was one of Toronto's best loved and most highly respected mayors. Howland's brother also served as mayor of Toronto, and today one of his nephews, William C. How-land, is chief justice of Ontario.

In 1900 Sir William Pierce Howland sold his home in Waterdown, thus bringing to an end the town's connection with one of Ontario's most illustrious families.

5

Dundas

Lieutenant George Rolph of the York militia was travelling on horseback from Detroit to Kingston during the days of the War of 1812. His horse had tired and so, seeing another horse grazing nearby, Rolph decided to change mounts. He promptly took down a fence and was busy saddling the fresh horse when its owner appeared on the scene. Not surprisingly the owner, Mr Lyons, a Dundas farmer, accused the young soldier of stealing his horse. 'No,' replied Rolph, 'I am only taking it. You take mine and charge the difference to the government.' So saying, he went on his way.

By the end of the war George Rolph had distinguished himself in battle and been awarded a silver medal for 'service to the British Army,' in particular for his action in the campaign which led to the surrender of Detroit. He returned to the scene of the incident with the horse to make his home. By 1821 he had become a barrister-at-law and, with his brother John, established what was for some years the largest law practice west of York. His abrupt manner, however, and his seeming arrogance did not endear him to the citizens of Dundas. Although he eventually won the grudging respect of his neighbours, he was disliked by most of them. This antipathy explains why Rolph was such a likely victim of one of the few 'tar and feathering' episodes in Upper Canada.

The incident occured five years after Rolph had settled in Dundas. On a June night in 1826 a group of men, their faces blackened, burst into Rolph's bedroom and dragged him from the house. They had expected to find him 'languishing in the arms' of a Mrs Evans, who had fled from the home of her abusive husband and, with her child, been given refuge in George Rolph's household. Undoubtedly the assailants were disappointed to find him alone in his bed, but, nothing daunted, these protectors of the town's virtue proceeded to strip Rolph, smear him with tar, and add the feathers from his own pillow. The half-conscious victim eventually found his way back to his house.

George's brother and law partner, John, advised him to do nothing about the assault for a while. He assumed that the culprits would be unable to resist boasting about the affair. This was indeed the case. By the following year three men, all leading citizens of Dundas, stood accused of the crime – Colonel Titus Simons (former high sheriff), his son-in-law, Alexander Robertson, and Dr James Hamilton. The plaintiff, Rolph, was clerk of the peace. For the defence were solicitor general Boulton, Allan Napier MacNab, and Alexander Chewett. The two latter defence lawyers, along with the editor of the *Gore Gazette* were known by many of the assembled crowd to have taken part in the contentious outing which caused the case to be before the courts. After long and complex proceedings, which were part of the Gore Assizes of 1827, Simons and Hamilton were fined £20 each. Undaunted, the two men sought contributions from residents of the town to pay their fines. They had, said one of the defence lawyers, 'attempted to vindicate the rights of an outraged community.' The matter remained before the courts for a possible retrial but was dropped by Rolph. He had been elected a member of the Legislative Assembly for Halton County in the mean time, this in spite of his notoriety (or because of it).

By 1832, George Rolph was sole head of his law firm, his brother having given up the practice of law to pursue his other interest, the practice of medicine. (During the years in which he combined the two functions John Rolph used to arrive in court with his saddlebag slung across his horse's back – one side containing legal documents, the other surgical instruments.)

Head of his law practice, clerk of the peace, MLA, George Rolph was still controversial. His opposition to the proposed Desjardins Canal in 1836 prompted an editorialist in the *Dundas Weekly Post*, 16 February 1836, to rail: 'let him shut himself up, bar himself forever within that cold and solitary abode of selfishness and caprice, which we believe, until it changes owners, will never in its most distant corner join fellowship with our town, or be the means of advancing her interests.'

That 'cold and solitary abode' was Rolph's first home, built on land purchased in 1822. The initial structure was log and it is reported that a log building behind the house served as a law office and even as Dundas's first court-house and jail. (Relocated, the latter building was later set afire by vandals.) The Rolph property encompassed much of present-day Dundas. Two 'lofty iron gates, handsomely finished, enclosed and surrounded by walls of fine stone,' created an impression not only of splendour 'quite worthy the entrance to a nobleman's mansion' but of aloofness. The house, which originally straddled Cross Street, was later moved to its present location at 43 Cross Street, on the east side of the road. Its initial shape and size have been altered. The southern portion of the building is the older, and the present house may be two separate buildings joined together.

Rolph married Georgianna Clement in 1836. Seven children were born to them. It was George's intention to create a private park surrounding his house, but after Georgianna's death at the age of thirty-five he lost interest in the scheme. Rolph died on 25 July 1875 at the age of eighty-one. His property was sold and the proceeds divided among the two sons and three daughters who survived him.

Of the three men who were charged with 'trespass and outrage' against George Rolph, one was not convicted. This was Alexander Robertson, son-in-law of Titus Geir Simons, the latter a former high sheriff of the Gore District and commander of his regiment in the War of 1812. Robertson built his home beside Lieutenant-Governor Simcoe's early road and today it is one of three fine pre-Confederation buildings in that area.

The Robertson home, called Foxbar, is located at 10 Overfield Street, just south of Governor's Road. The name derived from the family residence of Foxbar in Perthshire, Scotland, where Alexander Robertson was born in 1798, the son of Ross Robertson. Dundas's Foxbar is thought to be the home Robertson built for his wife, Matilda Simons, some time after their marriage in 1826. The building is an elegant hip-roofed stone structure with decorative brackets, central pediment with cornice, and three ornamental chimneys. The style would seem to date the house to the 1840s or early 1850s. If it was indeed constructed near the middle of the century, it may be the second Robertson home to occupy the site, and in that case the work of Alexander and Matilda's son, the Honourable Thomas Robertson, a prominent politician and lawyer. There is ample evidence that Alexander was in Dundas in the early 1820s, not the least of which is his part in the famous tar-and-feathering case. It is also noted, however, that in the 1830s he moved to London where he commanded the London cavalry during the rebellion years of 1837–8. He died in Goderich in 1855. The property then passed to his son Thomas, who by that time had been called to the bar. Subsequently, after business and political successes, Thomas Robertson was appointed to the Supreme Court of Ontario.

During Thomas's tenure at Foxbar many guests were welcomed and entertained there, but none more colourful than the Honourable T. D'Arcy McGee, 'cabinet minister, statesman, writer, orator and poet,' who was assassinated in 1868 as he left the House of Commons in Ottawa. On the occasion of his visit to Foxbar McGee gave poetry recitations and impressed the group with his sartorial splendour, the chief feature of which was his magnificent pearl-grey silk hat.

For nineteen years the Anglican churches in both Dundas and Ancaster were served by the Reverend William McMurray. Born in Ireland in 1810, McMurray came to Upper Canada as a young child.

Foxbar, 10 Overfield Street

The family settled at York, where William became a pupil of Dr John Strachan at the Blue School. After his ordination in 1832 McMurray was posted as a missionary to Sault Ste Marie on the north shore of Lake Superior, although neither the lieutenant-governor, Sir John Colborne, nor Bishop Strachan could tell him where the post was located. Since no survey of the territory had yet been made, not even the surveyor-general, Mr Chewett, knew its location. McMurray was advised to go to Detroit and ask for directions there. From Detroit he travelled north for a month by steamer, schooner, and canoe and eventually reached the area in which he would spend the next six years.

In 1833 McMurray married Charlotte, the daughter of John Johnston, a wealthy Irish trader, and his Indian wife. Charlotte, whose name in the Ojibwa language can be translated as 'the lovely maiden of the Sault,' accompanied her husband on his tours through the area, acting as his interpreter. About four years after their marriage the McMurrays met Anna Jameson, who in her book *Winter Studies and Summer Rambles* described Charlotte McMurray in a kindly yet somewhat patronizing manner:

I must confess the specimens of Indian squaws and half-cast women I had met with in no wise prepared me for what I found in Mrs. McMurray. The first glance, the first sound of her voice struck me with a pleasant surprise. Her figure is tall, at least rather above than below middle size, with an indescribable grace and undulation of movement which speaks the perfection of form. Her features are distinctly Indian, but softened and refined, and her expression at once bright and kindly. Her dark eyes have a sort of faun-like shyness in their glance, but her manner, though timid, was quite free from embarassment or restraint. She speaks English well with a slightly foreign intonation, not the less pleasing to my ear that it reminded me of the voice and accent of my German friend. In two minutes I was seated by her, my hand kindly folded in hers and we were talking over the possibility of my plans.

McMurray was revered by the Indians, who referred to him by his Ojibwa name meaning 'the lone lightning.' They were, however, direct in their responses to the missionary. On one occasion, after he chastised them for intoxication, a chief replied: 'My fathers never knew how to cultivate the land. My fathers never knew how to build mills. My fathers never knew how to extract the "devil's broth" from the grain. The white man makes it and brings it to us, and now blames us for drinking it.'

By 1835, after the appointment of a new lieutenant-governor, Sir Francis Bond Head, McMurray became disenchanted with the policies of the new administration. He felt that, because of the lieutenant-governor's view that it was useless to civilize the Indians, there would be less support for schools and other improvements. Fearing that he would now be placed in the distasteful position of having to break his promises to the Indians, William regretfully left the north in 1838 to settle in Dundas with Charlotte and their two sons. Another son and daughter were born to the McMurrays during their Dundas years. McMurray prompted the construction of St James Church, Dundas, and by 1843 was able to lay its cornerstone. In 1857 he left to become rector of St Mark's in Niagara-on-the-Lake. During his lifetime McMurray was instrumental in raising funds for the construction of Trinity College, which has a contemporary portrait of him. In 1878 Charlotte McMurray died at the age of seventy-one. Her husband lived until 1894.

Although it is known that the McMurrays lived in Orchard Hill at 190 Governor's Road during most of their Dundas years, it has been difficult to determine the actual builder of the house. The McMurray name appears nowhere on the land title; instead, it seems likely that the house was rented or loaned to the McMurrays by Manuel Overfield and his family. The land was owned by the pioneer Overfield family from 1820 until 1857, a period covering the years of the McMurrays' residence in Dundas. Giving credence to this theory is a passage from the will of Manuel Overfield, who died about six months after the McMurrays arrived. Overfield requested that his executors 'cause to be built ... a comfortable dwelling house and barn for the accommodation of my wife and family on lot 50, concession 1, Ancaster Township.' No one knows why Mrs Overfield and the family chose not to live in Orchard Hill, but it is assumed that they were satisfactorily located elsewhere in Dundas and therefore carried out the will's request and rented or lent the house to their rector. The 1851 census listed John W.G. Kern, born Canada West, aged thirteen, as living with the McMurrays and their four children. When William and Charlotte left Dundas in 1857, the title of the house shows that it passed to Kern. The arrangement, although presumably amicable at the time, ended in McMurray foreclosing on Kern's mortgage after the sale.

Whatever mystery surrounds the construction of Orchard Hill, the builder was obviously a person of taste, with knowledge of the styles of the day. The house is beautifully proportioned, its central gable emphasizing a graceful Palladian window over the entrance doorway. Originally a verandah enclosed the lower floor on three sides. It was later replaced by the present portico.

Behind Orchard Hill, at 192 Governor's Road, stands the third of the trio of pre-Confederation buildings by the old 1793 road. Called Ballindalloch, this house was built in the 1860s nearly a quarter-century after its two neighbours and exemplifies the change in architectural styles during that period. Ballindalloch is Italianate, its asymmetrical facade, ornate entrance, tall, slim windows, and heavily carved brackets all typical of a time when the simplicity and classicism of an earlier era were being discarded. Buildings had become more picturesque and ornamental, as had the furnishings within.

Orchard Hill, 190 Governor's Road

John Forsyth, the builder of Ballindalloch, named his house after his ancestral home in Scotland. Forsyth was a successful manufacturer of agricultural machinery and implements. By 1861 he had become a partner in Vulcan Works, one of only three factories in the world making screw machinery. Ballindalloch was purchased in 1872, after Forsyth's departure from Dundas, by the founder of the Dundas *True Banner*, James Somerville. He promptly renamed the house Uplands.

A colourful man, Somerville was active in politics as well as journalism. As editor of the *True Banner* he expressed his opinions in an aggressive and forthright manner so that, although his approach would seem intemperate today, there was no doubting where he stood on any issue. Obviously many readers agreed with his views, for he was elected mayor of Dundas in 1874 and eight years later became a member of Parliament. He died at Uplands in 1916. After his death his obituary stated: 'He had character. He was a broad

Ballindalloch, 192 Governor's Road

man. But he was a modest man. He made no big speeches. He had no poses ... We see his worth so plainly now. For many years we took it as a matter of course.'

Described with Victorian fervour as 'the jewel on the brow of Dundas,' a distinguished house sits in classical splendour overlooking the town from Cotton Mill hill. Mount Fairview, at 50 South Street, was built in 1848 for Hugh Moore on what was then the outskirts of Dundas.

Moore was a wealthy merchant whose general store stood at King and Main Streets. His wife, Jane Brock, was the daughter of Major Thomas Brock, a cousin of Sir Isaac Brock. A description of Mount Fairview in 1852 is contained in a letter from a schoolgirl who was visiting the Moores:

Mr. Moore lives on Mount Fairview, within the limits of the corporation, a most delightful spot, we can see the whole town and are still within four

Mount Fairview, 'the jewel on the brow of Dundas'

minutes walk of it. I never yet saw such scenery. The town is entirely surrounded by mountains and hills; ... the house is two storey with an observatory (from which we can see Hamilton). Galleries all around below and nearly so above. Drawing room below, wilton carpet, yellow and crimson satin sofa ... curtains all of the most exquisite New York workmanship, 700$ piano, you may judge of its beauty ... the school room is ... nicely carpeted, windows curtained, large table druggeted and two small tables and a piano in it.

Built of brick covered with stucco, Mount Fairview is square in plan. Four Ionic columns soar two full storeys to frame the south façade and support the hip roof above. The house is crowned with the belvedere mentioned in the letter as the spot from which one could see Hamilton.

The Moore's position and wealth did not spare them from the usual tragedies of life at that time. Of their ten children, three sons and a daughter predeceased them. Jane Moore died in 1890, her husband two years later at the age of 86. Moore's concern for his remaining children is shown in a codicil to his will added just two months before his death: 'with respect to the monies bequeathed to my son James F. Moore that in case he should marry, of the said monies $1000 should be given upon the death of my son to his widow ... and also $1000 to each of his lawful children.' James Frederick did die soon, a short three years after his father.

At about the time that Moore was building Mount Fairview the town fathers, after much wrangling and dissension, finally agreed to construct a town hall. Matters did not always proceed smoothly in council affairs, as the efforts of the first town council to incorporate make clear. Under the heading 'Incorporation of Town of Dundas' the *Dundas Weekly Post* of 11 January 1836 described their efforts: 'One who was half seas over, climbed onto the platform and solemnly sat in the chair. He sagely scrutinized the Acts of Parliament which were on the table, and then fell off the chair, after which he was hauled off the platform.' After this inauspicious beginning it is not surprising that it took another eleven years to achieve incorporation. At the same meeting George Rolph, whose presence seemed a sure guarantee of a contest of wit, was heard to comment upon the liberality of private individuals in Dundas which made incorporation unnecessary. This prompted the reply from the *Dundas Weekly Post*: 'It is a wonder that the word liberality did not freeze on his lips as it had long ago done in his heart.' When incorporation finally did take place, construction was begun on the Town Hall. Completed in 1849, it is one of the finest nineteenth-century municipal buildings in Ontario.

This stone structure on Main Street was built by contractor James Scott in the classical revival style according to plans drawn up by another Dundas contractor, Francis R. Hawkins. In a rather remarkable way the building managed to meet the requirements of virtually all the citizens of Dundas. Dignified, a symbol of the integrity of government which only the classical tradition could represent, it housed on the second level a ballroom, which also served as an opera house and hall for every imaginable civic event. On the first floor were the council chamber and town offices. In the basement butchers' stalls and farmers' stands lined the main corridor. In addition the basement contained a tavern – Alfie Bennett's Crystal Palace Saloon – and immediately across the hall was the town jail. Creative and pragmatic planning such as this is rarely found!

Town Hall, Main Street

Undoubtedly the most ardent supporter of the new Town Hall was a black man known only as Old Pomphrey. An escaped slave, he arrived in Dundas in 1843 via the Underground Railroad when he was fifty-eight. He worked at odd jobs, rang the town bell, served as town crier, and saved his money. When it came time to build the Town Hall, Pomphrey donated his life's savings – some $40 – towards its construction. It was sadly ironic, therefore, that he became the first occupant of the town jail. He was sent there for fighting.

In spite of their new building the council meetings continued in much the same manner. Only eight years after the hall was built, its designer, Francis Hawkins, appeared before council to defend his work on a school which he was building. The Dundas *Weekly Warder* reported on 3 July 1857: 'A more boisterous meeting of council never took place before and we sincerely hope for the honour of those sitting at the board never will again. The conduct was unbecoming in every sense of the word, and to publish in toto the doings would defile our Journal, disgrace the councillors and place them in a light, rather unfavourable before the eyes of their constituents.'

Less than ten years after building the Town Hall its contractor, James Scott, built a house for himself at 146 Park Street West. Both buildings attest to his skill. His stone house, built in the Gothic Revival style, without doubt the most popular style of the mid-century, is a prototype for many similar homes found in Ontario. Of particular interest is the central window above the entrance door, its graceful pointed arch echoing the gable above. Scott was able to employ the best of skills and materials for his home, owning as he did a planing mill and a thriving construction business. He was active in Dundas politics, becoming a member of the volatile town council in the 1860s. Later in that decade his cut-stone dwelling was sold to Andrew Graham, whose grocery business was located just west of Hugh Moore's merchant shop.

It is unusual to see the light-hearted effect of gables and bargeboard used in such a utilitarian building as a doctor's office or to think of describing such a pragmatic structure as an architectural gem. Such however is the case with the small board and batten building on Albert Street, once the surgery for several Dundas doctors. The structure was built in 1848 by Dr James Mitchell. Originally located on King Street, it withstood one hundred years of use

The surgery, Albert Street

on the town's main street before it was moved and restored in its present location. It is now part of the Dundas Historical Museum.

James Mitchell was a nephew of Egerton Ryerson. He studied medicine with Dr John Rolph and later served as a surgeon with the 7th Regiment, Gore District. In 1838 he married Martha McCay; letters in the Ontario Archives suggest that they had an adopted daughter, Minnie. James Mitchell died of cholera in 1854.

After Dr Mitchell died, his practice and the small surgery were taken over by his young partner, Dr James McMahon. As a boy of fifteen McMahon had studied with Mitchell, graduating later from the medical department of Victoria College in Toronto. He returned to Dundas in 1852, where he served the community both as a doctor and a politician, holding various civic offices and finally being elected for two terms as an MLA.

The house at the corner of Elgin and Victoria Streets (39 Elgin) is another fine example of Gothic revival architecture, with its asymmetrical arrangement of windows and doors and the vertical lines so typical of that style. The house is of frame construction with a stucco covering. It was built about 1860 by Thomas Wilson, who was born in Dunbartonshire, Scotland, in 1828. Thomas was the son of Charles Wilson, a distiller, and the grandson of a Glasgow manufacturer. In 1843 the Wilson family moved to Canada West, where fifteen-year-old Thomas trained with John Gartshore in Dundas. After twenty-five years with the firm Wilson purchased the foundry and machine works, which made mill machinery for most of the saw and grist mills operating in the province. Later the house on Elgin Street became the property of Thomas's son, Richard Todd Wilson.

Active in civic politics, Richard Todd Wilson served as mayor of Dundas for a short time (1891–2). His main interests, however, centred on his various business ventures, which included a grocery, wine, and liquor business, a coal-oil works, a flour and feed business, a mill, and a hotel.

One local legend concerns that part of Wilson's business which involved the distribution of barrels of liquor after they were unloaded on the docks of the Desjardins Canal. Apparently liquor from every shipment was mysteriously disappearing from the barrels en route to their destination. One day, unknown to Wilson, vinegar was substituted for the liquor. After that there were no more shortages and Wilson became known locally as 'Vinegar Dick.' He lived a long and full life, much of it in the Elgin Street house. In October 1926 the *Dundas Star* reported the Wilsons' celebration of their sixtieth wedding anniversary.

At 35 Cross Street, just south of the home of the redoubtable George Rolph, is a house that once belonged to an equally noteworthy if somewhat less controversial man, Thomas Howard McKenzie. A native of Fort George, Inverness-shire, Scotland, Thomas, following family tradition, was educated for the army. His father, James, was an officer in the Royal Artillery. Thomas came to Upper Canada in 1830 at the age of nineteen and settled in Hamilton. His thirst for adventure and willingness to work were both qualities which ensured success in the young country. Two years after he began work in Hamilton, he was sent to Preston to establish a business there for his employer, Colin, Ferrie and Co. By 1840 he was in Dundas with his own general store which specialized in woollen sales. He also bought and sold pork by the hundreds of tons. Reported to be one of the first dealers to pay cash for wool, McKenzie's sales exceeded

Wood-Dale, 35 Cross Street

£1,000,000 in his most profitable year. He attended the world exposition in London, England, in 1851 and saw blankets made by William Slingsby, manager of the Elgin Mills of Dundas, win first prize and therefore become the property of the queen.

McKenzie's quest for good wool took him to South Africa and his bent for adventure led him to Canada's Pacific coast. In 1834, in the company of a young friend and two Indian guides, McKenzie, then twenty-three, reached Rainy Lake after some time spent in explorations. On finding the Indians at war and a cholera epidemic raging the party decided that a retreat was in order and returned home. This was not, however, to be McKenzie's last taste of adventure. Throughout his life he was active in military affairs. He commanded a company in the 1837 rebellion and remained involved with the militia, attaining the rank of lieutenant-colonel in the Wentworth Regiment.

McKenzie married Dinah Sydney Smith, the daughter of John Sydney Smith, a surgeon who served in the Peninsular wars. The McKenzies had five daughters. Their Regency cottage, called Wood-Dale, was built in 1846. A verandah once stretched across the façade, its vine-covered treillage adding to the romantic appearance so important for this style. In 1876 a ballroom was added at the rear of the building, possibly at the urging of the five McKenzie girls.

Next door to the McKenzie house, at 31 Cross Street, stands Eastridge, the residence of Dundas druggist H.W. Ralph. This pleasing stone building is shown on an 1851 map of Dundas. It may, however, have been a single-storey dwelling at that time, for the mansard roof is undoubtedly a later addition. Ralph, along with his uncle, formed a wholesale drug company.

In the same year that Thomas McKenzie built his Regency cottage, an imposing classical revival house was erected across from it at 32 Cross Street. Its owner, William Notman, was a Dundas lawyer whose zest for the military made a visible – and audible – impression in the town. Notman was in possession of a 'six-pounder gun,' originally the property of Lord Selkirk, one of six such guns with which his lordship mounted a battery at the Red River settlement in 1816. According to the Dundas *True Banner*, the cannon became Notman's private property. He used it during the 1837 Rebellion when he was involved in the pursuit of William Lyon Mackenzie at Navy Island.

Returning to Dundas, Notman brought the cannon with him and stored it in his basement in order to have it at hand in case of need. The need seemed to arise upon every civic or public holiday, when the cannon was brought out and a salute fired. Each year without fail the cannon emerged on 24 May. Notman trudged up Cannon Hill at sunrise with his cargo and fired a salute to the monarch. The citizens of Dundas were, it seems, not always either impressed or amused. With an almost audible sigh the *True Banner* of 20 May 1859 reflected: 'The Queen's Birthday / We have as yet heard of no definite arrangements for a public celebration on the 24th but we suppose the "big gun" on the "brae" will proclaim the dawning of that auspicious morn; and that Colonel Notman and Captain Robertson will show our citizens their "soldiers" on parade.'

Notman had come to Canada at the age of sixteen. He studied law with George Ridout in Toronto and in 1827 started a law practice in Ancaster. Within three years Notman had suffered the loss of his only

32 Cross Street, home of William Notman and his 'big gun'

son. Just two years later his wife and two daughters died of diptheria, all within a space of four weeks. Notman was only twenty-seven at the time.

In 1835 Notman moved to Dundas. Eventually he remarried and became the father of a son, William, and two daughters, Jane and Mary. The Notmans lived for many years in the stately stone house on Cross Street. William Notman's military service spanned thirty-eight years. He was also actively involved in civic and political affairs, all of which he embraced with unbridled enthusiasm. At his death in 1865 the *True Banner* printed a lengthy obituary which began by stating that 'On Tuesday evening, William Notman was called from the scenes of time to the realities of eternity,' and continued by recalling the exploits for which he was famous, dwelling on the many appearances of the 'big gun.'

The event which caused Notman and so many other Dundas men to rally to the defence of the government, the 1837 rebellion, was largely the result of the actions of one of the town's first residents, William Lyon Mackenzie. Known widely as a publisher and journalist, politician and orator, Mackenzie began his career in Upper Canada in the retail trade. Born in Scotland and raised by his poor and widowed mother, the young Mackenzie entered the mercantile business and came to Upper Canada in 1820 with the son of his employer, John Lesslie. After a few weeks working on the Lachine canal, Mackenzie joined Lesslie in York in the 'book and drug' business. Shortly afterwards he and Lesslie moved to Dundas to open a new store. Their advertisement noted that Mackenzie and Lesslie were 'Druggists and Dealers in Hardware, Cutlery, Jewellery, Toys, Carpenters' Tools, Nails, Groceries, Confections, Dye-stuffs, Paints etc.'

While he was in Dundas, William Lyon Mackenzie is thought to have lived with Lesslie, although the exact location of the house they occupied is in doubt. Mackenzie's son-in-law and biographer, Charles Lindsey, notes that it was while he was living in Dundas that Mackenzie married: 'This event took place on the 1st of July, 1822, at Montreal. Miss Isabel Baxter, his bride, may be said to have been a native of the same town as himself, for she was born at Dundee and he at Springfield, a suburb of the same place. Though they both were at the same school together when young, they had ceased to be able to recognize one another when they met at Quebec. The marriage took place within three weeks from the first interview, a circumstance that accords with the general impulsive nature of his character. Of this union the issue was thirteen children.'

The trim little cottage at 31–3 Melville Street was for twenty years the home of a Presbyterian minister with the euphonius name of Mark Y. Stark. He arrived in Dundas in 1833 to serve as the first minister of St Andrew's Church. Ten years later, because of theological differences, Stark withdrew from the Established Church of Scotland. With two of his elders and over one hundred of his parishioners, he then formed the Free Church congregation called Knox Church. The pleasant house on Melville Street, purchased by Stark in 1856, became the rectory for that church.

Built during the 1840s by Alexander Chalmers, a saddle- and harnessmaker, the house with its neat peaked gable is typical of several trademen's homes in the area. A touch of bargeboard outlines the gable and a large door, well-fashioned and welcoming, serves as the focal point of the simple façade. When Mark Stark bought the

Kirkhill Cottage, 31–3 Melville Street

house he named it Kirkhill Cottage. It was here that he died in 1866.

Stark was a scholarly, well-educated man. He had travelled extensively through Europe and spoke several languages fluently. His interests included natural sciences and telegraphy but the driving force in his life was his church. On 22 April 1859 the Dundas *True Banner* stated: 'We have been requested to intimate that the Rev. Mr. Stark of Knox Church intends to give, during the summer months, a series of monthly sermons, especially addressed to the young – the services altogether on each occasion, not to exceed one hour.' It is not known to what extent the assurances concerning the length of the sermons attracted the young on those warm summer Sundays.

Sometimes a house contains details of construction which offer clues but no definitive answers about its history. Such is the case with the intriguing and unusual building at 11–13 Cross Street. Architectural details suggest that the house was built in stages

11–13 Cross Street

around a small central structure. Hand-hewn beams found under the plaster mark the initial portion. Five windows were incorporated in the second stage of construction, which provided more living space, and the third stage saw an addition at the rear, possibly a summer kitchen. Some time during the 1800s another two rooms were added to the south of the house, these with the high ceilings, ornate plaster mouldings, and fine wood trim of the period. Inexplicably, all the parts come together to form a unified whole, creating a charming and certainly unique building.

The 1851 map of Dundas shows the house as the property of Mrs Buckman and an 1868–9 directory again lists that lady, probably a widow, as the owner. The building later housed a funeral parlour. Today it serves Dundas well as a bookstore.

In the heart of Coote's Paradise stands a fine neoclassical house with its date, 1833, inscribed on the arch keystone. The hamlet with that memorable appellation was the tiny settlement which, when it grew, adopted the less memorable but more dignified name of Dundas – the latter in honour of Henry Dundas, secretary of state in the British government. Coote's Paradise was the point at which the first road commissioned by John Graves Simcoe, later called the Governor's Road, began. The village was originally named after Captain Coote of the 8th King's Own Regiment. Coote's Paradise was bounded by North, South, East, and West Streets, within which area the neoclassical structure at 30 York Street is situated. The stonework is partly cut and partly rubble and the door with its classical detailing still retains the original sidelights.

The building stands on what was the original Hatt estate. Richard Hatt, one of the town's first settlers and its principal founder, and his brother Samuel built mills. The Hatts' mill became the centre of the burgeoning community. Richard Hatt married in 1799. His bride, Mary Cooley, was the daughter of another pioneer, Preserved Cooley, whose unusual name was given to him because he was born during a raging storm at sea. In gratitude for their preservation the Cooley's named their son Preserved. Richard and Mary Hatt had eight children, the last of whom, Margaret Matilda, was born after her father's death in 1819. The fact that the York Street house stands on Hatt property and has such an early date makes it possible that the structure was built by the Hatt family.

The earliest remaining assessment rolls for Dundas carry the 1835 listings. At that point, two years after the house was built, the records list only two stone houses in Dundas. One, owned by William McDonald, innkeeper, had twenty-nine occupants – too many to squeeze into the house at 30 York Street. Thus it is probably the second stone house, listed as the residence of Daniel Campbell. His home was described as 'two storeys, on 1¾ acres with two additional fireplaces.' Also on the property were a merchant shop, a store house, two horses, one cow, and a pleasure wagon. Nine people lived there, three of them children under sixteen.

By 1849 the house was owned by a Mrs Coulson, who rented it to a number of tenants during the ensuing years. Although the building is sometimes called the Dundas Customs-House, it has been established that the customs-house was actually on Dundas Street on the direct route from the Desjardins Canal.

When William McMurray left his post as rector of the Anglican churches in Dundas and Ancaster, he was succeeded by the Reverend Featherstone Lake Osler. Son of a British shipowner and a former officer in the Royal Navy, Osler came to Dundas after twenty years spent in the townships of Tecumseth and West Gwillimbury. When Osler and his wife, Ellen Free Picton, emigrated to Canada in 1837, they did so in spite of assurances by the bride's friends that to go to Canada was absolute banishment. Their initial experiences would have only served to confirm the worst of these predictions about life in the wilderness. Osler's journals note that their first accommodation consisted of 'a sitting room and an apology for a bedroom' and later 'a hut in which cattle were kept ... the hut was surrounded by dead trees and, with the exception of wolves, no living creatures were within a third of a mile from us ... when Spring opened, even this poor accommodation had to be given up, a farmer needing it for his cattle.'

While he was in Tecumseth and West Gwillimbury, Osler provided much more than spiritual help to the settlers. He gave legal, medical, and financial advice. Appealing to friends in England, he procured eyeglasses which he gave to those who needed them most. He helped men to draw up a will after seeing widows left destitute when their husbands died intestate so that lands and possessions passed on to the eldest son. Keeping a fund of $200 so that settlers could borrow in emergencies, he recalled that 'every farthing ... was repaid.'

Eventually Osler was holding services in 'twenty different townships extending over 2000 square miles of country ... As there were few post offices through the country, I would give notice at the conclusion of the service that on that day six months ... I would be with them again to hold services and without any other notice the congregation would be waiting for me at the time specified ... I was frequently obliged to spend the night sitting on a bench' because of the vermin. When in 1840, his health broken, Osler left for a holiday in England, many came to see him on his way: 'Great was my surprise on reaching the village of Bond Head to find the whole place crowded with sleighs and wagons filled with people determined to accompany me for part of the journey. In all there were one hundred and ten vehicles of various descriptions forming the cavalcade.'

During his years as a missionary Osler instituted the first Sunday School picnic in Canada. Years later, when he was in Dundas, he introduced this popular event to his congregation there. The occasion was duly reported in the *Dundas Weekly Warder*, 3 July 1857:

30 York Street

PIC NIC

On Friday afternoon last, a large party consisting of the younger portion of
the Rev. Mr. Osler's congregation, together with their parents and numerous friends, joined in a Pic Nic having just met at the English Church at
about 2 o'clock, and after the Reverend Gentleman delivered a most appropriate and kind address to all present, they betook themselves to the grove
on the farm of Thomas Hatt Esq. and there enjoyed themselves under the
foliage of the spreading Oak and Maple until Sol had receded far in the
distance. The day was lovely, the countenances of all present were lovely,
the oranges and cakes most lovely and the attention of the young gentlemen present exceedingly lovely.

The Osler home in Dundas was the spacious brick house still
standing on South Street near Mount Fairview, overlooking the
town. It was built in the middle of the century by William Miller, a
lawyer born and educated in Niagara. Miller practised law in Dun-

Hill-Side Home, 29 South Street

das for eighteen years and then in 1853 was appointed judge of Waterloo County. The Oslers moved into the Miller house on their arrival in Dundas and raised their nine children there. One of their sons, Sir William Osler, became a legend in his own time. He died in England in 1919, his contributions to medicine unsurpassed by anyone of his generation.

At 29 South Street, across from the Osler house, stands a sedate Georgian building known as Hill-Side Home. Built in 1834, it was the home of Edward Lyons, who occupied the house until his death in 1890. A farmer, Lyons turned his hand to a variety of other pursuits, as, from necessity, did most settlers. Local records suggest that Lyons was a blacksmith, mechanic, and carpenter. He also owned a substantial amount of land so that in his will he was able to leave handsome bequests to his surviving children – four daughters, three sons, and the children of two daughters who, presumably, predeceased him. He left Hill-Side Home and all its contents to his third wife, Nancy. To sons John and William he left 'one spar of horses, one set of double harness, one lumber waggon, one sleigh, one plough and one set of harness to be chosen by them out of any such chattels as I die possessed of,' a valuable bequest, in addition to land and money.

Lyons was of Loyalist background and had acquired his land from the Crown. Perhaps his skill as a blacksmith was inherited from his grandfather, who, it is believed locally, was that unfortunate Dundas farmer whose horse was so arbitrarily commandeered by George Rolph as he rode through Dundas in 1812.

6

Ancaster

Customers who visited the Rousseau General Store in the village of Ancaster usually paid for their purchases in kind. Original ledgers from the 1790s and early 1800s show transactions such as John Rykman's purchase of tea, paper, nails, cheese, sugar, gloves, and whiskey in exchange for the skins of 52 martins, 1 otter, 2 racoons, several beaver, deer, and a small bear. Mr Totten paid for his rum and sundries by building chimneys, Jeptha Skinner traded butter for indigo and nails, and William Hambly covered the cost of 'spirits' by working as a surveyor. Other customers brought items for trade such as cabbages, wheat, and beehives or simply offered their labour at six shillings per day.

The Rousseau store had been opened in 1795 when its owner, Jean Baptiste Rousseau, settled in the village of Wilson's Mills (the name of the village was later changed to Ancaster). He was a fur trader, an interpreter for the Indians, and a fifth-generation Canadian. At his birth in 1757 he became the fifth in the family line to bear the name Jean Rousseau. His great-great-grandfather, born in 1570, had emigrated from Paris to settle at Trois-Rivières, Quebec, where he resided until his death in 1643. The Rousseau Papers, donated to the Ontario Archives by a great-grandaughter of Ancaster's Jean Baptiste, tell the fascinating story of the young man who became a fur trader, miller, merchant, interpreter, and a loyal friend of Joseph Brant.

Rousseau started in business at an early age. When he was sixteen, a contemporary remarked that the boy was 'beginning to speak the Indian language well and is capable of taking his father's place ... we flatter ourselves Sir ... that you will be glad for him to take his dear father's place in the King's service.' During the American Revolution Jean Baptiste Rousseau met and worked with Chief Joseph Brant while acting as an interpreter for the Six Nations Indians. The mutual respect that developed between the two men at this time continued throughout their lives. They later became business associates. Rousseau's ledgers show that Brant was one of the few customers at the general store who paid cash for his purchases of whiskey, blankets, and sundries.

When he was twenty-three years old, Rousseau wed Marie Reine Martineau. This was the first of four marriages for Jean, the other three to one woman. The young couple settled at Cataraqui but Jean continued to operate his trading post at the Humber River. After six years of this arrangement Marie, having met someone closer to home, wrote her husband a letter which outlined terms for a separation. She stated 'that I ... having frequently disagreed with my husband ... and at length finding that we could no longer live in unity ... have agreed ... to a mutual separation and to be no longer dependant on one another. And I do hereby ... promise and bind myself never to molest, trouble or injure him ... and further, I do hereby promise to pay unto the said Jean Baptiste Rousseau the sum of five hundred pounds of good and lawful money of the Province of Quebec should I fail in the above written condition.' Obviously a compassionate man, Rousseau returned Marie's dowery to her and, in a statement at the time, said: 'Although I ignore even the existence of my wife, I yet regard her as my wife. I recommend her to my executor, if she survives me. I beg him to do his utmost to lead her back to virtue, and to make her during her life, from my wealth, an annual pension income for life, as proof that I forgive her.'

Within a year, Rousseau met Margaret Cline, a young woman who had lost her parents, brothers, and all but one of her sisters during an Indian raid in New York State. Margaret and the surviving sister were rescued and raised by an Indian woman who had recently lost two daughters of the same age. Eventually the girls were purchased by Joseph Brant and taken to live as servants in his home. While on a visit to Joseph's sister, Molly Brant, Margaret met Jean Rousseau. They were married in an Indian ceremony that year.

As a Roman Catholic Rousseau could not obtain a divorce to marry Margaret. Thus he left his church, but he worried about the legality of the Indian ceremony. Therefore eight years later, shortly after they had settled in Ancaster, Jean and Margaret were married again. This second ceremony was conducted in nearby Brantford by an Anglican missionary who had not been informed of their previous marriage: 'Grand River, October 15, 1795. This is to certify that St. John Baptist Rousseau Interpreter in the Indian Department, and Margaret Clyne, formerly a Prisoner among the Mohock Indians were lawfully married at the House of Captain Brant on the Grand River in the Province of Upper Canada on the date above written by me. Robert Addison, Missionary to Niagara and to the Indians.' Finally, in 1807, after the death of Rousseau's first wife, Jean and Margaret were married again, this time legally. Their marriage licence referred to Margaret as a spinster, although by this time the Rousseaus had a sizeable family.

One of the few contemporary accounts of Mrs Rousseau is found in the diary of a Moravian missionary, Benjamin Mortimer. He suggests that, while Margaret's finer qualities may have been recognized by her husband, others saw her in a different light. Mortimer wrote that, when he stopped at their trading post, the redoubtable Mrs Rousseau refused him grain for his horses, although she admitted that there was plenty to spare. Other travellers reported similar treatment from the lady of the house. Her husband, however, was described as 'the genial Frenchman, Mr. St Jean.'

In Ancaster Rousseau became established in a variety of business ventures. He purchased mills, opened his store and a hotel, and also continued to serve his friends the Indians. During the War of 1812 Rousseau died of pleurisy while acting as an interpreter. It is a matter of some wonder that he lived long enough to see that war, for a doctor's records of 1799 list medicines prescribed for him at that time. They included 'calomel and julep, Hooper's Pills, worm powders numbers two and three, ipecac, sulphur, pink senna, rhubarb and Glauber's salts, etc.'

Two buildings on Ancaster's main street tangibly recall the Rousseau family, and, in addition, a mill stands nearby on the site of Rousseau's 1795 mill. The handsome stone house at 375 Wilson Street was built in 1848 by Jean and Margaret's grandson, George Brock Rousseau. Following family tradition, he too was a merchant and his imposing home reflected his importance in the community. Today it is the home of Canadian artist Frank Panabaker.

An old hotel, also built of stone, is situated across the road at 386 Wilson Street. This hostelry, which was built for George Rousseau, has been a landmark since the 1830s, its ornate bargeboard and finial adding grace to a solid utilitarian structure. The stables for the inn are adjacent, at 380 Wilson, and show a similar touch of ornamentation along the roof line. The 1830 hostelry was the third Rousseau hotel in Ancaster, the first two having been built by Jean Baptiste immediately north of the present post office. In the second of these inns the 1814 'Bloody Assize' was held in which nineteen men were tried for treason in the War of 1812. Of the group, fifteen were convicted and sentenced to be hanged, drawn, and quartered. Seven of the men received clemency, but the remaining eight met a grisly death. These wretched men were hanged at the same time, their heads severed and exhibited. The third Rousseau hotel, that standing today, had happier associations; it served as a centre for community activities for over one hundred years until it ceased to be used as an inn.

There has been a mill in the village of Ancaster since 1791, when

375 Wilson Street, home of George Brock Rousseau

Rousseau hostelry, 386 Wilson Street

Richard Beasley and James Wilson constructed what may have been the first mill at the head of Lake Ontario. The original name of the village, Wilson's Mills, was derived from their mill. It was into this milling operation that Jean Rousseau bought when he purchased the shares of James Wilson. By 1813 a stone grist mill had been built, and it served to house those prisoners awaiting trial at the Bloody Assize. After Rousseau sold his share in the milling complex, it passed through the hands of several owners, one of whom was Abraham Markle, MLA. He was among those charged with treason in 1814; had he not eluded capture, he would have been held in the mills of which he was part-owner.

In 1862 Alonzo and Harris Egleston purchased the property and within a year constructed the stone flour mill that stands today on lot 46, concession 2, Ancaster, just north of the village. At present the mill is still in operation, producing and selling stone-milled flour. Its use has been further enhanced by the addition of a restaurant

The Egleston flour mill, lot 46, concession 2, Ancaster

that overlooks the mill race. This addition, although contemporary in design, is sympathetic to the character of the early mill, thus creating a commercial operation that is both aesthetically pleasing and historically significant.

On Ancaster's main street is a small stone building that has also been successfully altered for commercial use. It is one of many examples in Ancaster of the local stonemasons' skill and the beauty of the material with which they worked. Once the home of a local tradesman, it now serves as a bookstore, its unpretentious exterior contributing to the unique nineteenth-century flavour of the village. This modest little house at 398 Wilson Street East was once the home of Adam Marr, a cabinetmaker who purchased the property in 1851 for £42.10. As was often the case, Marr combined his furniture-making with an undertaking business in a pragmatic attempt to operate both concerns efficiently. In 1875 Marr sold his building to James McElroy, a young Irishman who, according to census records, was also a cabinetmaker.

In mid-winter of 1868 smoke was seen billowing from the tower of St John's Anglican Church on the main street (Halson and Wilson Streets). This small frame church had been on the site for forty-two years, standing on land donated by the Rousseau family. Founded in 1816, the parish operated for ten years without a church building and then a frame structure was built to house both the Anglican and the Presbyterian congregations. It was known as a 'Free Church' during this period of joint tenure. The original indenture records the gift, in 1826, of some land plus £1000 from George Rousseau to 'the Reverend Ralph Leeming and others.' This ecumenical venture proved to be less than satisfactory for within a year friction developed between the two congregations. Church records from 1827 explain the rift: 'Whereas a church has been erected by Public subscription in the village of Ancaster ... under the style and title of a Free Church ... And whereas since the erection of said church for Divine Worship divers discords and disagreements arising from differences of opinion in religious matters ... have grown up and afford great annoyance to all concerned and which the undersigned ascribe to the extensive meaning and application of the term Free Church giving to every different sect an equal claim to its occupancy upon most occasions ... [this has led to] serious and alarming difficulties.' These difficulties were apparently so 'serious and alarming' that the congregations eventually agreed to disagree. The Presbyterians left to form St Andrew's and the frame church became the sole property of the Anglicans.

When the 1868 fire destroyed the frame building, the rector of St John's was Featherstone Lake Osler, the fourth man to hold that post at the church. The present beautiful stone building was built directly after the fire, during Osler's tenure. Osler had located his home in Dundas, a choice which his Ancastrian flock considered misguided. Their feeling of being overlooked may have had something to do with the fact that Osler's predecessor, William McMurray, had also chosen Dundas for his home. There was a small parsonage in Ancaster which had been built by the first rector, the Reverend Ralph Leeming, in 1820, but it was located one mile west of the village and was probably not considered suitable by either McMurray or Osler. In 1872 the answer to the problem of a suitable rectory in Ancaster was provided through the will of Leeming, who had left St John's because of ill health, intending to return to England, but

St John's Anglican Church and cemetery, Halson and Wilson Streets

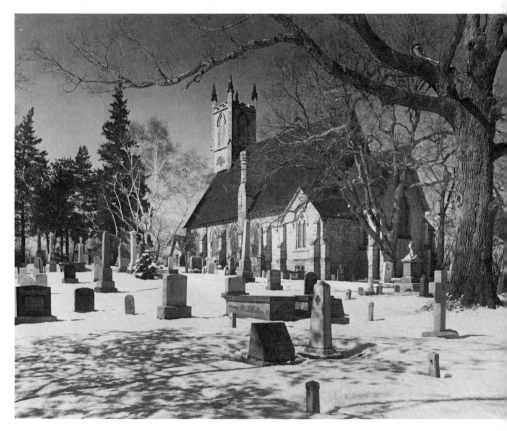

somehow was never able to bring himself to make the crossing. He returned to Ancaster in 1854, where he lived until his death in 1872. In his will Leeming left a bequest of $1000 for the purchase of a site for a parsonage, 'provided the said site is provided and money subscribed within 5 years of my death.' If this condition were fulfilled, Leeming directed that his executors 'pay over the sum of two thousand dollars to the wardens of said church to be used and applied by them in erecting ... such parsonage.' The rectory stands today at 21 Halson Street, a fine stone building that was completed about three years after Leeming's death.

The Township Hall, just east of St John's, is an equally important part of Ancaster's architectural heritage. Virtually all civic buildings of the time followed the dictates of the classical revival style and the Township Hall, constructed in 1871, was no exception. Built of stone and set well back from the street, this simple building possesses the innate purity inherent in the style and a dignity undiminished after more than a century.

When Dr Henry Richardson married Sarah Katherine Egleston in 1873, the young couple moved into their new house at 343 Wilson Street. The house was a gift from the groom's father, David Richardson. The Richardsons named their home Sunnyside, a somewhat frivolous name for what was an imposing and dignified structure. By 1881 two sons had been born to them but little is known of the family after that. The doctor died intestate in 1894 at the age of forty-nine.

From the centre of Ancaster the Sulphur Springs Road meanders down through a densely wooded valley to meet the Governor's Road on the west side of Dundas. Like a road into the past, Sulphur Springs Road seems almost untouched since the mid-1800s, when several families from Britain built estates nearby, recreating there the manor houses that they had known at home. On the north side of the road stands St Andrew's Presbyterian Church, home of the congregation that separated from St John's. Their first church, built in 1832, was later destroyed by fire and replaced in 1874 by the fine stone structure that is still in use today.

Milneholm, at 63 Sulphur Springs Road, is a Regency cottage located on land deeded to Lieutenant William Milne in 1822. Born in Scotland in 1766, Milne served in the British navy under Lord Keith, a relative of his mother's. His career took him to Alexandria, and

Township Hall, Wilson Street

while he was stationed there he carried dispatches to the sultan of Turkey. For this service he was rewarded with magnificent gifts, one of which was an Arabian horse. After the Peninsular War Milne retired from the navy and brought his wife and children to settle in Upper Canada. His wife, Elizabeth Gallwey, who had been born in Lisbon, Portugal, was, according to the dates on her tombstone, twenty-two years younger than her husband.

When the Milnes arrived in Ancaster in 1817, they built a log house on lot 43, concession 2, Ancaster and called their new home Springfield. Adding to his holdings, Milne purchased the adjacent lot five years later, and it was on this land that Milneholm was later built.

Milne died in 1826. His four children shared his extensive estate which included, as well as the Ancaster property, land in England, Ireland, and Pennsylvania. By 1832 a daughter, Maria MacKay, was sole owner of the Milneholm property, which subsequently changed

Milneholm, 63 Sulphur Springs Road

hands four times until it was purchased by her brother Alexander Stover Milne in 1846. In all probability it was Alexander who built the splendid Regency cottage that stands on the property today. Local records suggest that the builder was James Chep, Ancaster's postmaster, since he owned this acreage for four years in the late 1830s. At that time, however, Chep was living in a house on Wilson Street and was probably holding the land as an investment. In any event, given the propensity of military families to build in the Regency style, it is likely that Alexander was the man responsible for Milneholm. His father, an officer and a gentleman, would have approved.

Down the road from Milneholm stands a magnificent stone house that was built on the site of William Milne's original log house. It too was called Springfield by Henry Papps, the Englishman who built it in 1851. His son George recalled that the family had come from England in 1850 and that stone for the house was quarried from the ridge at the bottom of the road. Milne's log house was still standing at that time. George Papps stated that 'the spring in the ravine was a noted one and that the Indians came to it from great distances.'

For some reason Henry Papps sold Springfield just three years after it was built. The new owner was another Englishman, Thomas Bush, who after some years sold the house to William Farmer, Jr, an architect and engineer from New York City. It was the Farmer family who changed the name of the house to Brockton in honour of their ancestral home in Shropshire, England. During the years that followed Brockton evolved from the pleasant but unremarkable house that Henry Papps built into a magnificent, stately structure notable for both its size and its beauty. It is a far cry from William Milne's homestead, traces of which were uncovered by the Farmer family in later years. A pewter spoon, a brass watch chain, and other personal items were found, all tangible reminders of one of Ancaster's earliest settlers.

When Thomas Bush's daughter Ann Elizabeth became engaged to Dr Henry Orton, her father, who was then living at Springfield, built a home for the bride and groom on the western part of his property (lot 43, concession 2, Ancaster). The Ortons called their house Fairview because of the vista overlooking the hills of Dundas and West Flamborough. The house was constructed of the local stone so popular in the area and embellished with well-wrought bargeboard.

Henry Orton has been described by William Canniff in *The Medical Profession in Upper Canada* as being 'a keeper ever ready to assist and advise.' Dr Orton earned this reputation as he dispensed medicine from his office, a room that now forms part of the parlour at Fairview. He was the son and namesake of a doctor from Leistershire, England, who settled in Guelph in 1853. Henry Jr studied at Trinity College in Toronto and at Jefferson College in Philadelphia. He was so highly regarded by his patients that there were reported to be more than twenty local babies who were named Orton in his honour. His obituary spoke of him as 'foremost in every public charity and philanthropic enterprise.'

In 1873 Henry and Ann Orton lost their son Richard when he was seven months old. Perhaps for a new interest after his death, they traded houses that year with lawyer Thomas W. McMurray, who lived 'in town' at the corner of Wilson Street and Sulphur Springs Road. Tragedy, however, followed the Ortons. In 1878, their four-

Springfield, later renamed Brockton, Sulphur Springs Road

year-old daughter, Eleanor, died and four years after that Henry Orton himself died, 'from the effects of an injury caused by his horse taking fright, running away and dashing him against a tree.'

Further down Sulphur Springs Road stand the ruins of the Hermitage. This was once the home of George Leith, who in naming his estate was perpetuating the name of the first building on the property (lots 41 and 42, concession 1, Ancaster). The original Hermitage was built as a manse for the Reverend George Sheed, Ancaster's first Presbyterian minister. He died before his church was completed, but it is reported that his parishioners put boards over the unfinished floors so that his could be the first funeral in the church. The manse became the home of Colonel Otto Ives in 1833 when he brought his Greek bride to Ancaster. (Their coachman became the area's resident ghost after he hanged himself because of unrequited love. He is seen, it is said, wandering sorrowfully near Lover's Lane.)

Fairview, lot 43, concession 2, Ancaster

The Hermitage, Sulphur Springs Road, destroyed by fire in 1934

Leith bought the property in 1859 and built a new Hermitage for Eleanor Ferrier, his second wife. Only the shell of that building remains for it was destroyed by fire in 1934. Today, however, it is still possible to imagine the former grandeur of the Leith estate. The indestructable walls stand in the midst of beautiful parkland, now the property of the Hamilton and Region Conservation Authority. They tell the story of Leith, an aristocratic British immigrant, and his life in Upper Canada.

As the second son of a baronet George Leith was unlikely to inherit his father's title and estate, and thus he chose to come to Canada. The journals he kept during the years between 1834 and 1859 reveal a man absorbing impressions of his new country and show a certain amount of culture shock. He commented upon everything from the bad roads to the bad manners of the Yankees.

On his first trip to Upper Canada in 1834 Leith bought a farm near Hamilton. Two years later, while on a visit home to Scotland, he married Jemima Ramsay; he wrote in his journal on 14 January 1836 that he 'was married and reached Cupar about 10, the happiest fellow in creation.' The Leiths came to the farm near Hamilton and in that same year a son, John McDonald Leith, was born.

In his diary, Leith provided details of these eventful years:

1834
May 29. Went to the Park Theatre ... where I had the felicity of seeing a very pretty girl who had a few hours before received my money in a confectioner's shop, seated, full-dress, in the centre dress box and apparently perfectly at home.
July 7 [Hamilton]. Thermometer 92. Walked 24 miles to look at a farm.
July 9. The elections are going on over the whole country. People are as great fools on this side of the water as on the other about elections.
August 3. Exact statement of expense of settling on a farm of 100 acres within ten miles of Hamilton [including land, a log house, barn, stable, furniture, animals and farm implements] $1939.75.
August 13. We have been very much annoyed during the past week by a number of pigs. This morning, as I was chopping in one of the back fields, down came Mr. Law. I abused him about the pigs – he ditto; said if he had not been a magistrate he would have welted me ... He did not seem to relish coming to close quarters, but vapoured about pistols etc ... In the course of the morning sent him a challenge by Bruce, He accepted, and I started for Toronto to get my flutes.

August 16. After a good deal of jaw the seconds made up the row by recommending how to apologize, which he did fully. December 11 ... the present generation [the original settlers] may live comfortably enough because the generality of them bring their education with them but, from great difficulty, nay, almost impossibility, of realizing many dollars from farming, the next generation will be little better than the present race of Canadians and Yankees – mere drawers of water and hewers of wood with merely a common English education ... the ladies from home suffer from the climate and the incessant domestic drudgery to which the wife of every man no matter who he may have been at home, must submit.
1835
January 14. Started in the stage for Queenston ... Violent dispute the whole way to St. Catharines between a tailor-looking beast and a Methodist preacher about the universalism etc. Wished them both up to their necks in a horse pond.
March 19 [Boston]. I cannot say that I have seen four gentlemanly Yankees in the course of my perignations. All, for instance, in this house are just like our commercial travellers ... very spruce and neat in their dress, but not *gentlemen*. There is a want of blood.

Leith made one trip to Ireland. In spite of the condescending remarks about Canada in his journal, he obviously missed his new home:

May 31 [Ireland] ... unable to settle anything. Canada in my head the whole day long.
June 7 ... lay in bed dreaming of Canada.

After his marriage to Jemima in 1836 and on their return to Canada there is a gap in Leith's journals. At some point after the birth of their son Jemima died, and within a few years George Leith returned to Britain. In 1843 he married Eleanor Ferrier. For the next nine years George and Eleanor remained in Britain because of her father's illness and complications over the estate of George's father. During this time four children were born to them. Their fifth child, a daughter named Eleanor, was born in 1855 after their return to Canada. Leith's diary begins again in 1859 but with few entries. Leith lived at the Hermitage until his death at the age of seventy-five in 1887.

The stone Heslop house on Mineral Springs Road off Sulphur

Springs Road (lots 39 and 40, concession 1, Ancaster) was called
Woodend by its builder, John Heslop. A later owner called it Pine-
hurst. It has also been known as the 'murder house' since the day in
January 1891 when John Heslop, son of Robert Heslop of Northumberland, England, was shot and killed during an attempted bur-
glary. His wife and daughter were witnesses.

Heslop, a former reeve and warden of the county was at the time
serving as treasurer of the township. Because of this latter position
his assailants expected to find money in his house. After breaking in,
the four armed men were met by seventy-nine-year-old John Heslop himself, who 'sprang from his bed and stationed himself at the
top of the stairs, threatening the invaders with an upraised chair.
The prowlers demanded money, but he refused, then one of the men
shot and killed [him].'

The full story of the murder is told by T. Roy Woodhouse in
Ancaster's Heritage. He relates that four Indians were arrested,

Woodend, Mineral Springs Road

tried, and acquitted. Their trial occasioned much local interest because the four accused all admitted to being at the scene of the crime, then accused each other, and finally were given alibis by defence witnesses. One of these alibis became a byword in the area: some 'witnesses swore that all four of the accused were at Katie White's funeral, while others swore that they were not.' Thus in Ancaster anyone looking for an excuse for an unexplained absence would state 'I was at Katie White's funeral.'

The War of 1812 disrupted the lives of Upper Canada's hardworking settlers, for they had better things to do. In 1812 one settler, Adam Book, was starting to build a house on his farm south of Ancaster (lot 45, concession 4, Ancaster), but construction must have proceeded sporadically, for Book was called to serve with his militia unit at Lundy's Lane and Queenston Heights. Between battles he planted his crops and worked on his house.

Book house, lot 45, concession 4, Ancaster

Adam was the eighth child of John and Charity Book but the first to be born outside their German homeland. Like other Palatine Germans, the Books left their own country in order to escape the religious persecution that was rampant throughout much of Europe at the time. These German immigrants were often called Pennsylvania Dutch (*Dutch* in error for *Deutch*) because many of them settled in Pennsylvania.

While voyages to America from the British Isles were indeed hazardous and lengthy, those from Germany were even worse. In a history of his family Herbert V. Book states that the journey often took up to six months because there could be as many as thirty-six stops at customs houses on the Rhine, all of long duration and all requiring the travellers to support themselves financially while they were in port. Consequently in many cases the funds saved for the trip were spent before the trans-Atlantic voyage actually began. John and Anna Gertraute (later known as Charity) Book left Germany before Adam's birth in 1786 and just after the birth of their seventh child, Philippa, in 1785. They finally reached Canada when Adam was one and a half years of age. Three years later the family settled on land near Ancaster.

In 1812 Adam Book married Dorothy Shaw and the young couple began the difficult chore of establishing a home and farm during the war years. When the war ended, Book was able to devote all his energies to his farm. According to the census of 1851, he was living on his farm with his wife, Dorothy, and fifteen-year-old twins named Adam and Eve. At his death in 1869 Adam Book was able to leave his wife a prosperous farm and 'all stock, implements and the house.' His will, signed with an 'x' as his mark, provided that after Dorothy's death his two daughters, Eve and Maria (the latter either born after the 1851 census or living away from home at that time), 'should enjoy the said homestead, farm and premises as tenants in common or to receive and take rents and profits thereto, share and share alike.' The fine brick home that Book built for his family in 1812 is still lived in today by his descendants.

In the cemetery beside the Bethesda Church (lot 37, concession 4, Ancaster) are two gravestones whose admonitions give the visitor pause for thought. Marking the grave of 'poor Peter Shaver' is a stone bearing the inscription:

Come here poor sinner, cast thine eye
Then go thy way, prepare to die.

In like vein the gravestone of John Shaver states:

> Come here poor sinner, look and see
> What shortly must become of thee.

Mary Magdalena Shaver, John's widow, lived for forty years after his death. When she finally joined him in the cemetery her stone, in rather morbid fashion, was inscribed:

> I and my companion dear near forty years have been parted.
> I now lie with him in this cold bed to remain.

John Shaver, 'native of High Germany,' was one of four sons of Wilhelm and Katrinka Shaver, who had left Germany in 1765. John came to Canada after the American Revolution. He had spent the war years in New Jersey, where he fought for the British cause, serving with the Royal Regiment of New York and with Butler's Rangers.

The Bethesda Methodist Church (called the Shaver Church, as the family gave the land and money for its construction) was built in 1867. Family lore includes the story of Jacob Shaver, a descendant of John, who was one of the trustees for the new church. He boarded the stonemasons while the church was being built and also pledged $500 towards its cost. Jacob had faith but he had no cash on hand, so he planted barley on a field south of the church and a bountiful crop resulted. The crop was taken to a Dundas distillery and the money from its sale was donated to the church building fund. The abstemious congregation would have been horrified to know how Jacob earned his gift to the church.

The oldest of several Shaver houses in the fourth concession is on lot 36, the home of John and Mary's son Philip. The inscription '1835 Shaver' appears over the door of this pleasant two-storey brick structure, the date marking its completion. An old account book of Philip's records every item and every hour of labour that went into its construction. This detailed list, neatly headed 'An Account of Materials and Labour for Building of a House,' begins on 1 October 1833 and must be all-inclusive, since it even mentions a fifty-cent expenditure for sending and receiving a letter 'from States,' possibly for the plans.

The Shaver account books contain many items of interest. One of them, a recipe entitled 'Cure for Hydrophobia' (rabies), sounds like a remedy that would either cure or kill: 'One ounce pure copper filings; two ounces false tongue of colt, pulverized; two ounces of under jaw of a dog, burnt and pulverized. The copper to be taken fifteen minutes before the other in a little molasses. The tongue and bone to be taken in sweet milk.'

A neighbour of the Shavers who also came from New Jersey was Stephen Smith. In 1788, when he was twelve, he came to Canada with his parents. The Smiths settled first in Grimsby and then moved to Ancaster a few years later. Stephen and his wife, Mary Mann Silverthorn, purchased land (lot 42, concession 4, Ancaster) in 1801, shortly after their marriage. Nearby lived Stephen's father, John, and his brother Benjamin.

The daily journal kept by Benjamin Smith makes frequent mention of Stephen and their father, who is referred to as 'Dady.' Dady was a remarkable man, born in Ludgate Hill, London, in 1747. After

A Shaver house, lot 36, concession 4, Ancaster

settling first in New Jersey and then in Grimsby, he came to Ancaster in the late 1790s and began to build a new homestead at the age of fifty-one. (He sold his two hundred acres at Grimsby to Jonathan Woolverton for £40, five apple trees, and one spotted cow.) Dady lived to the age of ninety-eight.

There was little time in Benjamin Smith's life for extensive journal entries. His comments tended to be terse and to the point. The entry for 26 March 1800 said only 'Was my birthday 27 years Split stakes.' Equally brief was an entry for 11 October 1819: 'Nancy had a daughter at 5 o'clock. William and Jesse cradled [wheat].' There were, however, numerous references to Stephen and Dady which indicate that the family members assisted each other in establishing their farms: '1800 / January 6. Thrashed wheat at Dady's for Stephen ... / February 17. Thrashed wheat I and John Gordon. Stephens wheat ... / February 21. Cleaned up Stephens wheat all day.'

When Stephen Smith died at the age of sixty-five, his brother noted that date: '1842, September 8. I and Nancy went to Stephen Smith he died at half past 11 o'clock. It rained.' Stephen left ten children. His son William Mann Smith took over the homestead in 1845, purchasing it from his brother Allan, who had inherited the property. It was probably William who built the lovely brick house that stands there today. He kept the land until 1857, when it was purchased by other members of the family. At the same time mortgages totalling about £3000 were taken out, suggesting that the house could have been built during this period. Six years later William died intestate, leaving his wife Charity with eight children and an estate of $300.

It was not uncommon for men to die intestate, a situation that could cause numerous problems for the widow and children. When the Smiths' neighbour Philip Rymal lay on his death-bed in 1868, he stated to his son Eli that he had no will and had no intention of making one – a decision which is recorded in the settlement of his estate. In this case Philip was following the example of his son John, who had predeceased him nine years earlier. John left his widow Louisa an estate of $2500 with which to raise their 'eight children all under age.' Father Philip, however, left Eve Rymal, his widow, only $800 and the responsibility for seven grandchildren. At least she had the family homestead in which to house the children who were not yet independent. The house is a handsome stone structure that stands on the north side of Highway 53 (lot 40, concession 3, Ancaster). It was built in 1857 by Philip Rymal and his son John, both of whom were living there when John died two years later.

William Augustus Gott was a man of means. It is not surprising that he left a will, a document which reveals his wealth and provides a partial picture of his family. He was the son of Sir Thomas Gott of Kent, England. His mother was Dame Anne Gott, to whom he refers in his will as having bequeathed him her fine plate which he, in turn, left to his eldest son, William Charles.

In the early 1840s William Gott settled in Ancaster and purchased lot 43 in the third concession. Here he built a gracious one-storey house, simple in design, its central doorway enhanced by a fan transom. Gott named his house the Grove, a particularly apt name, for it stands in a grove of fine oak trees which shield it from the road. Situated on the western outskirts of the village, on the

Lot 42, concession 4, Ancaster, the Smith homestead

south side of Highway 2, the Grove is one of Ancaster's finest old homes.

Details of the Gott children's careers are found in William's lengthy will. He mentions 'my son William Charles Gott a lieutenant in the Honourable East India Company 56th Regiment of Native Infantry and now on service in the East Indies [1847], Augustus Grant Gott, now residing with me and my son-in-law William Green of Hamilton, merchant.' To his daughter Sarah Green, William left money for her 'sole and separate use free from the debts, control or engagements of her present or any future husband.' The Grove was evidently furnished with fine effects from England. Instructions were given for the disposal of paintings, linens, precious books, the plate, and other valuable possessions.

Sarah Gott, William's widow, died less than a month after her husband. Her own will mentions that any of her wearing apparel not wanted by her daughter should go to Mrs Allen, 'who has been

The Grove, lot 43, concession 3, Ancaster

accustomed to attend upon me.' Her most cherished possession, it seems, was the silver pencil case given her by her husband. She left it to her grandson, William Augustus Green, 'to whom I also give the sum of fifteen pounds for a watch so soon as he becomes old enough to wear one.'

Several years before the Gotts came to Ancaster, a solicitor from Hamilton built a small stone cottage on the other side of the village. He was Robert Berrie, a Scotsman, and his home, Mountain Park, was intended for use as a weekend retreat. It was admirably suited for that purpose, for his land (lot 48, concession 2, Ancaster) commands a magnificent view of the surrounding countryside. Berrie built Mountain Park shortly after purchasing the land in 1828. Eventually it became his permanent home and he lived there with his wife, Helen Eliza Butler, and their children.

Helen's grandfather was Colonel John Butler of Butler's Rangers, whose services to the Crown during the American Revolution made

Mountain Park, lot 48, concession 2, Ancaster

him one of the best known of the United Empire Loyalists. Her mother was Susan Hatt Butler, the second wife of the colonel's son Colonel Johnson Butler.

While he was living in Ancaster, Robert Berrie was active in local affairs and was instrumental in attempting to combat the cholera epidemics that swept through the country in the 1830s. As clerk of the peace for Halton and Wentworth Counties, he set in motion measures to clean up garbage and cesspools in an attempt to improve the deplorable sanitary conditions at that time. Perhaps it was cholera that caused the death of Berrie's own children. In any event, four of them died during that decade and in 1841 their mother also died, at the age of thirty-five. Shortly after her death Robert Berrie returned to his native Scotland, taking with him his only surviving child, a daughter. He gradually divested himself of his Canadian holdings, selling Mountain Park to William Coker in 1844 and finally authorizing Thomas Street in 1864 to sell or lease all the rest of his lands in this country.

Mountain Park eventually became the property of Andrew Robb in 1856. To the original cottage he added a larger stone house facing south to the Mohawk Trail. Robert Berrie's small home now forms the rear portion of the house. The result is a unique yet unified structure, its charm enhanced by the beauty of the site and by its melancholy history.

7

Brantford and Mount Pleasant

In a quiet section of Brantford, beneath towering trees, is a simple white frame church and a nearby tomb. Both have a history which is linked to events dating back to 1708 and the court of Queen Anne. The church, Her Majesty's Royal Chapel of the Mohawks, was built in 1785, a year after the land on which it stands was deeded to the Six Nations Indians for their services to the Crown during the American Revolution. In the shadow of the chapel lies the grave of Joseph Brant – Thayendanegea, war chief of the Six Nations, a man of 'animal courage,' an administrator influential in the courts of London, a warrior of absolute loyalty to the monarchy and to his people, a 'dread and terror' in battle.

In 1708 Thayendanegea's grandfather, also Joseph Brant, journeyed to England with three other sachems, or civil chiefs, from the Mohawk valley. With them was Peter Schuyler, a Dutch-American and a trusted friend of the Indians. The purpose of the trip, made at Schuyler's instigation, was to have an audience with Queen Anne. Schuyler hoped that by so doing he could impress the Indians with the power of the English and so secure their support in future struggles for land and supremacy in North America. The Indians, in turn, had two requests: that missionaries be sent to minister to their people, and that the sale of liquor to Indians be forbidden. Queen Anne complied with the first of these appeals, and within a few years a chapel was built near Fort Hunter in the Mohawk valley. Upon its completion in 1712 the queen presented her Indian subjects with a Bible and a set of rich communion plate. Some of these treasures are now in Brantford and some at the Tyendinaga Reserve near the Bay of Quinte.

The Indians kept their part of the bargain. They fought for the British during the Seven Years War (1756–63) and later in the American Revolution, under the leadership of Joseph Brant, grandson of the man who had met Queen Anne. The chaotic years that followed the revolution found the Indians in disarray, their homes and hunting-grounds lost. By the early 1800s many of them had followed Brant to Upper Canada.

Born in 1742, Joseph Brant grew up at Canajoharie in the Mohawk valley. He became a friend and protégé of Sir William Johnson, a colourful and influential Englishman who was superintendent for Indian affairs in British North America. It was Johnson who recognized young Brant's potential and sent him to be educated at Moore's Charity School in Lebanon, Connecticut. This school, which later became Dartmouth College in New Hampshire, was endowed by Sir William and a group of English gentlemen who supported the school at his urging. Both Indian and white children were enrolled so that each could learn the language of the other. In his two years at the school Brant learned enough English to work as an interpreter in the Indian department.

After his return to Canajoharie Brant married Christine, the daughter of a Mohawk chief. A son Isaac was born to them and later a daughter Christina. Two years after his wife, Christine, died from consumption in 1771, Brant married her sister Susannah, but she too died of the same disease within a short time. His third marriage was to Catherine, the daughter of George Crogan, an Indian agent. Catherine's mother was a Mohawk woman. Joseph and Catherine were married first in an Indian ceremony and later in an Anglican service that was conducted by Colonel John Butler. They had seven children.

In 1785, when the Haldimand Proclamation gave the Grand River tract to the Mohawks and 'such others of the Six Nations as wish to settle in that quarter,' Brant brought the Indian 'Allies of the Crown' to Upper Canada and the Brantford area. Their grant of land along the Grand River and stretching for six miles on each side was approximately 675,000 acres. In the ensuing years much of this land was sold by Brant to non-Indians, and this led to conflict with the government, for it interpreted the title to the land as one of trusteeship. In 1834, however, the Brant leases were officially confirmed. This was a pragmatic decision, for it would have been virtually impossible to revoke them on land which, in some cases, had been settled and farmed for nearly fifty years. So that the Indians' interests would be protected, the government seven years later established a reserve of 50,000 acres southwest of Brantford. This is Six Nations land today.

Shortly after Brant and his people arrived in Upper Canada Sir Frederick Haldimand arranged for the construction of the Royal Chapel that stands today beside the Mohawk Road. It replaced the chapel that the Indians had lost when they left their ancestral home. While much of the siding has, of necessity, been replaced over the years, some of the original boards remain. Originally the tower was at the opposite end of the chapel, with the main door facing the Grand River and the dwellings in the village. In 1829 the building was altered and the tower moved to its present location.

It is the interior of the chapel, however, that tells the story of the Six Nations. Their colourful history is depicted in eight stained-glass windows that provide a touch of splendour to the simple little

Her Majesty's Royal Chapel of the Mohawks, beside Mohawk Road

building. Adjacent to the altar is a coat of arms, carved from solid oak, the gift of George III. The Ten Commandments, the Lord's Prayer, and the Apostles' Creed, written in the Mohawk language, appear on tablets above the altar. Commemorative plaques and unique Indian beadwork all add interest to the chapel, but its principal treasures, the Queen Anne communion silver and the 1712 Bible, have been put in safekeeping. Outside, to the left of the tower door, is a chapel bell. Installed by Brant, it is inscribed 'John Warner, Fleet Street London, 1786.'

Canon W.J. Zimmerman, incumbent of the Royal Chapel since 1945, explains that the darkened corners of the Queen Anne Bible 'are a grim reminder of the days when the Bible was hidden away in a box along the Mohawk River' during the American Revolution. The Bible and the communion silver were brought to the new chapel by the Reverend John Stuart on his first visit in 1788, when the chapel was dedicated. According to Canon Zimmerman, 'Joseph Brant felt that a fitting service should be held. He himself and six braves paddled all the way to Kingston to bring back their beloved missionary of former days at Fort Hunter ... In this their hour of triumph he was to share as he had done so nobly in their hour of utter humiliation ... as they huddled together at Niagara Falls he had offered words of encouragement and hope.'

Because there were only travelling missionaries in the early years of its history, the chapel was without a regular minister until 1827. Canon Zimmerman quotes an early journal (1816) in which a visitor noted especially 'Aaron, a grey-headed Mohawk, who touched his cheeks and forehead with a few spots of vermillion in honour of Sunday.' A later visitor, Mr Mackintosh, reported in 1836 that the Reverend Mr Luggar was the first permanent incumbent and that he preached 'through the medium of an interpreter, who repeats in the Indian language every sentence pronounced by the Rev. gentleman. I was highly surprised at the happy memory which has been bestowed on the interpreter who, without the least impediment conveys the sermon to his country-men ... the canticles of the female voice were truly melodious ... the singers wore flowing mantles.'

Other original documents of the early 1800s provide glimpses of Joseph Brant's life. Early land records outline the sizable lands granted to him, 'his family and relations,' and mention also his sister, Molly Brant, the third wife of Sir William Johnson. She and her children received over six thousand acres in Kingston Township. In

1783 a 'Return of Loyalists on Carlton Island' indicated that her household consisted of fifteen people, including Molly herself, six children, servants, and four black slaves. Joseph visited his sister on occasion, and it was in her home that his friend Jean Rousseau met his second wife.

Brant was deeply concerned with the education of young Indian children. In an 1803 letter to Robert Nelles, a prominent settler originally from the Mohawk valley, he wrote: 'Dear Sir: I am extremely sorry of missing you yesterday when you passed here for I wish much to talk with you about the school which going to be kept at your place which reason I now send Jacob to know how many boys suppose you could board. I wish to know for I wish to send Jacob and Little Johnny [Brant's third and fourth sons]. I understand by the Reverend Mr. Philips that it must be stove gott for the school. I have one here that I could send for a while but the thing is how the stove to get there by sled ... Dear Sir I am yours sincerely, Joseph Brant.'

In his will Brant mentioned eight children and 'my grand-children by my son Isaac deceased, which said children as to this share of my estate, I adopt as my own.' Behind these words lay the tragic story of Brant's first son, Isaac, who, under the influence of liquor, attempted to murder his father. In the assault Isaac was wounded and later died. The council of sachems and warriors before whom Brant appeared gave their decision on Isaac's death in words of simple dignity: 'We have heard and considered your case. We sympathize with you. You are bereaved of a beloved son. But that son raised his parricidal hand against the kindest of fathers. His death was occasioned by his own crime. With one voice we acquit you of all blame.'

To his wife Catherine Brant left his 750-acre farm in Flamborough East, along with 'all my personal estate to be at her sole and entire disposal.' But after his death Catherine returned to the Mohawk village and the log house where they had once lived. She was seen in the Royal Chapel each Sunday, dressed 'in a black velvet skirt, black silk over-dress, a black cloth blanket and a black velvet cap with a fur band.'

Brant was sixty-four years old when he died in 1807, after a lifetime of service to his people. His dying words were 'have pity on the poor Indians.'

Nine years after Joseph Brant's death George Henry Martin

Johnson was born in the Mohawk village. His birth occurred in the house where his mother's parents lived, for tradition dictated that an Indian woman return home for the birth of her first child. Johnson's maternal grandfather was George Martin, a Mohawk chief. His maternal grandmother, Catherine Ralston, was a Dutch captive who had been raised as an Indian in the home of a chief. On his father's side George Johnson was the grandson of Jacob Tekahionwake (double wampum) who, at his baptism, was given the surname Johnson at the suggestion of Sir William Johnson, the friend and benefactor of Joseph Brant. Jacob's son, the father of George, was John Smoke Johnson, a warrior who had fought with Isaac Brock and who, according to his granddaughter Evelyn, 'with a young friend ... paddled swiftly and silently across the Niagara River and set the fire that burned Buffalo to the ground.'

George Johnson's lineage through his mother entitled him to inherit the chieftainship of the Mohawk people. He was educated in a Brantford school and became an interpreter for the government and chief of the Great Council of the Six Nations.

In 1845 George met Emily Howells, a young woman who had been born in England and emigrated at the age of eight with her father, stepmother, and two older sisters. Emily's father, Henry Howells, had been a Quaker but was forced to leave the sect when he married a woman who was not of the group. He came to the United States in 1832 to work for the abolition of slavery and Emily recalled his compassion in hiding runaway slaves who were fleeing north to freedom. At the same time Howell's intense religious fervour caused him to beat his daughters for almost any reason. As a result Emily spent as much time as possible away from home, visiting her sisters who had married after leaving England. Thus in 1845 she came to Brantford to stay with her sister Eliza and her husband, the Reverend Adam Elliot. Emily never returned to her father.

When Emily arrived in Brantford, George Johnson was living in the Elliot home, acting as an interpreter and assisting Adam Elliot in his work. Eight years later George and Emily were married, but only after Emily had spent the intervening period nursing her delicate sister and helping to raise the Elliot's four children. Ultimately Eliza and the oldest child died of consumption and the three other children died of scarlet fever. George and Emily's wedding was also delayed by the opposition of George's mother. She did not approve of her son's marriage to a non-Indian because this would prevent him from passing on the chieftainship to his son. Emily's other sister, Mary, was equally horrified when she was informed of the impending marriage, and her husband, the Reverend Vashan Rogers, refused to perform the ceremony.

Adam Elliot at least completely approved of the proposed marriage, which finally took place at Barriefield, near Kingston. George's mother later relented, and on the occasion of the birth of the Johnsons' first son, Henry Beverly, she brought the moccasins that George had worn as a baby to her daughter-in-law.

As a gift to his bride George built a beautiful house on land near the Grand River. He named it Chiefswood. There they lived for thirty-one years in a home filled with fine furniture, silver, china, musical instruments, and books, all of which helped to create the stimulating atmosphere in which the Johnsons raised their four children. The younger of their two daughters, Emily Pauline Johnson,

Chiefswood, the family home of poet E. Pauline Johnson, between Onondaga and Middleport

became famous as a poet and performer who, in her romantic and sensitive poetry, celebrated the rich traditions of her father's people. Wearing the full dress of an Indian princess, she gave readings across the country and eventually became internationally acclaimed.

Chiefswood stands today on the north bank of the Grand River, between the villages of Onondaga and Middleport. It is a handsome and dignified house of two storeys, finished in stucco. The front and rear façades are identical, with a projecting central bay flanked by French doors at ground level. During the summer months Chiefswood is open to the public.

Because of his prominence in the community Johnson and his wife entertained many distinguished guests in their home. Among them was the Prince of Wales (later King Edward VII), who made a brief visit during his historic tour in 1860. Alexander Graham Bell was also a frequent guest.

Johnson was a conscientious man and zealously patrolled the reserve to prevent infiltration by certain white men who were stealing timber and selling liquor. Twice he was viciously beaten by these ruffians and injured so seriously that he never fully recovered. His work for the government also caused him problems, for the Six Nations Council foresaw a potential conflict of interests. George's mother, however, held the hereditary right to nominate the chief and she insisted that a man must not be accused of neglecting his people's interests before there was any instance in which he had done so. This was accepted as a fair judgment by the council and Johnson never disappointed them.

Through the memoirs of Pauline Johnson's sister Evelyn another side of Johnson's personality is revealed. He was, it seems, a great admirer of Napoleon Bonaparte. Evelyn recalled that her father's lifelong respect for Napoleon produced some determined efforts to name his children after his hero. During the baptism of his first son Johnson passed a message to the minister requesting that the child be named Napoleon Bonaparte instead of the more prosaic Henry Beverly. Emily, fortunately, intercepted the message. Two years later, when their daughter Helen Charlotte Eliza (called Evelyn) was born, George lost his campaign for the name Josephine, but a second son, Allen Wawanosh, was given the nickname 'Kléber' after one of Napoleon's generals. Finally, with the birth of another daughter George realized his ambition. The baby was called Pauline, in honour of Napoleon's favourite sister.

If George Johnson and Emily Howells encountered family disapproval before their marriage in 1853, the pressure was even more intense for Peter Jones and Eliza Field, who were married ten years earlier. Peter, the son of surveyor Augustus Jones and an Indian woman, had fallen in love with and married the daughter of Charles Field, a wealthy English merchant. The diaries of the young couple, like the memoirs of Evelyn Johnson, give immediacy to their story, which began one hundred and fifty years ago.

Eliza Field, born in Lambeth in 1804, had been raised in a manner befitting a young lady of that time. She received all the benefits that a prosperous family could provide – good schools, tutoring in the arts, and extensive travel. Peter Jones, on the other hand, had spent the first fourteen years of his life with his mother and her Ojibwa people, constantly on the move in search of game. They faced a never-ending threat from starvation and from the white man's diseases to which they lacked immunity. Just to survive childhood was an accomplishment.

Peter's father, Augustus, was born in 1763 in Wales. As a surveyor he carried out the initial surveys of many of the townships in Upper Canada. He had 'two living wives – one Peter's own mother and the second his "legal" wife.' The woman he chose to live with was Sarah, not Peter's mother Tub-ben-Kangway. In Peter's words:

When about the age of nine years, my mother gave me away to an Indian Chief by the name of Captain Jim, who adopted me as his son. This Chief had lately lost a son bearing my Indian name and, taking a fancy to me, he applied to my mother to allow me to be placed in the room of his deceased boy. The application was successful and I was accordingly received into the family and treated as one of their children. Shortly after this adoption we left Burlington Bay for the River Credit; during this journey we suffered much from hunger and were obliged to cut down hickory trees; we then peeled off the bark and cut out chips, which we boiled in order to extract the sweet juice; this we drank and received much nourishment from it.

During the time I suffered much from cold and hunger. On awakening one morning I attempted to rise and walk out of the Wigwam, but was unable to stand upon my feet, the cords of my legs were drawn up and I was obliged to creep on my hands and knees. I remained thus crippled for two or three months.

That spring his mother came to get him. He 'greatly rejoiced to see my dear mother who ... carried me on her back to Stoney Creek, a distance of more than thirty miles through the forest. On the way we were fortunate enough to kill a groundhog – on which we subsisted.'

Fearing for his son's health, Augustus Jones took Peter from the home of his mother and in 1816 brought him to the Grand River. Here young Peter attended an English school and was converted to Christianity. He trained for the ministry, and by the 1820s he was working with the Mississauga Indians as one of the first Methodist preachers in Upper Canada.

A journey to England to raise funds for the Methodist Church exposed Peter to the zeal of the British for missionary work in the colonies. The trip was a success. He raised £1000 for the church and he met Eliza Field. There is evidence that, prior to meeting Eliza, Peter may have had another romantic attachment, which he terminated on the advice of the church. He spoke of that relationship in a letter to his brother John in 1830:

Dear Brother, Since I have been here, I have ascertained the mind and wish of Brother Case about changing my mode of life. He thinks that owing to the situation of things and my standing in the church that it will not do for me to think about getting burdened with a wife at present, and further he thinks that the person of whom I mentioned to him, would not be calculated for a suitable companion for many reasons. I am therefore under the necessity of requesting that you will inform Sister Anna to abandon all hopes of getting her desired object ... I shall always be happy to treat her as a sister in the Lord hoping that her disappointment (if it can be called such) will terminate for her present and future happiness. You can communicate this intelligence to Sister Anna in such a way as your wisdom may direct.

This early version of a 'Dear John' letter left Peter's brother with an unpleasant chore to perform, but the situation was evidently resolved for in 1833 Peter and Eliza became engaged. The young couple had overcome her father's concern, possibly because Peter had been invited to meet and talk with King William IV at Windsor Castle. Eliza, however, had to contend with the horrified reaction of relatives and friends and was herself shocked by their prejudice, which she charitably attributed to ignorance. Her father's initial approval was temporarily withdrawn when he learned that Peter's mother was one of Augustus Jones's two wives, and not his legal wife at that. It was only through the intervention of Egerton Ryerson, the first white missionary at the Credit River mission, that Field relented a second time. Ryerson accompanied Eliza to New York, where she and Peter were married.

Portraits of Eliza and Peter painted during their courtship in London and now at Victoria College, Toronto, show them to be an exceedingly handsome couple. Dr Ryerson described Peter as 'a man of athletic frame as well as of masculine intellect; a man of clear perception, good judgement ... a sound preacher, fervent and powerful in his appeals; very well informed on general subjects, extensively acquainted with men and things, serious without gloom, cheerful without levity, dignified and agreeable in his manners, a faithful friend, a true patriot, a persevering philanthropist.'

Jones was an advocate for his people and continually tried to secure aid for the Indians. His diary in 1828 recorded the difficulties he encountered with Bishop John Strachan and the Anglican Church. Strachan informed the young missionary that the government was not inclined to assist the Indians as long as they remained under the instruction of the Methodists, but should the natives come under the superintendence of the established church, then the government would give as much help as possible. Jones replied that 'their request would cause much dissatisfaction to the Methodists, as they claimed the Indians for their spiritual children.'

Eliza and Peter were ready for the difficulties which their marriage occasioned. Peter said that he knew of only three or four Indian men married to white women in 1843. Before their marriage he wrote to Eliza to tell her that the people whom she would meet thought it wrong for Indians and whites to intermarry. Eliza was immediately made aware of the fact that she was a curiosity. She wrote: 'I feel myself gazed on wherever I move.'

In Upper Canada Eliza's first home was 'one room which my dear husband calls his study with a bedstead, a writing desk, a table and a few chairs, Indian mats on the floor and ... an open fireplace.' During these early years she lost two children. As well, she struggled with her inability to speak the Indian languages, all the time viewing with dismay the prevalence of sickness and death among the native people. She knew also that many of the settlers were waiting for her marriage to break up. But the Indians were learning to love Eliza. She taught school and instructed the children in housekeeping, with emphasis on the merits of soap. Her father had manufactured this product, the use of which she believed was the first step in the direction of godliness.

Jones worked for many years to secure permanent title to the land on which the Credit River mission and the village stood. He visited England and had an audience with Queen Victoria to request the title. Difficulties continued until finally the Six Nations in Brantford offered the Mississaugas title to part of their land. At this point Peter and Eliza moved to Brantford where, in 1851, they built a fine brick home which they called Echo Villa. At last they were able to make use of the fine china and the Persian rugs that Eliza had brought with her from England.

Located at 743 Colborne Street, Echo Villa was probably a gift from Eliza's father, Charles Field. It is an impressive house, classical revival in style, its central door flanked by Venetian sidelighted windows. Patterned brick and a graceful Palladian window in the

Echo Villa, 743 Colborne Street

central gable add a touch of elegance.

Unfortunately Peter, Eliza, and their four sons had only five years in which to enjoy their new home. Peter's untiring efforts on behalf of the Indians had undermined his health and after a lengthy illness he died in 1856. His will made clear how very important his Indian heritage was to him. After leaving Eliza their home and bequeathing property to his four sons, he stated: 'and it is also my desire and request that after my decease one of my sons shall succeed to my office as a Chief of the Mississauga Indians ... and it is also my request that the said Indians will recognize my children aforesaid as being of their own people and belonging to the same tribe of which I am a member and that they shall share with them in their property both real and personal.'

Four years after Jones's death the *Brant Expositor* of 14 September 1860 reported that C.A. Jones, his son, spoke on behalf of the Mississauga Indians in the presence of the Prince of Wales. There were many identical orations on that day – the young prince was addressed, and probably bored, by numerous dignitaries, including the mayor of Brantford, the county judge, the mayor of Simcoe, and the presidents of the St George's and St Andrew's Benevolent Societies. To them he gave a set reply, similar in each case. To the son of Peter Jones, however, he gave personal thanks in reply to the following sincere words of welcome: 'Great Prince. We are glad that our much loved Queen and your August mother has so kindly given her consent that you should visit her people on this side of the great waters and we admire your ready compliance with her wishes and ours, in venturing your precious life to the dangers of the great deep ... we are thankful that the Great Spirit has taken you under his care and brought you safely amongst us ... Our love and devotion to the great British Chiefs has grown stronger.'

On 17 January 1854 the Brantford *Conservative Expositor* reported that the citizens of that town had gathered to celebrate an event of enormous significance – the arrival of the first train, marking the official opening of the Brantford to Buffalo rail line. The railroad era had begun. This stirring event was heralded by the 'firing of cannon and every demonstration of joy that could possibly be indulged in.' Such unbounded rejoicing naturally called for a show of official approbation and so parades and speeches were duly arranged. The parade consisted of the 'Sons of Temperance, the Odd Fellows and the Fire Companies.' It formed in front of the Town

Hall and, led by the Brantford Philharmonic Band, marched to the railroad depot. The speeches which followed were not to the liking of the *Expositor*'s reporter, who commented that 'during the welcome the Mayor, in comparing the President of the Railroad with a Roman conqueror, blushed and stammered so outrageously that the miserable apology that he made for a speech ... was so laughable that few could preserve their gravity.'

Although the speeches were a failure, the railroad was not. It brought prosperity and growth to Brantford. To Henry Yates, one of the founders of the Great West Railway, it brought wealth and the ability to build for himself a grandiose Tudor villa. Yates called his house Wynarden but it became known locally as Yates's Castle. It stood, in anachronistic splendour, beside the railway tracks that had made its construction possible.

Yates must have seen Wynarden as the realization of his every dream and fantasy. Built of yellow brick and stone, the house incorporates an astonishing number of architectural features which combine to form an ornate but imposing structure. In its day it was surrounded by terraced gardens and a high stone wall. A tunnel linked the house to servants' quarters and a small private school; four greenhouses, carriage houses, and stables also stood on the property. On the exterior of the house a stone crest is inscribed 'H.E.Y. 1864' (Henry and Emily Yates and the construction date). Wynarden was equally opulent on the interior and no expense was spared in its treatment. The architect, John Turner, created intricate ceiling designs and continued throughout with equally ornate and costly finishes. The house was equipped with speaking trumpets, dumb waiters, a ventilation system, and bathrooms with hot and cold running water. Today, the house at 75 Sydenham Street, is in a state of deterioration and only an imaginative eye can detect the magnificence that was once Yates's Castle.

In choosing architect Turner to build his castle, Yates selected the man whose name had recently become known for his design of the Brant County Court House at 80 Wellington Street. The Court House was, of course, classical revival in style, its design inspired by the Palazzo de' Medici in Florence. When it was constructed in 1852, it consisted only of what is now the central section and it housed the court-house, jail, county offices, and a law library. In 1861 the wings were added.

John Turner was born in Wales in 1806. He trained with the

Cubits of London, a prestigious architectural firm. Following his marriage to Elizabeth Marsh of London he emigrated to Brantford where, by 1832, he had completed the design for his first building, a frame Anglican church. When he died in 1887, his obituary noted that he was 'one of the oldest residents of Brantford. He came here when the now prosperous and densely populated city was a scattered village ... The professional work of Mr. Turner speaks for itself ... the Brantford Court House, the St Thomas Court House, Walkerton Court House, [the first] Union Station, Toronto, the Institute for the Blind, Brantford.' He designed, as well, several of Brantford's churches.

At the time of his death Turner made his home on Nelson Street. His will instructed that 'the house and lot now occupied by myself and family as a homestead' be left to his daughter Edith May Turner and to his wife Elizabeth Ann, 'to have and to hold ... as joint tenants and not tenants in common.'

Brant County Court House, 80 Wellington Street

The census for 1861 lists Charles Duncan, dry goods merchant, aged 29, born in Scotland, and his wife, Jane, aged 25, born in New Brunswick. The Duncans were living in a two-storey brick house, a house that stands today at 96 West Street. The dry goods firm mentioned in the census became Charles Duncan and Sons Ltd, a store that sold fine furniture and china. The success of the business no doubt accounts for the way in which the Duncan house was embellished over the years. What was basically a simple rectangular structure with a projecting central bay (not unlike Chiefswood) became a striking and impressive building enhanced by a magnificent verandah with ornate treillage that stretches across the façade. Interior details were handled with equal lavishness and in succeeding years the Duncans added elaborate mantelpieces, stained glass, and in the parlour a decorative hand-painted ceiling replete with cherubs. This latter addition to the decor was executed by their daughter, novelist Sara Jeannette Duncan.

One of five children, Sara Jeannette grew up in Brantford and initially became a journalist writing for newspapers in Canada and the United States. At the age of twenty-seven she embarked on a world tour accompanied only by another young woman, an unusual venture for the time. Her observations were published in Canada by the *Globe* and later came out in book form. In 1891 she married Everard Charles Cotes, curator of the Indian Museum in Calcutta; after that time she lived in India and later in England. Her literary achievements include nineteen works of fiction, of which her novel *The Imperialist* is of particular interest in Brantford. Written in 1904, it is the story of a small town called Elgin which is undoubtedly modelled after the Brantford that Sara Jeannette remembered. In his introduction to the 1971 edition of the novel Claude Bissell writes: 'She was in many ways the freshest and liveliest voice raised in that time.'

Throughout her life Sara Jeannette Duncan kept in close touch with her sister and three brothers in Canada. Her home in England became a centre for many of the literary and political figures of the time as well as for visiting Canadians, to whom she always offered a warm welcome. She died there in 1922 at the age of sixty-one.

Not far from the Duncans' splendid home stood the Kerby House which, when it was built, was the largest hostelry in Canada. It was called 'a new hotel for the new age,' and its construction in 1854 greeted the railway era in Brantford. A year before James Kerby completed his hotel, he sold some of his extensive land holdings, including part of lot 1 on the west side of Dumfries Street (now Brant Avenue). About five years later a pleasant brick house was built on the property in a style known locally as a 'Brantford cottage.' Like other vernacular houses, the cottage at 36 Brant Avenue combines elements of Georgian simplicity and balance with a few classical details and a touch of the picturesque. With few exceptions the combination works well.

Efforts to determine the origins of the storey-and-a-half cottage at 36 Brant Avenue indicate that the builder was Benjamin Munn, who purchased the property in 1868 for $2300. He promptly took out a mortgage for $1725, which suggests, although it does not prove, that he built the house shortly thereafter. The four previous owners had held the property only briefly.

Another of Brantford's many vernacular cottages is at 89 Charlotte Street. The first owner of the land and possibly the builder of

Duncan house, 96 West Street

the house was Daniel Costello. On his death in 1892 he left his widow, Maria, the following bequest: she was to receive half of his personal effects plus $365 per year, presumably so that she could spend one dollar every day on something other than necessities. The remainder of his money was left for the support of his grandchildren. The Charlotte Street house, like the many other 'Brantford cottages,' was probably built in the 1850s or 1860s when the town's prosperity began. Whatever their history, the presence of these cottages adds charm to Brantford's older areas.

An entirely different type of house can be seen near the northern outskirts of Brantford at 191 Balmoral Drive. This beautiful frame house is Myrtleville, homestead of the Good family. Built by Allen Good in 1838, it was recently given to Heritage Canada by his descendants so that its preservation would be assured. In addition, in an act of remarkable generosity family members have left with the house many of the heirlooms that they had owned for genera-

36 Brant Avenue, a 'Brantford cottage'

tions. These treasures all help to make Myrtleville, which is now open to the public, seem more like a home than a museum.

Good was an Irish merchant and banker who, having heard of opportunities with the newly opened Bank of British North America, emigrated to Montreal and took a post with the bank in 1836. With Good were his wife Eliza and their three children (a fourth was expected soon). The family sailed first to New York and then began the four-hundred-mile trek to Montreal, travelling by stage and sled. They brought with them their linens, sterling plate, and treasured books. Eliza remarked that 'the travelling is worse than you can form the distant idea of ... imagine us on a frame like a large piano box, dragged over holes of snow by two horses where every minute you fell up and down.' At one point in the journey, according to the Goods' oldest daughter, Allen remonstrated: 'Now Bessie, my heart, we must expect the ups and downs of life.'

Good's banking career ended after a conflict with Peter McGill,

Myrtleville, 191 Balmoral Drive

president of the Bank of Montreal. By this time Good had purchased land near Brantford and he and Eliza decided that they were better suited to a life of farming. They stayed in Brantford while their house was being built, and work proceeded haltingly, for it was the time of the Rebellion of 1837 and the workmen were periodically called away to serve with the militia. When it was completed, Myrtleville was a house of quality and timeless charm, well designed and well proportioned. Originally stuccoed, it was sheathed with clapboard about thirty years after it was built. On the main floor the parlour and diningroom were backed by the kitchen, pantry, and a bedroom. Four more bedrooms and a nursery upstairs accommodated the Good's ten red-haired children.

Allen Good never achieved financial success in spite of his hard work and for many years the family struggled to make ends meet. Visitors to Myrtleville today, however, benefit from the Goods' misfortune. Since the family could not afford to replace the original furniture at the time when excessively ornate late-Victorian pieces became popular, the house retains most of the beautiful furnishings so treasured by Allen and Eliza Good.

The family's journals reflect many aspects of life in rural Upper Canada. Mention is made of marauding bears and rattlesnakes, and of the ever-present fear of the typhus and cholera epidemics that ravaged the country. Any illness caused great concern and was often treated at home by blood-letting. The plight of Irish refugees was of particular concern to the Goods, who housed their countrymen whenever possible. Education was a happier experience, enriched by the presence of tutors in the household.

The Good journals tell of a murder that took place on their property and of the trial and conviction of two men, who were later executed at a public hanging. The full details were recorded in the *Brant Expositor* of 10 June 1855:

On Monday evening, people began to pour into the town and the whole night long the streets resounded with the tramping of feet. We are told by a tavern-keeper on the Burford road that as many as 600 teams passed his house during the morning. They came from the east, west, north and south and the adjoining counties of Oxford, Norfolk, Haldimand and Waterloo contributed their quotas of sightseers. There were present great numbers of women both young and old but to the credit of the Brantford female population be it said, they in general staid at home ... The execution took place on schedule with the two criminals in clean white shirts and trowsers making a confession to the assembled crowds before they were hanged, while standing with a rope around their necks and with their hands pinioned. Hymns were sung while the bolt was drawn and after 20 minutes they were pronounced dead by strangulation ... the spectacle being over, the immense crowd quietly dispersed.

Life at Myrtleville continued in a less spectacular fashion. While Good entered into local affairs and travelled, Eliza found enough to occupy her time with their ten children. She found companionship, too, in the company of neighbouring families. Speaking of the Ewings and Smiths, she said: 'We are three close neighbors which is very pleasant as bad neighbors on a farm are most disagreeable.'

Allen Good died in 1876, his wife twelve years later. While they may not have achieved all the goals they set for themselves when they came to Canada, their contribution through their children and

Bell house, 94 Tutelo Heights Drive, the birthplace of the telephone

through Myrtleville was an important one. Their home stands today as a tangible reminder of this legacy.

In the same year that Good died, another Brantford resident was embarking on a venture that was to bring him fame throughout the world. His name was Alexander Graham Bell. Recalling that day in the summer of 1876 when he sat in Mr Ellis's store in the village of Mount Pleasant, Bell said that he waited 'with the receiver and my watch in my hand.' After a preliminary humming the words 'To be or not to be' were heard distinctly, transmitted by means of Bell's new invention, the telephone.

Graham Bell's father, a world-renowned expert in the sound and speech process, brought his family to Canada in 1870 after losing two sons to tuberculosis and being advised that Graham's health was also threatened. On their arrival the Bell family stayed first in Paris with an old friend, the Reverend Thomas Henderson. They soon purchased a home in Brantford at 94 Tutelo Heights Drive, and here Graham lived with his parents for a year before leaving for Boston to teach at a school for the deaf. While in Boston he worked in the evenings on the electrical experiments which culminated in the invention of the telephone.

Each summer Graham returned to his parents' home in Brantford. Here he had a favourite spot by the cliff at the rear of the property which he called his 'dreaming place.' At Tutelo Heights in the summer of 1874 he showed his father the results of his electrical experiments and during that summer the basic concept of the telephone was born.

The surroundings were ideal for his work. The Bell home was set back from the road in a quiet location. The cliff which provided the 'dreaming place' has eroded over the years, and in 1925 the house, called by the Bell family the 'old homestead,' was moved 80 feet from its original site. At that time a basement was added and the beautiful lattice work across the verandah was built. The ornate trelliage is an outstanding feature of the homestead, although it does conceal the French doors on the façade which were part of the original construction. These doors and the peaked gable above were the central features of the house as it was originally constructed for Robert Morton in 1858. The building is open to the public.

Beside the Bell house is the Brantford home of the Reverend Thomas Henderson, the friend with whom the family stayed when they first came to Canada. This modest frame house, originally situated on Sheridan Street, served as the first telephone business office in

Canada. It, like the homestead, is in fine condition, its small-paned windows intact. Also like the homestead it is open to the public.

Alexander Graham Bell said that 'Brantford is justified in calling herself the telephone city because the telephone originated there ... the telephone was invented in Canada. It was made in the United States.' Three crucial trials took place in 1876: the first call from Mount Pleasant; a second call from the homestead to a location in the city at a distance of three miles, for which experiment stovepipe wire was strung from tree to tree; and the first long-distance call, to Paris eight miles away.

In 1877 Graham married Mabel Hubbard and the couple stayed in the homestead before leaving on a trip to England to introduce the telephone there. Melville Bell sold the Tutelo Heights home in 1881 and moved to the United States to be near his son. Graham had a summer home in Cape Breton, where he made the experiments in flight which then held his attention.

Henderson house, which served as the first telephone business office in Canada

When Alexander Graham Bell first heard the words 'to be or not to be' spoken over the telephone, he was in Wallace Ellis's store in the village of Mount Pleasant, a few miles southwest of Brantford. Ellis and his daughter were there with Bell, as were William Biggar and his son James – all descendants of Mount Pleasant pioneers.

Wallace's ancestor, Henry Ellis, had come from the Mohawk valley to Upper Canada in 1798. After spending the winter in Niagara, he and several other families travelled to Ancaster, where they purchased provisions and continued on in their search for land. Ellis, it is said, hoped to find a place equal in beauty to his ancestral home in Wales called Mount Pleasant. Eventually the little group settled on a site near the Grand River which they leased from the Six Nations Indians. According to local legend, the annual rent was one peppercorn. A survey taken seven years later showed that among the families living there were those of Henry Ellis, Abraham Cooke, and Robert Biggar.

Although he and his family had been in Upper Canada for the previous ten years, Biggar did not settle in Mount Pleasant until 1816, the year that his name appeared on the survey. He was therefore too late to have a say in choosing a name for the village. But a few years later, when the settlers were naming the small community at Brant's Ford, Biggar attempted to have that village named after him and his old home of Biggarstown in Scotland. He was opposed by a miller, Mr Lewis, who opted for Lewistown and a Mr Reville who wanted the place to be called Birmingham after his home town. Biggar must have sent word of his intentions to Scotland, for in 1827 he received a letter addressed to him at Biggarstown, British North America.

The Biggars built a fine brick house, now called Tall Trees, on lot 10 in Mount Pleasant. Robert's wife, Mary, lived for only ten years after their arrival in Mount Pleasant. Her death and Robert's are marked by two stones which lie in a private cemetery near their home. His stone reads 'In memory of Robert Biggar, native of Scotland, died April 23, 1836, aged 76.' His wife's stone is inscribed 'Mary Lauder (wife) died 1826, Feb. 10, aged 62.'

To his many children and grandchildren Biggar left generous bequests of land. A codicil to his will suggests, however, that he was a keen student of human nature. He directed that, should any one of his heirs feel inclined to dispute his or her portion of the estate, that share should revert to the remaining heirs. This no doubt assured that any dissension in the family was halted before it began.

One of the Biggar children, Hamilton, was a minister in the Episcopal Methodist church at Rice Lake. He established the mission for the Chippewa tribe. Hamilton Biggar's bride was Eliza Racey, daughter of Squire James Racey, a prominent pioneer of Mount Pleasant, who had come to Upper Canada from England in 1803. Eliza's interest in the Reverend Hamilton Biggar caused her to take an intense interest as well in attending his Methodist meetings, much to the distaste of her Anglican father. She was said to have devised a means of leaving home for the meetings by first tossing her bonnet and cape out of the upper window and then appearing below for a stroll, only to dart out, pick up the appropriate clothing from below her window, and leave for church. The couple finally eloped in 1832, but they seem to have been welcomed back, as their nine children were made to feel at home in Mount Pleasant.

Of the first settlers who came to Mount Pleasant in 1799, one man

Tall Trees, lot 10, Mount Pleasant

achieved considerable financial success. This was Abraham Cooke, storekeeper and postmaster, described with parochial hyperbole as 'Mount Pleasant's Merchant Prince.' Cooke may have attained this lofty title as a result of the attention he received after building his imposing home, Brucefield, on lot 7, Mount Pleasant.

The first guest to be received at Brucefield was James Bruce, eighth Earl of Elgin and governor-general of British North America. The year was 1849. Lord Elgin, whose tenure of the office of governor-general was marked by violent political upheaval, was faced with the task of implementing the principle of 'responsible government' in Canada. It was a challenge he attempted to face with skill and diplomacy, but of course there were those who disagreed with his approach. His support of the Rebellion Losses Act that year brought forth a storm of Tory opposition and bombastic editorial comment in the press.

Since the newspapers of the day were never reluctant to voice an

Brucefield, lot 7, Mount Pleasant

opinion with no pretense at objectivity, the visit of Lord Elgin to
Mount Pleasant produced some entertaining rhetoric. The *Hamilton
Spectator* for 29 September 1849 reported: 'Since this day week the
Governor-General has emerged from his seclusion at the falls and
made a dash into the country by the Grand River ... his Lordship has
taken all the villages on his route and carefully avoided the cities and
towns ... At Mount Pleasant His excellency lodged with Mr. A.
Cook, an untra-Radical of course and in the morning His Excellency
with great condescension named Mr. Cook's nameless residence
'Brucefield' – a silly piece of egotism which can only excite the pity
of sensible men ... the world is tolerably well satisfied that Lord
Elgin is no more a descendant of the Bruce than is the gentleman
whose house he named.' Another paper, the *Provincialist*, also
reported the governor-general's visit but from a different viewpoint: 'September 27, 1849 ... His Excellency slept on Tuesday night
at the house of Abraham Cooke Esq. of Mount Pleasant ... [In

Townsend house, Mount Pleasant

Brantford ... he was] entertained by His Worship the Mayor ... Dr Digby, who is a Tory. Indeed we understand the Tories of Brantford appeared in full dress and acted like gentlemen on the occasion.'

Abraham Cooke died on 30 September 1864, leaving Brucefield, 'the homestead where I now reside,' to his wife, Eleanor, and after her death to their son Abraham B. Cooke. It is now a nursing-home.

More than twenty years after Brucefield was built, a wagon-maker and blacksmith in Mount Pleasant built a fine red brick house a short distance to the north where the road curves into the village. According to the Mount Pleasant Tweedsmuir History the owner of the house, Alvah Townsend, was 'quite incensed when he found that the builders had not used the same type of stairway as they built in Cookes's Georgian mansion.' The exact construction date of Townsend's house is not known but a total of $4000 in mortgages was taken out in 1863, suggesting that the house was built shortly thereafter.

The Townsends obviously required a sizeable house, for by this time their family included eight children. Census records reveal that Townsend came from New York State, his wife Sarah from Ireland. By 1871 six of their children – all in their twenties or thirties – were still living at home. Alvah was then sixty-four years old, weary Sarah fifty-seven. In 1883 the Townsends sold their house to Duncan Marquis and his wife for $10,000.

The most architecturally interesting house in Mount Pleasant is one of three octagonal buildings built there in the late 1850s. These buildings were designed according to the theories of an eccentric American, Orson Squire Fowler, whose architectural philosophy inspired the construction of a multitude of octagonal structures throughout Ontario. The three octagons in Mount Pleasant were the Nelles Academy, the Stowe Brothers Carriage Shop, and the Richard Tennant house. Their owners must have agreed with Fowler, who claimed that an eight-sided building promoted all manner of benefits to the occupants, including good temper, even for those yet unborn.

The Tennant house is a particularly fine example of the style, its high, steep gables and the lantern above providing it with a rather raffish and playful appearance. A verandah originally surrounded the house and its loss deprived the building of a certain sense of stability. Gone too are the lovely gardens and the stone wall that one enhanced this still unique building. It is now a restaurant.

Richard Tennant died in 1878 and was buried in the cemetery

beside All Saints Church, a short distance south of his house. His gravestone records his birthplace as Yorkshire, England, and his age as fifty-three at the time of his death. In his will he left all his estate to his wife, Caroline, who was buried beside him ten years later. Nearby are the graves of other early settlers, many of whom helped found All Saints. Built in 1845, All Saints is a fine example, in its simple beauty, of vernacular church architecture. Three years after its construction the Reverend A.N. Bethune described it as 'a neat edifice of wood, painted completely without and partially within.'

Five years after Tennant's death, his octagonal house was sold to James Knight Goold. Goold was an officer in the British army, and he and his wife, Charlotte, had lived in Bermuda, Barbados, and Halifax until Goold retired and moved to Mount Pleasant, a move that was probably prompted by the presence of relatives in the area – Goold's in Brantford, his wife's in Toronto.

Octagonal house of Richard Tennant, Mount Pleasant

Charlotte von Moll Goold's grandfather was William Berczy, a talented artist, whose paintings hang in the National Gallery of Canada. A man of courage and vision, Berczy was the leader of a group of German immigrants who eventually settled in Markham Township in the 1790s. His son Charles, the father of Charlotte Goold, was postmaster of Toronto from 1839 to 1853, president of the Consumers' Gas Company, and a director of other business concerns.

James Goold's will, written in 1915, listed bequests to eight children and grandchildren. He mentioned specifically that his daughter Harriet was to receive the 'tapestry picture of the Ascension,' and added 'I give to my said daughter and my grandaughter Lillian V. Goold the use of my dwelling house for six months after my decease with the sum of four hundred dollars for their living expenses during such term.'

One of the other two octagonal buildings in Mount Pleasant was

All Saints Church, Mount Pleasant

the Stowe Brothers Carriage Shop. The building has since been demolished, but the Stowe name is remembered in the annals of Canadian medical history. Emily Howard Jennings Stowe, the wife of John Stowe, became the first female doctor in Canada.

The Stowes had settled in Mount Pleasant at about the time that Richard Tennant was building his octagonal house. John developed tuberculosis and thus, after their third child was born, Emily taught school in order to support the family. In the mid-1860s her application to the University of Toronto's School of Medicine was rejected because of the prevailing feeling that women were 'frail tremulous creatures, given to weeping and swooning and fits of the 'vapours' ... and totally incapable of facing the hardships of life.' Emily then left her family in the care of her sister and entered the New York Medical College for Women, graduating in 1867, at which time she moved to Toronto. Thirteen years passed before the medical establishment granted her a licence, although she practised successfully without one during this time, while the Council of the College of Physicians and Surgeons apparently turned a blind eye to this infraction. During these years she purchased a house on Church Street in Toronto and continued to support her husband while he studied to become a dentist.

In 1883 the Stowe's daughter, Augusta Stowe-Gullen, became the first woman to graduate in medicine in Canada, thus fulfilling a prophecy made by her mother twenty years before. After being denied entrance to the university, Emily Stowe had stated: 'Your senate may refuse me entrance but the time will come when you will be compelled to open your doors to women students.'

8

St George to Thamesford

It was an age when 'civilized and enterprising men came to a howling wilderness.' These are the words of the Reverend William Wye Smith, son of a pioneer of Beverly Township, early resident of the St George area. In his unpublished memoirs Smith speaks of those who starved to death, those who supported life on 'cow-cabbage and dandelion leaves boiled into greens,' those who were killed while clearing the land. Tales of the 'howling wilderness' are found in the atlases which cover the counties of Wentworth, Brant, and Oxford. Through these three counties Dundas Street passes north of or between the larger communities such as Brantford, Paris, and Woodstock; it and the parallel route, highway 99, make their way through small villages such as Troy, St George, Princeton, Copetown, Lynden, and finally Thamesford, just east of London, at which point the routes have united to become highway 2. In the nineteenth century all these villages and others nearby supported mills, related trades, and artisans.

The country was indeed rough. In Beverly Township in Wentworth County the Beverly swamp was legendary: it was composed, according to accounts of the time, of rattlesnakes, mosquitoes, black-flies, and quicksand. A Brant county atlas contains tales of pioneers who pitted their muscle against a wolf or 'clutched a bear by his shaggy mane with one hand' while dealing it a mortal blow with the other. Such lore has no doubt benefited with the passage of time. The muscles and the deeds grow larger, yet when the atlases were printed in the 1870s, they recalled the years of the early 1800s and the men who remembered those days were still alive to tell the tales. The isolated communities along the Dundas were peopled by sturdy men and women, and some of their houses remain to recall their lives.

The Mannen homestead is located on lot 3, concession 1, Flamborough (formerly Beverly), Wentworth County. The fine two-storey brick house which stands on the property today was not built until 1844, the year marked in date-stones under the eaves. Exactly fifty years earlier John Mannen was engaged in clearing his land. He was killed by a falling tree while performing his settler's duties, clearing the Governor's Road in front of his lot.

Mannen, formerly of the British army and serving in the United States, received his land in 1794. At the age of thirty he and his wife, Elizabeth Cooley, began wilderness farming in Upper Canada. Their Crown grant was not approved until 1818, fifteen years or more after they had settled the land and built their first log house. It is believed that John, the ancestor of a family who settled throughout

Mannen house, lot 3, concession 1, Flamborough (formerly Beverly), Wentworth County

Ancaster and Beverly Townships, was dead before his grant was confirmed. His family stayed on their land. By 1848 an assessment roll notes that they had constructed a substantial two-storey brick house. Its hand-made bricks were made from local clay.

John and David Mannen, sons of the pioneer, both farmed on lot 3. It is believed that David was the builder of both John's house and his own. The assessment rolls do not mention the two-storey building until 1848; however the property would not have been fully assessed until construction was completed.

The Mannens were survivors. After the pioneering years they experienced relative prosperity. By 1851 their farm was producing wheat, barley, oats, potatoes, turnips, hay, wool, and maple sugar in large quantities and supporting sheep, cattle, and pigs. In his will, dated 1872, John Mannen gives a picture of his thriving farm, mentioning in bequests to his wife, Hannah, various outbuildings, horses, and carriages, as well as numerous household effects. In an unusually specific bequest John leaves Hannah 'one third of the fruits in my homestead orchard to be selected annually by her by alternative choice, one tree to be chosen by her to every two trees to be chosen by my son Benoni ... until the whole of such fruit is annually divided.' Having decided which tree was hers and which Benoni's, Hannah could ride off on her horse which, the will notes, was to be kept in her half of the driving shed.

According to local legend, the Mannens assisted escaped black slaves as part of the Underground Railroad. One such slave, who was trapped in a well which was being dug on their land, spent two days at the level of eighty-eight feet before he could be rescued.

Directly north of the Mannen property, on Dundas Street just west of the village of Troy, are two houses built by the descendants of men who were successfully cultivating the land just after the War of 1812. Their names were Lawrason and Blasdell. The great flexibility in the spelling of names at this period has given rise to a good deal of confusion. The Lawrason name is also spelled Larison and Laurason on early records. The John Larison listed as having cultivated twelve acres by 1816 is probably the John Laurason listed in 1819 as poundkeeper in Beverly. By 1833, when Thomas Lawrason purchased lot 5, concession 3, Beverly, Wentworth County, the spelling had changed again.

The red brick house on the Lawrason property today is at least the second to be built on that site, for early assessment rolls list

Thomas's house as frame and under two storeys. Once again it is clear that prosperity attended upon years of hard work. By 1869, when the next generation passed on the land, the family fortunes included other real estate and personal assets. John Purvis Lawrason, Thomas's son, was able to provide for his mother, his wife, Sarah, and his six sons and three daughters. The legacy of the homestead was of prime importance. It was left to Sydney Lawrason with instructions to the executors to 'direct my son ... in the management of the property.' There is mention of wagons, horses, various sets of harness, barns, and other outbuildings, as well as cash and real estate. Sydney was to remain custodian only as long as he was 'managing the property right' and properly providing for his grandmother, mother, and brothers and sisters. If he failed in his responsibilities, the executors were directed to take charge. The hard-won legacy was not to be dissipated.

Although Sydney received the residue of his father's estate, the homestead site went to the eldest son, James Miller Lawrason. He inhabited the red brick house which had been built in 1857. In *The Pioneers of Beverly* John A. Cornell notes that James Lawrason was a 'fine hunter and kept honey bees.' He 'caught racoons to make coonskin coats and carriage robes.' On the occasion of Brantford's becoming a city he drove 'in a two-seated democrat ... having a fine coonskin robe hung over the back of each seat, causing much comment.'

Many insights into life in Beverly are contained in William Wye Smith's notes. Not only was starvation a constant fear, but shelter and travel were problems. The fine houses which remain in the area are the second or third to be built by a family. Sometimes a family had to live 'under blanket tents for two months; till they got up houses for shelter.' These first houses of log were sturdy but low. Smith remembers 'one so low that as the farmer swung his axe to chop wood the upswing could be seen over the top of his house.' For practicality, however, 'there is nothing warmer than a log house when it is new and well "daubed."' As the settler's first duties were completed, there began to be time to improve the log house. 'A log house with up and down partitions is the first stage towards opulence and luxury.'

The frame house on lot 3, concession 3, Beverly Township was built by Jonathan Blasdell. The building, called Poplar Grove, is not listed on assessment rolls until 1847, but census records show Blasdell to have had thirty acres under cultivation as early as 1839. Presumably he was renting the land from the owners, the family of William Baldwin of York. One of the Upper Canadian families of position and wealth, the Baldwins bought land in a number of townships as an investment, a common practice, and rented it to settlers. Waiting until he had legal title to the land, Blasdell then constructed the frame building still standing there today. It is believed locally that the house served at one time as an inn.

A descendant of Isaac Blasdell, Jonathan came from one of the first families to settle in Beverly. Isaac is said to have walked from his home in Beverly to Toronto at the age of fifty-two to get Bibles for a Sunday School. The roads being poor, he went through the bush and returned the same way. He camped for part of the night by a fire but woke to see the eyes of wolves gleaming in the dark. Fending them off, he finished his journey in safety.

Jonathan Blasdell died in 1849, five years after he received title to

Poplar Grove, lot 3, concession 3, Flamborough (formerly Beverly)

the property on which his frame house stands. The cemetery in nearby Troy, the largest village in Beverly, shows that he and his family were subject to the almost universal grief of the time – the loss of infant members. Here are buried with Jonathan and his wife, Catherine, two of their children, aged fourteen and four, and 'Little Eddie,' the son of another member of the family.

Hard as life was, there had to be room for a robust sense of humour. William Wye Smith relates incidents which took place near his St George home. 'Bees' or work parties for every task from barn-raising to quilt-making occurred frequently. The ultimate refinement of the bee was held by one farmer, who invited the local settlers to a 'dung-frolic.' This supposedly lively affair turned out to be a party to get help in moving the manure out of the back field.

Smith also commented sorrowfully on the frivolity and lack of attention to work that he found in the youth of the mid-1800s. He noted that 'the young bloods all rode on horseback ... A favourite 'badge' as it might be called of the young bloods ... was in winter a red worsted 'muffler' round the neck; worn quite loose with the long ends hanging down the front. Sunday afternoon was the chosen time for their Knight-errantry. And they went by on their creaking saddles, with their horse curvetting and prancing. From this sight Smith derived the moral that 'pride and conceit grow in the woods, as well as in the populous city.' To his satisfaction Smith was able to record that he had lately seen an older and wiser version of one of the 'young bloods,' now married and with a farm to work: 'I remember meeting, in a new township, twenty years after, one of the most exquisite of the Exquisites of my boyhood. But what a difference ... to see him in the nearest village with flannel shirt sleeves and not even a collar on ... Such are some of the revenges of time.'

Just east of St George stands a graceful stone building (lot 1, concession 3, South Dumfries, Brant County), its ornately carved verandah highlighting the front façade and contrasting with the ivy-covered walls. This is the Nixon homestead, which was built by Charles Nixon, grandson of the pioneer of the family, Allen.

Originally from Ireland, Allen Nixon served with the British army in the United States during the Revolutionary War. He came with other Loyalist families to the Grimsby area at war's end. Allen and his wife, Mary Moore, had established a good farm near Grimsby and were operating a blacksmith shop serving the British troops in the War of 1812 when both contracted cholera. They died within a week of each other.

Four years after Allen and Mary's death their fourth child, Robert, married Elizabeth Corwin. Robert, an officer in the 4th Lincoln Regiment during the Mackenzie rebellion, farmed at Grimsby. When he died in 1852, Robert left a will which showed once again that the two major goals of the early settlers were to purchase land and to provide a legacy for their descendants. Robert had accumulated land in Oakville, part of which he left to his wife, Elizabeth, and part to his daughter Eliza. To his five surviving sons he was able to leave land spread throughout South Dumfries, Brantford, and Grimsby Townships. He charged his third son, Dennis, who inherited the homestead in Grimsby, with the role of being 'at all costs and charges in bringing up and educating and clothing all my children until they reach the age of twenty-one years' and of caring for his

Nixon homestead, lot 1, concession 3, South Dumfries, Brant County, east of St George

mother 'as long as she remains my widow.' This concern for younger children was common in wills of the period. Life expectancy was short and families large. Often when a man died, he left young children or infants whose upbringing fell to an older brother, the new head of the family.

To his oldest son, Charles, married and away from home by the time of his father's death, Robert left land in Brantford Township and land 'adjoining his own farm to hold to him, his heirs and assigns for ever,' plus £75 'one year after my death.' On his South Dumfries land Charles Nixon began construction of his stone home, Woodview Farm, which was completed in 1854. Here he moved with his wife, Mary Corson, and their son Henry Robert, six weeks of age at the time of the move. The lovely red brick cottage to the east of the homestead was built for Henry Robert and his bride in 1880. On his father's death Henry Robert moved into Woodview Farm. Later, the homestead became the residence of his brother the Honourable Harry C. Nixon, who became the thirteenth premier of Ontario in 1943. His son, Robert Nixon, great-great-grandson of the original settler, Allen, now occupies the house. Robert was leader of the Liberal party in Ontario from 1967 to 1975.

The War of 1812 had involved the Nixon family as it did most who settled the land in the early 1800s. The task of cutting a farm out of the wilderness and keeping it worked to prevent the forest from reclaiming it was a full-time job for an entire family. It was therefore with no joy that the pioneer heard of impending battles which would take him away from the land. William Wye Smith brought the subject down to basics when he recounted how the news of the war was brought on foot to the St George neighbourhood. 'John Buckberry, well remembered about St. George, told me when I was a boy about the excitement when the war with the United States broke out in June, 1812. He had the alarming news, and was tearing along the concession, shouting the word to the neighbours, as he passed rapidly on foot. He passed a field where an old neighbour was sowing buckwheat. Buckberry hailed him from the roadside; "The Americans has declared war." The old man dropped his seed-bag, and held up his hands in astonishment at such rashness and thoughtlessness. "What do they mean?" cried he "declarin at this time o' year, when everybody is busy sowing their buckwheat."'

South and west of the main intersection in St George, in a wooded setting, stands a building which dates from just after Confederation, a station-house which was built for the Brantford, Norfolk and Burwell railway, which opened in 1876. The rules for construction of rural stations were that costs must not exceed $450. Sturdily built for that price, this station survived a move from its original site after its closing in 1973. Its roof was removed and the whole building transported to the present site, which was originally part of Old Grove Farm, the property of the Howell family of St George. When it was built, the station-house represented the end of an era, and when it was moved, it became one of a very few such buildings to be restored and used as a residence. Now transformed, each of the rooms is serving a new function; the baggage-room of its railroad days is a hall, the freight shed a livingroom, the loading-platform a sunroom, the coal-bin a kitchen.

The construction of the railroad marked the end of a period. Because of the relative difficulty of transportation in pre-railroad

Converted station-house of the Brantford, Norfolk and Burwell railway, St George

days communities were by necessity almost self-sufficient, and very much under the influence of the first settlers in the areas, their ideas and their habits. The broader influences felt after the opening of the railroad were seen in a variety of ways, one of which, mentioned by Smith in his memoirs, might not be the first to spring to mind. This was a change in courtship patterns: 'before the Railways, young men in the county seldom went beyond their own township for a wife. Nay, a young man was rather thought to be despising our own girls if he went into the foreign territory of another township to get a wife.'

Just east of the railway station in St George stands a white frame house (lot 8, concession 2, South Dumfries, Brant County). The title to the land contains the names of both Nixon and Lawrason. Although one of the most important legacies left by a pioneer was his name, tradition and sentiment produced a profusion of descendants with identical Christian names, thereby creating massive confusion. In 1822 this lot was purchased by Robert Nixon. If this was the Robert Nixon who was the father of Charles of Woodview Farm, he purchased the land at the age of five. This being unlikely, it must have been the Robert who was the son of John, brother of Robert of Grimsby. This confusion is minor compared to that which sets in regarding the Lawrason name. The land was sold in 1845 to John Lawrason who built the present frame building. He was the son of Captain John Lawrason, who served in the War of 1812, was commended for 'steady and soldier-like conduct,' and married the daughter of his commanding officer, Major Titus Simons of Dundas. Captain John Lawrason was the son of Miller Lawrason, a Loyalist, BUT was he the same John Lawrason/Larison/Laurason who was the father of Thomas Lawrason just down the road. It is probable, but still lost in the mists of genealogy, that John and Thomas, whose houses stand today at lot 5, concession 3, Beverly, and lot 8, concession 2, South Dumfries, were brothers. So rests the matter!

There is absolutely no confusion concerning the building located west of the Lawrason house, about a mile east of the junction of highways 24 and 5. It is the family home of Adelaide Hunter Hoodless, founder of the Federated Women's Institutes of Canada. The pleasing frame building was bought by David and Jane Hunter in 1851. Adelaide, born in 1858, was their thirteenth and last child. Married to John Hoodless in 1881, Adelaide had four children. The

Women's Institutes were formed as a direct result of a tragedy which occured eight years after the marriage. The fourth Hoodless child died at the age of eighteen months after drinking impure milk in his home. Adelaide felt responsible for his death and began to crusade for better education for rural women in the science of home-making. Hearing her speak, Erland Lee of the Farmers' Institute of South Wentworth urged her to attend and speak at a farmers' meeting. This she did, noting that she 'hoped farmers would devote as much thought to the diet of their children as they did to that of their animals.' The result was that one hundred and one women and one man (Erland Lee) met in 1897 and the Women's Institute was born. Local reports commented on the fact that, when they were asked to vote on the matter, the women cautiously put up their hands – they were unused to being in the position of making a judgment on a public matter.

From this beginning the idea of the Women's Institutes was

Home of Adelaide Hunter Hoodless, junction of highways 24 and 5

exported, first to Great Britain and then to other Commonwealth countries, and finally the Associated Country Women of the World was created in 1933. In 1959 the Federated Women's Institutes of Canada purchased and restored the house in which Adelaide Hoodless was born and opened it to the public. This memorial is a fitting one for a woman who said: 'A nation cannot rise above the level of its homes.'

The impact of Thomas Hornor in Oxford County began when he was chosen by Lieutenant-Governor John Graves Simcoe as part of a 'grand design' for the settlement of western Ontario. Intent upon making London the capital of the area, Simcoe wanted settlers in this relative wilderness and he wanted them quickly. Since the United Empire Loyalists had settled on the lakefront lots, Simcoe chose as settlers men who were established merchants in the northern areas of the United States and set up a scheme whereby chosen men would get proprietorship of a whole township if they would settle the area. Hornor, through the influence of his uncle, Thomas Watson, came to the area to supervise the development of Blenheim Township. The wilderness he came to was served only by the rough track which Augustus Jones had started to blaze for Lieutenant-Governor Simcoe, which was to be the road which connected Burlington Bay and London. Jones had blazed a direct line through the forest from Coote's Paradise, or Dundas, to the Grand River.

When Simcoe left Upper Canada, his scheme collapsed. Hornor, however, remained in Blenheim Township. Since he had plans for a mill site, he returned to New York State to purchase the necessary supplies. By 1797 the Hornor mill was established and Hornor was the first permanent settler in Blenheim Township.

Born in Bordertown, New Jersey, in 1767, Thomas Hornor was the son of John Hornor, a man who had been instrumental in the founding of the College of New Jersey, an institution first built in Elizabethtown but later moved to Princeton. Thus the village in Oxford County which grew up near Hornor's mill came to be known as Princeton. It is located on the Governor's Road between Paris and Woodstock.

Three years after settling in the township Hornor joined the York militia, and in 1812 he reaffirmed his loyalty to the Crown by enlisting seventy-five Indians to fight for General Brock at Detroit. Hornor was commissioned as a colonel in 1822 and was a member of

Parliament for Oxford County for many years. This indomitable pioneer died in 1834, a victim of the cholera epidemic.

Thomas's son, Henry Clifton Hornor, farmed on land not far from his father's mills. Early in the 1850s he built an impressive stone house (lot 9, concession 1, Blenheim Township, Oxford County) which overlooks the Governor's Road. He had little time in which to enjoy his new home, however, for he died during the summer of 1853, leaving his wife, Elizabeth Charlton, to raise their four young children.

Since her husband had died intestate, Elizabeth Hornor had to apply to the courts to be named guardian of her own children. Because all women had dower rights, Elizabeth would have received the interest on a portion of Henry's property, but the bulk of his estate went to the children, and Elizabeth was custodian of it only. In her application to the courts Elizabeth promised that, when the children reached the age of twenty-one years, she would render to

Hornor house, lot 9, concession 1, Blenheim, Oxford County, near Princeton

them 'a true and just account of all goods, money, interests, rents, profits or property belonging to the said children ... and thereupon without delay deliver and pay over to the said children respectively the properly sum or balance of money which may be in hand ... belonging to them respectively.'

The first services held for the Anglicans of St Andrews (now the town of Thamesford) were conducted in a sawmill. Here in 1845 the powerful William Bettridge of Woodstock preached in John Finkle's mill. Later the parishioners were known to worship in the offices of local Anglicans and failing that in available barns. They were even said to have met in the Methodist church. Finally, on land donated by Miss Vansittart of Woodstock, they built a church, a harmonious work in stone on Dundas Street. As the land was donated, so were the stone and the lumber. The tower and bell were added for Queen Victoria's silver jubilee.

The growth of the congregation must have had much to do with

St John's Anglican Church, Thamesford

the personality of the first rector, William Brookman, a man of many parts. He was the editor of a journal, in which at his death he was praised by one of his editorial associates. Writing under the pen name of Mark O'Bown, Brookman had 'sent many a whimsical comment and many a keen letter to the correspondence column.' He was called 'a man of unique mind, of the broadest culture ... The sinner was a little dearer to him than the saint.' In closing the writer drew an appealing description of Brookman as a man with 'a brilliant mind streaked with a quaintness which made conversation with him a delight.'

9

Paris

'If a man had good breeding, he would show this by his deeds, rather than through his ancestors, who are like a field of growing potatoes – the best part of them underground.' These words, not surprisingly, were spoken by a Yankee. His name was Hiram Capron and, like many Americans who pioneered in Upper Canada, he was not impressed by those members of the British upper classes who arrived at the same time but demanded respect solely by virtue of their station in life and their ancestral heritage. Capron's ire was directed at one particular Englishman, William Holme, a wealthy gentleman who dealt with Capron – and probably all the Americans he encountered – in a patronizing and disdainful manner. It was an attitude which did little to promote good feeling between the two men.

William Holme was the first settler to arrive at the Forks of the Grand, a picturesque spot at the confluence of the Grand River and Smith's Creek. Here in 1819 he built a log house and proceeded to purchase more land, his aim being to establish a substantial estate and become one of the first of the gentleman farmers in this promising location. Wilderness farming, no easy task, may have proved more difficult than Holme anticipated. After nine years he sold his land to an eager and persistent Hiram Capron, who, although still a young man, was able to raise the $10,000 that Holme demanded for his land, buildings, and the rights to exploit the extensive gypsum (plaster of Paris) beds on the south bank of Smith's Creek.

Born in Leicester, Vermont, to an adventurous pioneering family, Capron was a fifth-generation American, the great-great-grandson of Banfield Capron, a youthful English stowaway who landed in

Rhode Island about 1674. Banfield's sons and their sons inherited his enterprising spirit and each, in turn, pushed on to new frontiers. So when young Hiram, at the age of twenty, left home to seek his fortune he was following in the family tradition. He moved to Upper Canada, and in 1822, with two of his partners, George Tillson and Joseph Van Norman, built a furnace on the north shore of Lake Erie. Two other partners gave financial backing and Capron was superintendent of the operation. Not only was the furnace a financial success, setting Capron's fortunes in motion; it was also a place of fascination to the whole area. According to Donald A. Smith's *At the Forks of the Grand*, the local residents 'came to exchange farm-produce for iron ware and other manufactured articles; and, if they were so inclined, they came to take part in the dances that were frequently held nearby. Often a young man, if he was in a courting mood and wished to please his girl, would take her for a visit to the Furnace.'

From the day in 1823 when he first visited the Forks of the Grand, Capron dreamed of founding a town on the site, for he was enthralled by the beauty of the valley, which he described as: 'bounded on two sides by bold uplands, clad with forest verdure; the river flowing gently past on the other side, shut in by precipitous banks covered with luxurious vegetation. The river here, too, flows in graceful curves, and divided by pleasant islands, is lost to the eye amid the lovely woodlands.' Obviously Capron had the soul of a poet but he was also a pragmatist. When in 1828 he purchased Holme's property, the furnace, established only five years earlier, was already a successful business producing stoves, kettles, and metal products.

In the spring of 1829 Capron moved his family to their new home – Holme's log cabin – and hired a surveyor to lay out a town site. Writing to his brother, Capron explained: 'I have had a surveyor employed to lay out a town-plot, which is nearly completed. I will shortly send you a beautiful plan of said town, which I intend to call Paris, being built upon a plaster bed, which lots I am offering gratis to actual settlers.' By the following year Capron had built a large dam and had set about making improvements to the Governor's Road, which by this time had become so overgrown that it was almost impassable. Again in a letter to his brother he said: 'We are now trying to raise money to open the Governor's Road which forms my southern boundry lines ... which, if we get opened will bring the greater part of travel west by my place.'

By 1830, with his village beginning to grow, Capron also found time to begin construction of a new house for his family. He built on a site which commands a view of the river that so inspired him. His simple house stands today at 8 Homestead Road, little changed on the exterior from the day it was built. Dormers now provide light on the second floor and a portico at the front entrance is a recent addition.

During the years that followed Paris grew and prospered. The founder of the town prospered as well, mining and grinding gypsum. He became known to everyone as 'King' Capron. Unlike some successful and wealthy men (in 1856 his holdings were estimated to be worth $250,000), Hiram Capron was loved and respected by the town and by his employees. He was unfailingly generous and, although not affiliated with any church, he gave money and land to Paris's churches, helped to establish a library, and frequently

Capron house, 8 Homestead Road

offered monetary help to the needy. The *History of Brant County* notes that Capron was 'remembered by all as keen, shrewd, generous under a mask of reserve.' His employees were surprised to find that they were treated as friends and welcome to eat at his table.

In 1823 Capron had married Mary De Long, the daughter of a Quaker family in the Norwich district. To them were born five daughters and two sons, Banfield and William. Mary Capron died in 1853 and, some time between that year and the 1861 census, Hiram married again. His second wife, Charlotte, was about sixteen years his junior. Capron died in 1872 at the age of seventy-six, leaving Charlotte and his daughters the income from his plaster mill. His son Banfield received a substantial amount of land but William was left only one lot with a strange proviso attached to that small bequest. If at the time of William's death he did not 'leave more than one lawful child him surviving,' his inheritance was to pass to Banfield and his sisters. William died three years after Hiram. Only one child did survive him, and the terms of the will were carried out. The reason for this unusual clause in the will is unknown.

A few years before the death of his first wife, Mary, Capron had built a new house in the classical revival style at 191 Grand River Street North. It was called 'the stone house.' Its pilastered corners, five bays, and finely worked interior details were altogether a fitting dwelling for the leading citizen of the town. Unfortunately, although this magnificent house still stands, only parts of the original are visible. When John Penman bought the property in the 1880s, his enthusiasm resulted in a rash of exuberant Victorian additions to the exterior, a plethora of towers, arches, gables, and pillars, while similar profusion of details were added on the interior. At this time the building received the name Penmarvian.

Capron may have been spurred into construction of his second home when he saw the house his neighbour, Norman Hamilton, completed in 1844. Hamilton Place is impressive, not only because it stands on a commanding site, its classical design dominating the area, but because it is sheathed in a veneer of cobblestones, a medium in which Paris's masons established their supremacy during the period from 1838 to 1860.

Described in the *History of Brant County* as a 'pushing, independent, success-at-any-price Yankee,' Hamilton came to Paris in 1831. Aggressive he may have been, but his enterprises benefited every farmer in the area – he made whiskey and raised pigs. In the pioneer economy, when most farmers grew grains, there was sometimes a surplus of that commodity above the farmer's needs if his farm was well established. Hamilton would take grain, turn it into whiskey, and give the farmer cash plus some of the whiskey. If the farmer had a surplus of pigs, Hamilton would purchase them for his pork-packing plant. According to Smith in *The Forks of the Grand*, the pigs were fed on the discarded mash from the distillery, with the result that 'the happy porkers gorged themselves on the rich mash as though it were ambrosia ... they seemed more like Greek heroes reclining upon beds of asphodel than gross swine wallowing in the mire.' The interlocking nature of Hamilton's business ventures so benefited him as well as the community that by 1844 he was able to build Hamilton Place, a testimony to his success.

A native of New York State, Hamilton grew up in the village of Mendon, not far from Rochester. This could be one of the reasons that he chose to build his house of cobblestones, for Rochester was

Hamilton Place, 165 Grand River Street North

the centre of cobblestone construction in America. Another determining factor was the presence in Paris of a master stonemason, a man who had learned his craft in his native New York State and who became responsible for making Paris the cobblestone centre of Ontario. His name was Levi Boughton.

Although the use of local stone was one of the most common and inexpensive of building methods, cobblestone-work required the selection of small, oval stones which were laid horizontally with a ridge of mortar projecting between the courses. In the finest examples, such as Hamilton Place, several years would have been spent in assembling the best and smoothest stones of the right size and considerable time in laying them. The result was that cobblestone-work was expensive even though the stones were available in the river beds at hand. In Hamilton Place the elliptical stones are placed at right angles to the wall, with only the ends projecting from the thick bed of mortar, resulting in a veneer that is nearly six inches in depth. The surface resists weathering well as is shown by the fact that the building is in excellent condition one hundred and forty years after it was completed.

Hamilton retired from his distilling, pork-packing, and milling businesses a few years after building his house and devoted the remainder of his life to community and philanthropic pursuits. He married three times. At his death in 1874 at the age of sixty-seven, he was survived by his wife and a daughter who was probably an infant at the time. Since the census of 1871 makes no mention of either a wife or a daughter, it would appear that he acquired both after his sixty-fourth year. In his will Hamilton left funds to ensure that his daughter would be provided for 'in a manner befitting her station.' Even her spending money was mentioned in the will: it ranged from $25 per year at the age of twelve to $100 per year at the age of twenty. At twenty-one she was to receive $2000 yearly as pocket-money.

Eventually Hamilton's daughter Elizabeth inherited the fine house her father had built, and she lived there for many years with her husband, Paul Giovanni Wickson, a noted artist during the early years of this century. The large belvedere atop Hamilton Place served as his studio, and no artist could have asked for a better location in which to work, for it is filled with light and commands a view of the entire valley in every direction.

When mason Levi Boughton built Hamilton's house, he had been resident in Paris for five years. A native of Albany, New York, he lived for a time near Rochester and then moved to Paris in 1839. The first cobblestone building he constructed in Paris was St James Anglican Church at Burwell Street and Grand River Street South. The stonework is a mixture of field and cobble, the stones rougher and less carefully matched in size than in his later work. Boughton and his workmen were to refine their art over the next few years. The irregularity of the stones and the colours of the field variety create an interesting blend of textures which has its own appeal. In 1863 a chancel was added to the original structure of St James. Fieldstone was used for that addition, probably to avoid the expense of matching the cobblestone veneer on the nave.

The architectural order of the church building itself belied the somewhat less ordered state of affairs existing within. Generous gifts from Great Britain had made construction of the church possible. The £500 which had been donated for the building came from parishioners in Scotland and Ireland and from a personal appeal made to the Duchess of Leeds by the mother of Charles Dickson, recently settled in Paris. Shortly thereafter, in response to her son's request, the good lady herself arrived in Paris, possibly to supervise construction and ensure that the conditions of the gift were met. The terms, which were quite specific, were set out in a letter to Mrs Dickson from Bishop John Strachan, who was in receipt of the money: the church was to be Episcopal; it was to be built of stone; it was to be called St James Church; the Reverend Mr O'Neil was to be given first offer of the post. The first three conditions were easily met. The man who accepted the position as rector, however, was William Morse. It was a decision he lived to regret.

The young rector arrived in 1839 and a year later revealed some of his problems in a letter to Bishop Strachan. Many of these problems seemed to centre on Mrs Dickson: 'February 7, 1840 ... Immediately on my arrival here I was grieved to find a spirit of bitter animosity prevailing between Mrs. Dickson and a few others of the church people about matters regarding the church, then in contemplation.' Morse noted that Mrs Dickson had also involved herself in other disputes outside the church – obviously she had not been idle since her arrival in Canada. 'The young man to whom Mrs. Dickson has been attached since the death of her husband is the eldest son of the party whose side she took in a local dispute,' – this action, according to Morse, seemed to 'feed the flame of contention.' He observed that most of his parishioners were already feuding with each other and with Mrs Dickson about 'breachy oxen, right of ways, trespass etc' to such an extent 'that the Disputants could not assemble to worship God under the same roof.'

The officious Mrs Dickson was only one of Morse's problems. Before his arrival the parishioners had agreed to contribute to his support. By the time Morse had settled in, however, the situation had changed. He explained to Bishop Strachan that many 'refused to attend the service lest they should, as they expressed themselves, "have to put their hands in their pockets."' Given this state of affairs, it is something of a miracle that the Anglicans in Paris ever managed to build their lovely church.

Unhappily the saga continued after the church was completed, for five years later Morse was still explaining his case to Strachan. As he noted, it had been necessary to buy a horse, since he served the parishes in Galt and St George as well as Paris. This horse must be

St James Anglican Church, Burwell Street and Grand River Street South

fed, shoed, and stabled. Having left England with church funds for travel and having stretched those funds to include purchase of the horse, he now had £27 on which to eat and live for a year. This included £5 which his parishioners at St George had given him – presumably Galt did not pay him either. In spite of Strachan's promptings, matters did not improve, and in 1845 the Reverend A.N. Bethune noted the 'stagnant condition of things.' By 1848 Morse had returned to England, a move which prompted Strachan to write of his displeasure in a letter to one of his clergymen, suggesting that many of the people in England who sponsored missionaries to Upper Canada were poorer than some of the Canadians who benefited from their generosity. Needless to say this situation was not unique to Paris. It was a struggle for many clergymen to make their way unless they had a private income. Many ministers in Canada, including Bishop Strachan, supplemented what income they received by speculating in land. Perhaps this way of overcoming dependence upon parsimonious parishioners occurred to the impecunious Morse as well, for by 1851 his name is listed on the title deed to the home of Asa Wolverton in Paris as providing funds for a £500 mortgage to Wolverton's land! Morse was either investing from abroad or had returned to give the colonies another chance.

Across the road from St James, at Church and Burwell Streets, is an unusual cobblestone building which served as both home and dispensary for druggist Samuel Souden. Only the street façades display cobblestone-work while the other walls were built with the less expensive fieldstone. A door set into the rounded corner of the building undoubtedly led to the business premises.

Little is known of the Souden family other than what can be found in census records spanning a period of thirty years. These records show that Souden was born in Scotland and that in 1851 he was forty-five years old and lived in a two-storey stone house. With him lived his wife and three children, George, Anne, and Sarah. Ten years later the census shows that another son, Samuel, had been born and that the family was still living in the cobblestone house. By the time that the census was taken in 1871, Souden had died and his widow, Elizabeth, was living with their son George on a farm in South Dumfries Township. With them were Sarah, young Samuel, and Eva, a baby of five months, who had obviously been born within a short time of her father's death.

It seems likely that Levi Boughton started to build his own house not long after completing work on the Souden building. In spite of the fact that Boughton gave Paris its unique architecture, there is remarkably little known about him and his family locally. The census records provide some personal details. The first is that Boughton was thirty-five years of age when he settled in Paris. By 1851 he and his wife, referred to only as Mrs Boughton, aged forty-two, had seven children ranging in age from twenty to two. They are recorded as living in a lathe-and-plaster house. The census-taker noted, in addition, that the Boughtons were still constructing their house and that 'the unfinished house is what is called coble work – a handsome building.' This fortuitous note by the recorder serves to date the house. Young Levi Boughton, following his father's trade, is listed as mason and plasterer, aged eighteen, born in the United States. He no doubt assisted his father in the construction of their homestead. It lacks the expert touch of some of the elder Boughton's other work so perhaps he left work on the family home to his son,

Home and dispensary of druggist Samuel Souden, Church and Burwell Streets

who was learning the trade.

By the time of the 1861 census Levi's affairs appear to have prospered, for at this point he had completed most of his best work in Paris. This time Mrs Boughton's name, Lydia, is revealed, and it is clear that the four eldest children have left home. One more daughter, Delila, has been born. Levi has acquired one horse and one cow plus two pleasure wagons. He owned an acre and a half of land and his business was worth $6000.

An example of the best of Boughton's work can be seen in the home of another American settler, Charles Mitchell, also from New York State. After spending four years in Hamilton, Mitchell arrived in Paris in 1836. Like Hiram Capron, Norman Hamilton, and most of the other immigrants from the United States, Mitchell brought with him a respect for the classical mode of architecture, a style which was felt to embody the federalist principles of their native country. When in the 1840s Mitchell decided to build a house, he naturally

Mitchell house, 16 Broadway Street

chose the classical revival style.

Set on a high foundation, the building at 16 Broadway Street is square in plan with a low hip roof, resulting in a shape approximating a cube. Like all buildings of this style, exterior appearance was the prime concern. The availability of light to the interior was of secondary importance and the layout of the rooms received scant attention. In the Mitchell house light for the second-floor rooms was provided through the roof lantern and by small windows at floor level. On the exterior these eyebrow windows are set in a wide, flat cornice and are covered with cast-iron grillework.

Mitchell owned a carriage-making business with a blacksmith shop attached and also operated a fanning mill. According to the 1851 census, the output of the factory in the previous year was fifty-five carriages, with a total investment of £2000. Charles, his wife, and their four children lived in their dignified home until 1858, when they moved to a farm just west of town. Twenty years later, after

Home of farmer George Brown, near the Golf Links Road

the death of his wife, Mitchell moved back into Paris, where he resided until his death in 1882.

Mitchell's obituary appeared in the *Brant Review*, 24 November 1881. It referred to him as 'an old residenter well-known ... and much respected.' Mitchell's will directed that a marble or granite pillar, 'costing not less than three hundred dollars,' be erected as a memorial for himself, his wife, and their two daughters who died in childhood.

One of the finest cobblestone buildings in the Paris area stands near the Golf Links Road, a few miles north of the town (sub-lot 1, concession 3, South Dumfries). It was the home of George C. Brown, a young farmer and another American immigrant. He purchased his property in 1854 and immediately mortgaged it for £2000, suggesting that construction of the house could have started almost right away. A second mortgage, dated 1862, may mark the end of the construction period. A span of such length is not improbable for the construction of this house, considering the high quality of the cobblework. By this date local masons had mastered their craft. The water-washed round and oval cobblestones, combined with a sprinkling of small fieldstones, have been set in the mortar with skill and precision and produce a warm and richly textured veneer. Here the cobblework, which in Paris is often seen in buildings constructed in the classical revival style, is equally at home in the simple style of the Ontario cottage with its familiar transom and sidelights by the entrance door and two flanking windows on each side. This well-formed building was, according to the 1861 census, occupied by Brown, his wife, Ann, then aged 35, and their two children, Helen and Charles.

Not far from the Brown farm (three miles north of Paris, east of Highway 24A) is the Paris Plains Church. Here, cobblestone works just as well in a simple Gothic revival building, its arched door and windows appearing subdued by the neatness of the cobble method. Since the church was built in 1845 using volunteer labour supplied by the local farmers, there must have been by this time a sufficient number of skilled masons in the area to produce work which rivalled Boughton's work in town. Here the round or oval stones are laid diagonally and are predominantly grey in colour with occasional brown and yellow tones.

Five rows of neatly laid cobblestones, tipped with precision slightly to the left, pose and at the same time elucidate a mystery. They are found in the Matthew Deans house (lot 36, concession 2, South Dumfries) on Silver Street, north of Paris. These five rows at the base of the building are laid in a distinctly different manner from that employed for the rest of the house, where the arrangement is random. Clues to this mystery are found in the title to the property. Matthew Deans purchased the lot in 1858 from 'William Dickson the younger,' and, while he was living in a temporary home on the southwest portion of his land, he commissioned the most skilled of Paris's masons, Levi Boughton, to construct his homestead. Boughton's death-date is uncertain, although we know from the Paris census records that he was living in 1861. It is therefore probable that Boughton began construction of the Deans house after the desired stones of perfect symmetry had been located but that he died before the building had been completed.

Matthew Deans came from Paisley, Scotland. In 1828 he married Mary Connel. Twenty-three years later the census notes that the

Paris Plains Church

couple were living in a single-storey log house with eleven children, three servants, and an Indian. Deans was already farming lot 36 at that time, possibly renting the land which he eventually purchased, while he lived with his closely knit household of seventeen persons in the one-storey log house.

On Deans's death in 1876 the fourth of his sons, John, inherited the house, farmed the land, and with his wife, Isabella, raised a family of seven children. The younger Deanses lived for twenty-three years in their substantial cobblestone home. On his death John's obituary described his life in terms which would apply to many of those whose whole energies were spent in working the land: 'he lived a quiet life and therefore refused any municipal position and devoted himself to his occupation'; his death 'produced considerable surprise and universal regret.'

Since he was the owner of two sawmills, it is not surprising that Asa Wolverton built his dignified classical revival house of wood, referred to as 'lathe and plaster' – the latter material so readily available in Paris. Born in the southern United States, Wolverton came to Paris in the 1830s. His brother Enos founded the village which is called Wolverton. He, like Asa, was a miller and therefore largely responsible for the prosperity of that settlement. Asa's house at 52 Grand River Street South in Paris is a 'split-level' dwelling with two storeys at the roadside or front façade and three facing the river. The pedimented verandah at the front has its counterpart on the river side of the building. An unusual feature is the connected group of outbuildings attached to the main house which composed the storerooms, carriage house, and barn. This arrangement, while common in the New England states and the Maritime provinces, was unusual in Upper Canada. Built after Wolverton had purchased his lot from Hiram Capron in 1851, the house was constructed during the height of cobblestone-work in Paris and therefore utilized the talents of Boughton and his masons in two features – a garden wall and a compact and attractive smoke house. Although Wolverton was financially successful at the time his house was being built, he nevertheless took out a mortgage to assist with construction costs. It is this £500 mortgage which was held by the Reverend William Morse, whose fortunes seemed to have taken an upward turn since his days as rector of St James Church across the road.

Before moving into their new home Wolverton and his wife,

Juliet, may have lived in the neat frame cottage immediately to the south at 60 Grand River Street South, for interior details suggest that the frame building is the older of the two. Both houses were owned by the Wolverton family. Like its larger neighbour, the single-storey frame building is built on the banks of the Grand River and graced with a verandah which affords a striking view of the valley below. According to local legend, Wolverton built this house for a son. Neither census records nor Asa's will, however, mention any children; they refer only to Juliet's 'heirs and assigns.' Perhaps the son predeceased Asa or alternatively was Juliet's son from a prior marriage.

Wolverton died towards the end of 1861 when he was fifty-seven years old. His entire estate was left to Juliet. Since no other residents are mentioned, it appears that Asa and Juliet lived alone in

Asa Wolverton's house overlooking the Grand, 52 Grand River Street South

Wolverton's cobblestone smoke-house

their imposing home at 52 Grand River Street South. Juliet later married John McElroy and in 1867 sold the house.

Each pioneer community has its particular atmosphere as the result of accidents of settlement patterns. Paris has two distinct features. The first is the unique quality of its architecture. The second is the presence of more than the usual number of Yankees. The quality of brash enterprise found in the Americans, so often the subject of disparaging comment by visitors and immigrants from the British Isles, had its virtues. Hiram Capron summed up what was the attitude of most of his compatriots when he described his own departure from home. He left 'with only the clothes on my back, and my hands and head. Thus my stock of trade was small, but I had one capital chance – the whole world lay before me to operate in.'

Capron's fellow-Americans brought not only their enterprising spirit but some of the most colourful and memorable names to be recorded in their new communities. The Capron account books list

60 Grand River Street South

some of these: Zacharias Clump, Cephus Church, Ransom Rounds, Hesekiah Nelson, Trueworthy Smith, Abel Mudge, and Increase B. Coon.

10

Woodstock

The settlement of Woodstock in the 1830s was influenced by a policy formulated thirty years earlier by Lieutenant-Governor Simcoe and by the presence of three remarkable English immigrants, all of them clever, articulate entrepreneurs, who might also be described as powerful, adventurous, and, on occasion, devious.

In 1793 Simcoe decided to locate the provincial capital on the Thames River and to name the new town London. This decision gave new importance to areas previously considered less attractive and also promoted the allocation of large tracts of land to men with proven leadership ability whose conservative political views reflected those held by the government. Although these plans did not develop as Simcoe had envisioned, the philosophy behind them affected settlement in the area in later years. By the 1830s the rebellious proposals of William Lyon Mackenzie and the general political unrest caused the government actively to encourage British immigrants to take up land in the relatively unsettled areas near London. The three influential men who arrived in Woodstock between 1832 and 1834 were, therefore, most welcome – they were Captain Andrew Drew, RN, Henry Vansittart, vice-admiral of the Blue, and the Reverend William Bettridge, a former interpreter for the Duke of Wellington.

Born in London in 1777, Henry Vansittart came from a family that had owned a fleet of merchant ships in Holland. Having supported William of Orange, the Vansittarts settled in England, where they enjoyed the good will of King Charles II and prospered in their new home. As a young man Henry Vansittart joined the Royal Navy and rose through the ranks to commander (after brilliant action at the Cape of Good Hope), rear admiral, and eventually vice-admiral of the Blue. At this exalted rank he retired. Although personally prosperous, Vansittart was anxious for the future of his two younger sons and so his thoughts turned to Upper Canada. In due course the family settled at Woodstock but not before the way had been opened by an emissary, Vansittart's former midshipman, Andrew Drew. Their partnership, which began amicably and with trust, ended in bitter division. It affected the settlement and even the location of the town of Woodstock.

In the spring of 1832 Andrew Drew arrived in Canada with a new bride and £1800 of Henry Vansittart's money. He was forty years old and, by all accounts, an impressive, energetic man. Behind him was a distinguished naval career and this, along with his charm and the Vansittart wealth, helped to ensure his warm reception when he landed at the town of York. Land negotiations began at once and soon the Drews were at the site of Woodstock on lands which included the north and east portions of the present town. Already settled in the area were two other military men, Lieutenant-Colonel Alexander Whalley Light and retired naval Captain Philip Graham, the first of the aristocratic British immigrants who were to play such an influential role in the future of the fledgling community.

Almost immediately the Drews started construction of their home, a Regency cottage that they named Rathbourne. It is a remarkably beautiful house, situated on a site just north and east of the village. The Duke of Northumberland is reported to have visited there and referred to the Drew home as the finest he had yet seen in Canada. The house stands at 735 Rathbourne Ave. It is still surrounded by its original verandah and still imbued with that air of picturesque serenity typical of the style. It is in superb condition today as a result of the care with which the family of the present owner has restored and maintained it.

Drew's home was undoubtedly a source of satisfaction to him. His financial dealings were equally rewarding but always complex. Although there is no evidence to suggest that he was dishonest, his endeavours on behalf of the partnership were complicated and seemingly beneficial to himself rather than to Vansittart. His personal dealings left him in possession of prime land around the town site (which he had also helped to lay out) while the investments he made for Vansittart were not as advantageous or as suitable. John Ireland, in his article *Andrew Drew and the Founding of Woodstock*, states: 'an admiral might well be disturbed to find that he owned shares in a backwoods tavern. The partnership funds had been spent with nothing to show for it except land in Drew's name.' Even the site which Drew had selected for Vansittart's house was 'on land in which he had no evident interest.' A bitter feud developed between the two men.

The quarrel between Drew and Vansittart was an acrimonious one and lasted for several years. Even the church was involved in their dispute. Vansittart had contributed funds towards the construction of an Anglican church in Woodstock, but Drew claimed he had supplied additional money needed for the completion of the new building. When the congregation of Old St Pauls Church refused to pay Drew what he felt was owed him, he locked the church and the congregation was forced to hold services in a nearby log building. The Reverend William Bettridge, a friend of Vansittart's, no doubt added fuel to the fire for, according to Ireland, he was 'most autocratic, a great insister upon his rights and in money matters even

Andrew Drew's Regency cottage, Rathbourne

more greedy and devious than Drew.' He had the distinction of 'being the only man ... whom Drew actually hated.' On one occasion Drew referred to Bettridge as the 'greatest hypocrite who ever escaped the gallows.' These gentlemen, it should be remembered, were among those who were expected by the government to set the standards for the community.

In spite of his failings Drew was an able administrator. He served as a magistrate and was local agent for the Bank of Upper Canada. During the Rebellion of 1837 he led a group of militia men to Navy Island, where Mackenzie and his followers had fled. Drew was charged with the task of sinking the Caroline, the rebels' supply ship. On 23 December 1837 Drew wrote to the Honourable Peter Boyle de Blaquiere of Woodstock to send without delay 'all the pikes you have, as we are about to organize a party of boarders ... for we are on the march for Chippawa to dislodge Mackenzie, and our present intention is to attack Navy Island where he is posted with 1200 men and 13 pieces of cannon.' After the successful completion of this mission Sir Francis Bond Head praised Drew, stating that prior to the attack the captain had called for 'a few fellows with cutlasses who would follow him to the devil.' Drew was presented with a sword worth a hundred guineas.

In 1843 Drew left Woodstock. It is believed locally that his departure was prompted by three attempts on his life. He was stationed for a time in the West Indies and later in South Africa, where he served as naval storeskeeper. A letter from there to his friend Admiral Augustus Baldwin revealed an appealing aspect of his character. He remarked that he had 'a good appointment and we are all enjoying ourselves but it is not a sinecure: working hours from 7:30 to 6:00. We have only three of our children with us – Caroline, Andrew and a troublesome little snip ... the youngest and consequently a spoiled child.' Ireland has remarked that in many ways Drew was typical 'of the men who founded the cities of Ontario. None were particularly noted for their scruples. All were primarily interested in their own advantage. Nonetheless, in a sense they built Ontario and ultimately Canada. It may be a pity that they were not candidates for a halo, but nation builders are rarely saints.'

Although Drew carried out the initial survey of the site of Woodstock, Henry Vansittart is generally recognized as its founder, for it was his wealth and prestige that provided the impetus for its growth. Vansittart first arrived at Woodstock without his wife,

Mary Charity, for, because of her ill-health, he had been forced to leave her and their children in Saratoga. He left little else behind, however. His entourage which included the Reverend Bettridge and his wife, Mary Hounsfield, was accompanied by a remarkable amount of baggage. Along with furniture, china, delicate crystal, and silver, the vice-admiral brought with him the rigging for a ship, as well as a shipwright to build the vessel. (Vansittart, knowing that he would be living near the Thames River, expected it to be the size of its British counterpart and wished to have his own ship for transportation. The size of the river was only one of the disappointments he encountered in Upper Canada and the ship was never built.) The procession passed by the home of farmer John Galbraith of Blenheim Township on 20 June 1834 on its way to Woodstock. The sight was so impressive that Galbraith noted in his journal: 'Nineteen or twenty wagon loads of Admiral Vansittart's baggage went past who is going to settle near Archibald Burtch's' (Burtch was Woodstock's first settler).

Only two weeks after his arrival in Woodstock Vansittart's wife died and he was left with their four young children to raise. He had to deal as well with the many problems resulting from his partnership with Andrew Drew. Probably as a result of these pressures his own health failed and he suffered a slight stroke. Within two years of his wife's death he decided to remarry. His family and friends were scandalized not only because his bride was much younger than he but because she was from a lower social class, and also illiterate. Anna Jameson, who visited Woodstock that year, remarked: 'The Admiral, no longer young, has recently astonished the neighborhood by marrying a very, very young wife of a station inferior to his own. His good sister has come out to countenance him and his menage, a proof equally of her understanding and affection.' It is also believed that Vansittart's family urged him not to take his young bride into his home but to lodge her instead at a local hotel.

The vice-admiral's new wife was Isabella Stevenson from the township of Bexley. Her father, John Stevenson, managed Vansittart's extensive holdings there. The 1851 census showed that Stevenson, his wife, Mary, and their four other children were then the only people living in the entire township since, 'owing to a want of roads and distance from mills, the settlers have all left but one family.' Isabella and Henry Vansittart were married there, and their home near Balsam Lake was apparently a seasonal residence.

In *A Gentlewoman in Upper Canada* Ann Langton wrote that she attempted to visit the couple there in 1840 but was 'unhappily frustrated due to a thunder storm.'

Vansittart's sister, Caroline East, was obviously a lady of stamina and courage for she was sixty-five years old when she arrived in Woodstock, hoping to prevent her brother's marriage. In spite of her failure in this matter, she remained in Canada, possibly to supervise the upbringing of the Vansittart children. Her brother built for her a substantial brick home called Eastwood. It stands today, just east of Woodstock (lot 8, concession 1, Blandford), in the area where Vansittart settled after he had rejected Drew's choice of a building site. Since the deed to the land on which Eastwood stands shows that Vansittart settled 'Caroline Anne East, widow' on the property in 1839, the house was probably built shortly thereafter. The deed lists Vansittart as 'Rear Admiral of the Red,' a confusion of colours on the part of the registry office of the day!

Eastwood, the home of Caroline East, lot 8, concession 1, Blandford

Caroline East, who was renowned for her beauty, was a wealthy woman in her own right and naturally played a leading role in the social life of Woodstock. When the first horticultural society was formed in 1852, Mrs East was the hostess, her orange and aloe trees reportedly attracting much attention. When she died six years later, the *Ingersoll Chronicle*, 21 May 1858, announced her death 'At Bisham Cottage, near Woodstock (the residence of her nephew J.G. Vansittart Esq.) ... in the 84th year of her age, Mrs. Caroline Ann East, relict of the late Augustus Henry East, second son of Sir William East Bart.' She was buried in the family vault behind Old St Paul's Church. Many years later, when the vault was opened, it was discovered that her coffin had been broken open at some point. The rector at that time, the Reverend John Morris, stated that the entry was no doubt the result of widespread knowledge of her great wealth and the hope of finding valuables which had been buried with her.

The indomitable Mrs East was predeceased by her brother, who died in 1843 after a fall from his horse while riding on the Governor's Road. In its laudatory obituary the Woodstock *Monarch*, 16 March 1843, stated that Henry Vansittart was a man for whom 'it was his daily work and delight to do good ... there was a manner in conferring his favours which gave a tenfold value to them: *he* appeared the *obliged*.' The article went on to state that he was survived by three sons, two daughters, his sister, two brothers, and a cousin. No mention was made of his wife, Isabella.

Whether or not Isabella Vansittart was recognized socially, she was very much alive. Her husband's will, written before their marriage, left his 'intended wife' considerable property in Bexley and elsewhere. Codicils to the will after the marriage show further bequests to 'my dear wife Isabella' and indicate that Henry left her well provided for. She remained close to her own family and records of land transactions show that by 1868 she was living in Port Hope, probably to be near her sisters Sophia Molson (who had married Thomas Molson of the brewing family) and Charlotte Orr (married to the manager of the Molson distillery in Port Hope). Sophia's marriage to the elderly and ailing Thomas Molson was met with as much dismay by his family as was Isabella's by the Vansittarts. Isabella is last recorded (in 1872) as living in the township of Egremont in Grey County, still described as 'widow of the late Admiral Henry Vansittart.'

The minister who conducted Vansittart's funeral was, of course, his good friend William Bettridge, the controversial gentleman who came to Woodstock with Vansittart and remained as rector of Old St Paul's Church for the next forty years. Bettridge had served at St Paul's, Southampton, and no doubt named his new post after his English church. Behind him was a career in the military that was by no means ordinary, but then neither was the man. He had served in Flanders under the Duke of Wellington. Anxious to take part in a battle at Quatre Bras, he left his regiment and so, after the battle, was arrested. Later, when the Iron Duke was seeking an interpreter to interrogate the French prisoners, he learned that Bettridge, then in a cell, spoke eight languages and so the headstrong young man was made the duke's official interpreter. Later he was rewarded with the post of town major of Brussels. When the war was over, he was offered the position of chief of staff of the Greek army. He declined and instead entered the ministry.

Old St Paul's Church, Dundas Street

Bettridge was a scholar and a gentleman who, in spite of his over-bearing manner, was probably well suited to serve the somewhat aristocratic settlement of Woodstock. Many of his parishioners were retired military men who, with the exception of Andrew Drew, were not unduly offended by his officious approach. In any event, Bettridge managed to get things done.

When the differences between Drew and the congregation had been sorted out – Drew received free rental of a pew and a free burial vault and so turned over the key – the church doors were opened. Within three months of his arrival in Woodstock Bettridge wrote of his congregation in a report to Sir John Colborne: 'A motley but very interesting group presents itself to the eye on leaving church. There are indeed no splendid equipages to attract "the idiot eye of gaping wonder" but every species of vehicle.' He noted that his church was 'crowded with people, some from a distance of 10 to 20 miles,' and that his Sunday afternoon scripture lessons were widely attended by children and adults. In conclusion Bettridge added: 'We hope soon to have the honor and Christian Satisfaction to see Your Excellency amongst us with Lady Colborne,' whom he described with a certain obsequiousness as 'your Spiritually-minded Aide-de-Camp, this excellent help-mate.'

By 1838, four years after St Paul's was constructed, church-warden Peter Boyle de Blaquiere wrote to the bishop in Montreal that 'a substantial and commodious brick church has been erected ... principally by the liberality of Rear Admiral Vansittart of the Navy ... the said church is pewed and furnished with a reading-desk, common prayer, Bible, a pulpit, a communion table and vessels for the same.' Today the church looks much as it did at that time and the old pews are still in use. It stands on the north side of Dundas Street near Huron Street on a site chosen by Drew. Legend has it that Drew, in gratitude for the birth of his first son, placed a rock on that spot and vowed to build a church there. Given Drew's propensity for profit-making decisions, the tale seems somewhat unlikely.

Bettridge's success at Old St Paul's faltered temporarily in 1840 when a furor developed over his possible misuse of church funds. The rector had taken a journey of seventeen months' duration to Great Britain in order to raise money for the church in Upper Canada. Because of Bettridge's eloquence and enthusiasm more than £3000 was realized, but a problem arose when, on his return, it was discovered that he had spent more than that amount while travelling.

The matter was so controversial that a commission was set up by the Bishop of Toronto and records of its seven-day hearing appear in the Strachan Papers. When he was asked to supply a detailed account of his expenses, Bettridge showed amounts such as £108 for conveyances during a period of two hundred days. He was unable to account for more than one-third of the money spent. The commission ordered him to repay the money, he refused, and the matter was sent to the Archbishop of Canterbury, who ordered Strachan not to pursue the matter. So unhappy was Bishop Strachan with this decision that for several years he refused to visit the Woodstock church. Four years later feelings were still running high. The bishop, who had finally visited Old St Paul's (but in Bettridge's absence), wrote to the wilful rector and recommended 'a sojourn near the sea [for] the state of your nerves.' Bettridge's nerves seemed steady, however, and he remained a driving force in the community until his retirement in 1874. He died five years later, in Strathroy, at the home of his son.

While Drew, Vansittart, and Bettridge were involved with social and financial pursuits, not to mention their continual squabbling, life went on in a more prosaic way for Woodstock's less prominent citizens. Among them was schoolteacher Henry Izzard, whose contribution to his community was less dramatic but nevertheless worthwhile. He lived with his family in a pleasant brick house at 146 Vansittart Avenue. Izzard purchased the property from Richard Rawlings in 1853 and during the next six years placed four mortgages on the land totalling more than $1500. It seems reasonable to assume that the money was being used to finance construction of the house. Built as a Regency cottage, the Izzard house was undoubtedly once surrounded by a verandah onto which French doors opened from the front rooms.

The census records of 1851 state that Izzard, who was born in England, was thirty-three, and living with his wife, Pamela, twenty-three years old, and four children. The oldest of the children was Henry, who was thirteen and no doubt the product of an earlier marriage. By 1871 nine more children had been born to Henry and Pamela. In that year eleven of their progeny were still living at home, their ages ranging from twenty-four down to two years. The Izzards had, not surprisingly, sold the cottage on Vansittart Avenue in 1861 to Charles Whitehead, no doubt to seek larger quarters for their growing family.

Izzard supported his family as a teacher in Woodstock's first common school (tuition 2 shillings, 6 pence, per quarter). He later became principal of the West End School. According to *Bits and Pieces, A Montage of Woodstock, Ontario*, the West End School was built 'to relieve pressure on the common school.' The cost of these schools was about $7000 each, and 'they were built for service not for looks. Heat was supplied by huge box stoves and on cold days it was necessary for the students to continually change places in order that at least once during the day they would be warm.'

The Izzard's Regency cottage, now tastefully restored, is one of many fine houses that grace Woodstock's impressive, tree-lined Vansittart Avenue. Across from the Izzards lived Thomas Scott, a druggist, who, with his wife, Helen, and a son, Alfred, occupied a modest frame house at 123 Vansittart. This house is difficult to date but the census of 1861 shows that Scott was living in a 'frame and brick two storey house' in that year. He had purchased the property

Izzard cottage, 146 Vansittart Avenue

two years previously and may have built an addition to an existing smaller house. Of particular interest in the interior is a triple fireplace which serves three rooms, having three flues in a central stack.

In 1867 the Scotts sold the house to another druggist, James White, who in turn sold it the following year to his brother Alexander. Born in England, but of Scottish descent, Alexander White was a manufacturer. He died when he was about forty years old, leaving his 'Homestead' to his 'dear wife Elizabeth' and after her death to his three children, David, Walter, and Alice. The house remained in their family for many years.

Across from the Whites, at 84 Vansittart Avenue, is a tall brick Italianate villa, one of many such houses that once provided a certain elegance in Ontario's urban centres. Like its counterparts throughout the province, it is irregular in plan, with paired round-headed windows, ornamental brackets supporting the roof, small balconies, and a watch tower – altogether a fitting house for one of Wood-

123 Vansittart Avenue

stock's most prosperous merchants, Thomas Parker. Born in England, Parker came to Canada as a small child with his parents John and Jane (Harrison). The family settled in Peterborough, but when young Thomas was eighteen, they moved to a farm in Zorra Township, near Woodstock. Five years later Thomas returned to Peterborough, where he studied at Mr Wilson's grammar school in the winter and worked in the lumber business during the summer. By the 1850s Thomas Parker was in business in Brantford and Hamilton. He then moved to Woodstock where he formed a partnership with John D. Hood, and in 1859 he married Hood's sister Annie. According to *Men of Canada*, Parker continued in business until he had 'realized a competency.' He sold his business and retired, devoting the rest of his life to civic pursuits. In the late 1870s he served as mayor of Woodstock for two terms. He was a founder and first president of the Board of Trade, now the Woodstock District Chamber of Commerce.

Italianate villa of Thomas Parker, 84 Vansittart Avenue

A year after their marriage the Parkers became parents of twin girls, Annie and Jessie. The sisters never married and the Parker house, built four years after their birth, was their home for many years. Their names appear in the 1916 *Woodstock Social Register*, a publication which indicates that the social niceties of the day were strictly observed. Ladies were 'at home' to receive visitors at certain hours each week or in some cases once a month, and the extent of the register suggests that the remainder of their time was spent in returning these calls. The Misses Parker of 84 Vansittart received on the first Friday of each month. Mrs Alexander White, across the street, received every Wednesday. In total there were 373 listings in the register, enough to occupy the most socially ambitious of Woodstock's citizens.

Woodstock produced many colourful individualists, one of whom was lawyer John Ford Maddock, who lived at 195 Vansittart Avenue. His house, built in 1840, has been radically altered but it is still of interest because of Maddock and the 'duel story.' In 1851 the census showed that John Maddock, who was born in England, was at that time forty-three years old and living in a single-storey frame house. With him were his wife Sarah, four sons, and three daughters. The 'duel story' concerns one of his daughters and her hot-tempered father. When the Maddock girl in question developed a skin infection, Maddock called in Dr Watt to prescribe treatment. The unfortunate doctor made the mistake of putting a name to the condition, calling it scabies. When informed of the diagnosis, Maddock was insulted and enraged. He set out with an axe to find the doctor but, unable to locate the offender, the still furious father challenged Dr Watt to a duel. A suitable time was arranged and seconds selected. The participants were in place and ready to proceed when a warrant for their arrest was delivered by an officer who bore the splendid name of Constable Snarey. Shortly thereafter both families moved from Woodstock – the Watts to Niagara and the Maddocks to Australia.

Another of Woodstock's more interesting men was George Alexander, Oxford County's first senator. His home, called Rokewood, stands at 479 Wellington Street North on a height of land that overlooks the site of an early curling match. As was often the case, the Alexander house was built in two stages. The older section, dating from the 1840s, was a small dwelling to which the main body of the house was added in 1873. The name of the builder and the date 'D. McKay '73,' is etched in a brick on the house.

Born in Banffshire, Scotland, in 1814, Alexander attended Aberdeen University before coming to Canada to settle and farm near Woodstock. He married Mary Cecilia, daughter of Colonel Alexander Whalley Light. By 1851 they were the parents of two children, Denham, three, and Mary, one. In that year the Alexanders were living in a brick house, presumably the one that stands today at the north end of Wellington Street.

In 1858 Alexander was elected to the Legislative Council of the Province of Canada for Gore Division and he sat until Confederation. He was called to the Senate in 1873. When he died thirty years later, the *Woodstock Daily Sentinel-Review*, 14 October 1903, recalled the triumph of his first election, when he defeated James Cowan of Galt: 'his election by a small majority was a great surprise ... [and] ... celebrated by a huge procession with banners flying ... There was subsequently an immense demonstration and bonfire on the Victoria Park here when an ox was roasted and dis-

Rokewood, home of Senator George Alexander, 479 Wellington Street North

tributed amongst the crowd.' In describing his years in the Senate the obituary stated that 'in later years [he] was not on friendly terms with some of his Conservative colleagues notably the late Senator McPherson and the late Senator George W. Allan. The causes of these differences arose from the failure of the old Upper Canada Bank for which Senator Alexander, who was understood to be a heavy loser, blamed the two Senators named ... the late Senator was a man of fine appearance and good education. His knowledge of German which he spoke fluently was one of no little service to him in his political aspirations among the Germans of Oxford and Waterloo.'

In a speech at Stratford in 1885 the aging senator stated that he was no longer seeking political office but spoke with fervour against the prime minister:

He is one of the most remarkable men of the age. He is perhaps the most highly gifted of all the public men which this dependency of empire has yet produced, combining in himself all the qualities which make a man powerful and popular. For a long period of his life he was considered the highest authority upon questions of constitutional law – but not now! ... The Right Honourable Gentleman's prominent infirmity [is] the lust of power, which of late years [has] become with him so absorbing a passion as to engulph any higher principle of life ... The first minister appear[s] to be intoxicated by the world's adulation ... he acts as a man in his phrenzy ... He forgets that we are a people of limited numbers and limited wealth, struggling into existence by very hard toil. He forgets the depressed state of the maritime provinces and the limited resources of the Province of Quebec and that they will never submit to heavier financial burdens ... we behold him with his all-confident majority, rushing through with break-neck speed.

He was speaking of Sir John A. Macdonald.

A report by Dr Adam Ford, quoted in *Curling in Ontario 1846– 1946*, describes one of the first curling matches recorded in the province, which was held near Alexander's home in 1849:

Scottish curlers had settled in Zorra township and had evidently played the game somewhere up in that township. Mr. George Alexander ... heard of it and had them come down and curl on the river near his place ... The stones were flat boulders picked up in the fields, weighing about, I should say, fifteen to twenty pounds each, with no handles, the players bringing their stones in bags. The stones were pitched along the ice as a ten-pins player tosses his ball along the alley ... Mr. Alexander had a lunch sent out in hampers and a bottle of something that they said smelt of the rafters. Keener curling I never saw and there was a rare mixture of Scots and Gaelic ... Mr. Alexander brought out Colonel Light, Captain Graham and other friends to watch the game in the afternoon. When the game was over we all went down to Hell's Tavern and dressed for supper by throwing our bonnets and plaids on a table in a corner and running our fingers through our hair. There was haggis and beef and greens and more of the stuff with the taste of the rafters. Someone sang Hurrah for the Thistle and we all joined in the chorus till the ceiling shook ... somehow I have ever since been proud that I was a boy from Zorra.

When Alexander married Mary Light in 1847, he put in her name more than two hundred acres of land immediately north of Woodstock. This generous gift was part of the marriage settlement. Rokewood was built on this property, as was another impressive house that was in all likelihood constructed at about the same time.

435 Devonshire Avenue

We do not know why, since they were living in their Wellington Street home, the Alexanders would build such a sizeable second house on their property if they were not planning to live in it. Perhaps for a time they did.

The second house on the Alexander property stands at 435 Devonshire Avenue. It is a solid, good-looking building, certainly a house of the calibre that one might expect the future senator to erect. The title to the property reflects much of the history of Woodstock. The land was originally owned by Andrew Drew, who in 1834 sold it to Admiral Vansittart; he in turn sold it to the influential Peter Boyle de Blaquiere. Vansittart's son Henry was the next owner, and it was he who in 1845 sold it to George Alexander. Two years later the property was given to Mary Alexander, and it remained in her name for the following twenty-two years, with her father and other prominent men named as trustees. In 1867 eleven acres and undoubtedly the house were sold to George Kirton, a Woodstock photographer. The true story of the Devonshire Avenue house and of who built it may never be known. Unquestionably it invites further research.

One of Woodstock's most noteworthy residents was Lieutenant-Colonel Hugh Richardson, a man who achieved national attention as the presiding judge at the trial of Louis Riel. His impressive brick home, built in 1847, stands at 419 Vincent Street. Richardson was born in 1826 in London, Upper Canada, the son of Richard and Elizabeth Miller Richardson. At the age of twenty-one Hugh Richardson was admitted to the bar and for the next twenty-five years he practised law in Woodstock. Obviously an ambitious man, he became reeve of Woodstock at the age of twenty-five, served as mayor in 1864, and from 1857 to 1862 was the crown attorney for Oxford County. The 1861 census found him living in his Vincent Street house with his wife, Charlotte, and their five children. In the mid-1870s Richardson went west, where he became legal adviser to the lieutenant-governor of the Northwest Territories, living first in Battleford, Saskatchewan, and later in Regina.

In his introduction to *The Queen v. Louis Riel* Desmond Morton said of Richardson: 'Since 1880 he had presided over the police court at Regina and if liquor offences were the most common item on his docket, he had already convicted an Indian for cannibalism and two half-breeds and a white man for murder.' His address to the jury at the Riel trial 'was a cautious speech, by a man well aware that better legal minds than his own would be searching his words for the chance of a mistrial.' In handing down the sentence Richardson solemnly remarked:

Louis Riel, after a long consideration of your case, in which you have been defended with as great ability as I think counsel could have defended you with, you have been found by a jury who have shown, I might almost say, unexampled patience, guilty of a crime the most pernicious and greatest that man can commit. You have been found guilty of high treason. You have been proved to have let loose the floodgates of rapine and bloodshed, you have, with such assistance as you had in the Saskatchewan country, managed to arouse the Indians and have brought ruin and misery to many families whom if you had simply left alone were in comfort, and many of them were on the road to affluence. For what you did, the remarks you have made form no excuse whatsoever ... All I can suggest or advise you is to prepare to meet your end.

Judge Hugh Richardson's house, 419 Vincent Street

From 1897 to 1898 Richardson was administrator of the Northwest Territories. He died at Ottawa in 1913.

The Oxford County Jail, built in 1837, is very much a part of Woodstock's past. It has been the subject of great interest in recent years because, like other early buildings that have seemingly outlived their usefulness, it faces possible demolition. Fortunately, as a result of protests from both architectural and social historians as well as from local enthusiasts, its existence now seems assured. The pleasing appearance of the building belies the many dramatic events that took place behind its walls.

If Woodstock has produced more than the average number of talented entrepreneurs, adventurers, and local characters, it has also had its fair share of bizarre murders and hangings, five of which took place in the jail on Buller Street. Perhaps the most grotesque of these executions was that of Thomas Cook, a blind labourer from Innerkip, a village northeast of Woodstock. He had murdered his

Oxford County Jail, Buller Street

wife in 1862 and was hanged that same year in front of the jail so that a bloodthirsty public could witness the spectacle.

In the census taken the year before the murder Cook was listed as an Englishman, aged 46, blind, and living in a single-storey log house with his wife, Bridget, who was also English. The same census showed two Cook children living with the family of Joseph Brown, a man whose name appears in the report of the hanging. He was, it seems, a special constable and the one to whom the dead man's coffin was delivered. He is mentioned as a relative of Cook's first wife. The newspapers of the day gave the trial and execution extensive coverage, describing both in horrifying detail. The *Canadian Illustrated News*, 20 December 1862, noted that both the Reverend D. McDermid and the Reverend William Bettridge counselled the condemned man in prison and that 'he freely confessed his guilt, acknowledging the justice of his sentence and expressed his readiness to suffer death.' Cook thanked his counsel, the ministers, and the jailors but refused to see his children. He would never have killed Bridget, he claimed, if he had been sober. The lengthy article about the hanging described Cook's horrible end: '[Cook's] fall being so great and the man's body being in a diseased condition, the vertabrae and muscles connecting the head with the shoulders gave way, and, terrible to relate, the head rolled off while the body fell with a heavy plunge into the interior of the scaffold ... For a few minutes the body lay as it fell, the authorities apparently shrinking from the task of touching the murderer's remains.' And so ended the last public hanging in Woodstock.

It was nearly twenty-eight years before another man met his death on the gallows in the Woodstock jail. His name was J. Reginald Birchall, a man of some charm, who had posed in Woodstock as Lord Somerset and was later convicted of the murder of Frank Benwell, one of two young Englishmen he had lured to Canada by offering to teach them farming. Birchall was described by J.W. Murray, the detective who solved the murder, as 'handsome and easy in manner, with a certain grace of bearing that was quite attractive ... clearly he was a man of the world, a gentleman.' Consequently the Birchall trial aroused avid interest in the press. He was, according to the Woodstock *Weekly Sentinel-Review*, 19 September 1890, 'by far the most cheerful, vivacious and sprightly prisoner that has been confined within the grim and lonesome walls of the County gaol for many a day.' Birchall managed to be the centre of attention even in jail – he was voluble and entertaining, he tried to cheer the other prisoners, he read voraciously and drew numerous sketches which he used to decorate the walls of his cell so that 'it might with a few changes be taken for the editorial "den" of the sporting editor of a daily newspaper.'

The trial was held in the Town Hall but the premises could not accommodate the throngs who wanted to follow the proceedings. G.T. Blackstock, defence counsel, was frustrated because Birchall 'continually sent them on wild errands for an alibi and each time it was supposed to be the truth but proved otherwise.' The prosecutor was Britton Bath Osler (brother of Sir William Osler and son of Dundas's Featherstone Lake Osler), one of Canada' greatest criminal lawyers. On 14 November 1880 a remorseless Birchall went to the gallows. His last words, spoken to his wife, were 'Goodbye, Flo dear; be brave.' There were three subsequent hangings in the jail, the last in 1954.

Town Hall, Dundas Street

The Town Hall, scene of the Birchall trial, was built in 1852, a year after Woodstock was declared a town. It is located on Dundas Street at Finkle. It was modelled after its counterpart in Woodstock, England, and its simple dignity still adds grace to the downtown area. Five years after its completion the town received a gift and a glowing tribute from one of its native sons, W.S. Light of Lyte's Carey. His gift, 'the Royal Arms of Great Britain and Ireland cut in stone [was] to be erected in such suitable locality as the Mayor and Council deem expedient.' This coat-of-arms is mounted on the wall above the front entrance to the Town Hall to commemorate the fact that Woodstock had reached, according to Mr Light, 'that rank among the towns of Western Canada to which she is so justly entitled in consequence of the vast and extensive strides which she has within the last few years taken.'

The names of Light and Lyte's Carey had been known in the town since 1830, two years before the arrival of Andrew Drew. Colonel Alexander Whalley Light received a military grant of nine hundred acres adjacent to the town site so that the future town was completely encircled by his holdings and those of Philip Graham and Andrew Drew. This situation, needless to say, provided the three astute gentlemen with the certainty of future profits. Like so many of his peers, Colonel Light had a cosmopolitan and adventurous background. Born in India, he was the son of an Englishman from Lyte's Carey, Somerset, who was with the East India Company. As a boy of twelve Light enlisted in the army and saw action in many parts of the world. He fought at the Battle of Waterloo, retired afterwards on half-pay, then emigrated to Canada to face further challenges. His home, also called Lyte's Carey, was eventually destroyed by fire, but an octagonal barn now marks the site of the original estate.

This barn, although not built until the latter part of the nineteenth century and not by the Light family, is interesting in its own right. The fad for octagonal houses was prevalent throughout Ontario in mid-century, but for some reason octagonal barns did not appear on the scene until the 1880s and 1890s. As noted earlier, these structures were based on the theories of Orson Squire Fowler, an eccentric American who believed that octagonal buildings produced for their occupants both psychological and physical benefits. Presumably these benefits applied to farm animals as well. Still in good condition, the octagonal barn can be seen south of the Dundas

Road, off Valleyfield Drive (lot 27, concession 1, East Zorra).

The military career of Captain Philip Graham, the third of the trio whose land holdings surrounded Woodstock, rivalled his neighbours' in scope and variety. On his death in 1849 the *British American* for 30 June reminded its readers that Captain Graham had seen brilliant action while in the Royal Navy, including one encounter in which a slave schooner was seized in the face of no fewer than five armed pirate vessels and 'ten thousand armed natives and twenty guns.' Having survived this event, the intrepid Captain Graham went on to serve under Lord Nelson and, according to this account, 'under the Royal Standard he was willing to bleed and die.'

One of the many Woodstock legends concerns an event closer to home, when Graham, travelling with his men on the Niagara River, was advised by a crew member that they were about to enter the rapids above the falls. The captain, incensed by this breach of authority, shouted 'Silence, or I will blow your brains out – it is for

Octagonal barn, lot 27, concession 1, East Zorra

me, not you, to give the orders.' Drawing on his oar, the crewman replied: 'If I am to go over the Falls, I may as well go without brains as with them.' Apparently he survived to tell the tale.

It is understood locally that the Graham family lived for a time in the brick house at 770 Dundas Street East. Certainly the house was built during Graham's lifetime but his name does not appear on the title. Perhaps the family rented the premises. When Graham died he was survived by his wife, Mary, and seven children. The *British American* noted that he had 'left a numerous family unprovided for; two of his sons are at an age to bear commissions in the army and imbued with their father's spirit. We trust that these sons of such a sire may not long remain neglected and unemployed.'

Few of Woodstock's pre-Confederation houses were built of stone but one exception is a small house at 301 Ingersoll Avenue. Although modest in size, the rich colours of the stone and the pleasant proportions of the house combine to produce an unusual but satisfying

301 Ingersoll Avenue

structure. A search of the title suggests that the house was built in 1867, shortly after the property was purchased by John and Bridget Havener. Census records of six years earlier reveal that the Haveners were Irish, that they were, in that year, parents of four children under sixteen years, and that they owned one cow and one horse. John's occupation is not listed. Three years after purchasing the property the Haveners sold it to one Thomas B. Carr, who in turn sold it in 1878 to James Sutherland – probably the Woodstock merchant who became mayor in 1880 and later member of Parliament for Oxford North and minister of public works.

Woodstock boasts its share of the small vernacular houses that were so prevalent in nineteenth-century Ontario. Typical of the style is the pleasant brick house that stands at 140 Graham Street. It was built by barrister Henry Burkett Beard, an Englishman, who purchased the property in 1843 and no doubt built the house shortly thereafter. In 1866 Beard sold the house to Andrew Ross, who at the

140 Graham Street

time of the 1861 census was listed as deputy sheriff. Ten years later Ross sold the house to 'Margaret McKay et al,' and it was this sale that gave the house its chief claim to fame, or rather notoriety. Mrs McKay, a widow, took in boarders, the best-known of whom were Mr and Mrs J. Reginald Birchall. Their unsuspecting landlady would have known the couple as Lord and Lady Somerset, and she may well have been among the many in Woodstock to whom the Birchalls owed money, for they left behind them a trail of unhappy creditors.

Of the many individualists who added colour to life in nineteenth-century Woodstock, none was more remarkable than the legendary 'Klondike Joe' Boyle. Although he was not born until the year of Confederation, no history of the town would be complete without mention of his name. Boyle was born in Toronto but later joked that 'he took his family to Woodstock when he was a mere four-and-a-half years old.' His years there were a springboard to a life brimfull of challenges, intrigue, and danger, far from the relative tranquility of western Ontario. Boyle's careers as a sailor, boxing promoter, prospector, and entrepreneur culminated in heroic action during the First World War when, at his own expense, he took a fifty-man machine-gun detachment to England. He later became an intelligence agent for the British, formed an espionage ring, and, after a series of adventures each more hair-raising than the last, saved the Rumanian archives and crown jewels and removed the Rumanian treasury of $20 million from Moscow to Jassy in bushel baskets. When he died in 1923, Boyle was described as Canada's greatest hero and adventurer. The Queen of Rumania provided his grave with a cross and a ground stone on which were words from a poem by Robert Service: 'A man with the heart of a Viking, and the simple faith of a child.'

11

London

In 1831 Colonel Thomas Talbot, the autocratic patriarch of some six thousand settlers near Lake Erie, wrote of the fledgling town of London and of its imposing new court-house, a turreted and crenelated fortress that stood in incongruous splendour on the banks of the Thames River. Surrounded as it was by a handful of small frame structures and by muddy, stump-strewn 'streets,' the court-house made an immediate impression on visitors, who, claimed Talbot, described it as 'the finest building in the province.' These remarks were quoted by William Lyon Mackenzie in 1833; had he known, however, of the drama that would be played out in that court-house a few years later, Mackenzie might well have added a few words of his own.

During the months that followed the ill-fated Rebellion of 1837 many of Mackenzie's followers were rounded up and sent to stand trial in the London court-house. There, while waiting for their fate to be decided, these unfortunate souls languished in the jail that was housed in the basement of the building, enduring conditions not dissimilar to those of a medieval dungeon. In 1834, when the court-house was only five years old, a committee had been set up to investigate conditions in the jail. It reported that the 'state of the gaol ... is such as to demand earnest and immediate consideration' and went on to disclose that: 'All the cells on the lower storey are imperfectly ventilated as is evident from the impure and unwholesome smell proceeding from them ... The sitting room intended for the use of the prisoners during the daytime is much too small for the purpose, being but 12 feet square and is at all times subject from its vicinity to the privy to the most offensive smell. This is more especially the case in wet weather when the flood rises and overflows the floor of the room.' Conditions had improved not at all when forty-four rebels were incarcerated there in 1838. Of these men, six were found guilty of treason and hanged publicly in front of the court-house. The remainder were exiled to Van Dieman's Land (Tasmania).

The human tragedy inherent in political uprisings and in their aftermath was revealed in a letter written by one of the condemned men to his wife:

London, 27th January, 1839

Dear Wife,

I am at the moment confined in the cell from which I am to go to the scaffold ... I am permitted to see you tomorrow ... I wish you to think of such questions as you want to ask me as I do not know how long you will be permitted to stay. Think as little of my unhappy fate as you can, as from the love you bear to me and have ever evinced I know too well how it must affect you ... may God protect you and my dear child and give you fortitude which is the gift of Him our Lord who created us. That this may be the case is the prayer of your affectionate husband.

Joshua G. Doan

On 6 February 1839 Doan was hanged. According to the London *Gazette*, he 'met his fate with a good deal of composure – shaking hands with the clergyman, the sheriff and his clerk and with his companion on the drop [Amos Perley] – who also performed the same ceremony. At length the drop fell, and they were both launched into eternity without a struggle.'

The court-house and jail where Doan and his fellow-prisoners spent their last days was built between 1827 and 1829, its construction providing the impetus for London's growth. With political and financial support from the influential Colonel Talbot it was decided in 1825 that London, then little more than a clearing in the wilderness, would become the centre of government for the district, owing to its central location. By 1829, when the magnificent court-house had been completed, it immediately becoming a landmark for miles around. In the fall of 1828 John Cole, an early resident in the area, wrote: 'There is a court house and gaol under it built this summer in the village only 2 miles from me that is 50 feet wide, 100 feet long, and fifty feet high all of brick, and you may guess that it cost something.'

Middlesex County court-house and jail, Ridout Street at Dundas Street

The construction of public buildings frequently causes controversy and the London court-house was no exception. The main objections to it arose from its cost, which came to £4050 (including the expenditure of £14.12.7 for a privy, a sum which a few of the locals felt extravagant). The building was rectangular in shape, with four octagonal towers marking the corners. Stone was used to build the basement and the prison cells, but the rest of the structure was brick, which was mortared over and marked with squares to resemble stone. Above it all, from a flagpole on the roof, flew the Union Jack.

Most of the cases tried in the new court-house were of a trifling nature, with penalties ranging from fines to imprisonment and, on occasion, flogging. Even the stocks were used for a while until a humane magistrate ordered that they be thrown into the Thames. The real excitement, however, centred on public executions, and these events always brought large crowds of onlookers and a resultant festive atmosphere to the town. The first murder trial to be held in the new court-house occured in the summer of 1830 when Cornelius Burleigh was convicted of murdering Timothy Pomeroy, a sheriff's officer. Burleigh (as one report put it) 'gained the dubious distinction of not only being the first, but also the second man to go to the gallows in London. The rope broke on the first try.'

Burleigh's execution was bizarre from the moment it began. While standing with the rope around his neck, he was forced to endure hearing his 'confession' read to the waiting crowd by his spiritual advisor, the Reverend James Jackson, who quoted Burleigh as saying: 'I was often found in the merry dance and lost no opportunity of inducing thoughtless and unguarded females to leave the paths of innocence and virtue ... I now bid farewell to the world and to all earthly things, at the age of 26, and I sincerely hope that all of you who behold my disgrace will take warning by my untimely end and avoid the snares into which I have run ... and with a sincere desire for the happiness of all I leave behind, I say, "Farewell."' The onlookers were, no doubt, enthralled.

The unhappy story of Burleigh does not, however, end with his execution. Once dead, his body was placed on a table in the court-house square and, while the crowd looked on, a group of doctors and medical students proceeded immediately to dissect his remains. At that time cadavers of convicted criminals were the only ones legally available for medical research. The unfortunate Burleigh achieved even more notoriety, for his head was claimed by one of the students – a young American named Orson Squire Fowler. In later years, as we have noted, the eccentric Fowler gained fame for his philosophical and architectural theories about octagonal buildings, but at the time of Burleigh's death this indefatigable American was pursuing an interest in phrenology. He felt that criminal tendencies could be determined by the size of various bumps on the skull and hoped to prove his point by using Burleigh's skull as his prize exhibit. This he did for several years, zealously promoting the pseudo-science of phrenology through his writings, publishing, and lecturing. Sometime in the 1880s, when Fowler paid a return visit to London, he presented the well-travelled skull to the Harris family at Eldon House, just up the street from the court-house and jail. It is now on display there, a gruesome reminder of a colourful chapter in London's history.

During the aftermath of the Mackenzie rebellion prisoners continued to be housed in the damp and crowded cells under the court-house. Finally, after a grand jury presented a scathing report on the filth, water, and fumes in the place, a new jail was built adjacent to the court-house and prisoners were transferred to it in 1844. This new building served, for well over a century, as the jail for Middlesex County. Few changes were made to the court-house until a substantial addition was built in the late 1870s. The original building was gutted, and the east wall was demolished. The building was doubled in size, the addition being made on the east side of the original building; this addition included the central tower on the present-day front (Ridout Street) elevation. The court-house had barely been completed when it was called upon to house the hordes of reporters and spectators who came to attend the trial of the men accused of murdering the Donnelly family of nearby Lucan. Two trials were held, the first ending in a hung jury, the second acquitting the accused, possibly because the jurors were afraid of reprisals. During the years that followed minor changes were made to the interior of the building, and in 1911 a law library was added to the south elevation. The old court-house remained in use until the mid-1970s, when it was replaced by a new building across the street. The original turreted structure, once described by Anna Jameson as 'the glory of the towns-people,' was retained and restored. Now housing Middlesex County municipal offices, it is open at specified times to the public.

One of the people who played a significant role in the turbulent early years of the courthouse was James Hamilton, who was appointed sheriff of the London District in 1837. Because of the political unrest at the time one of his first duties was to arrest anyone suspected of harbouring rebel sympathies. It was a chore he found distasteful for, because of the hysteria that prompted this search, many men were wrongfully arrested and imprisoned, spending months in the London jail before they were finally acquitted. In the next year the sheriff was scouring the countryside again, this time in order to find jurors for the forthcoming treason trials. According to a bill he submitted to the governor-general, Lord Elgin, in 1851, he travelled over twelve hundred miles to round up these jurors and he was still, thirteen years later, trying to obtain £14.3.0 as 'additional compensation' for the expenses he incurred in 1838. The sheriff's most difficult duty, however, was supervising the execution of the rebels convicted of high treason.

Sheriff Hamilton was born in 1792, a son of the Honourable Robert Hamilton, who had settled near the Niagara River prior to the immigration of the Loyalists. The sheriff, like so many others at the time, speculated in land, one of his ventures being the development of a subdivision in southwest London. His partner was builder Robert Carfrae, and the two men submitted their plans for the area in 1849. Shortly thereafter Hamilton built for his family a substantial frame house at 198 Elmwood Avenue. It is evident that the house was built before 1851, for Hamilton mentioned it in the will he wrote that year and again when he insured the house for £600 two years later. Some time after the turn of the century the frame siding of the house was covered with brick and, possibly at the same time, the house was turned on its foundation so that it now faces south instead of east, as it did when the sheriff built it.

Hamilton was married to Catherine Warren, the mother of his children Henry and Catherine, but evidently he was married twice, for his will refers to his wife, Margaret, and to a stepson, Alexander D. McLean. When Hamilton died on 28 March 1858, he had not been living in the Elmwood Avenue house for some time, having sold it four years previously to Alexander Kirkland for £750. In her diary Amelia Harris of Eldon House commented on the sheriff's death and his funeral three days later: 'the shops were closed during the procession, which was very large, as he was much respected. He took cold the night Maggy McFarlane drowned herself. He was all night searching for her and her death preyed upon his mind.'

Hamilton's partner in his real-estate venture was Robert Car-frae, a carpenter and builder who was one of the first people to settle in London. A native of Leith, Scotland, Carfrae arrived first in Toronto, where others of his family had already become established and had developed close ties with members of the Family Compact. Young Robert, however, decided to launch out on his own, arriving at the London townsite in time to find work on the courthouse, which was then under construction. He was twenty-two years old.

The astute Scot recognized London's potential and chose to stay and take part in the development of the town, which experienced a period of rapid growth after the courthouse was completed. It proved to be a wise decision, for Carfrae eventually became a prosperous land speculator. His business concerns must have kept him busy, since he was almost fifty years old when, in 1853, he finally married. A few years later, probably around 1860, he built a house, a

Sheriff Hamilton's house, 198 Elmwood Avenue

simple vernacular cottage at 39 Carfrae Street. Built of brick, the house is deceiving in its appearance, for the simple exterior belies the generous proportions and handsome detailing found within. Carfrae obviously put his carpentry skills to good use when it came time to build his own house.

When he died in 1881, Carfrae bequeathed his house and the bulk of his substantial estate to his wife, Sarah Louisa, as long as she remained his widow. In the event of her remarriage, however, the money was to go to the Baptist church and the house would revert to Carfrae's nephew, Hugh, 'should [the trustees] deem him worthy of it but not otherwise – of which they shall be the only judges.' Sarah Carfrae, who did not marry again, was able to live out her life in Carfrae Cottage. When she died in 1902, the house was inherited by Hugh and it remained in the family until 1944.

In his later years Carfrae told of the day in 1827 when he first arrived at the new settlement on the Thames. He stopped at a cot-

39 Carfrae Street

tage to enquire of the owner, 'How far is it to London?' and the man replied, 'Why you are in it!' Carfrae would not have had to ask that question had he arrived even eight years later, for by that time the court-house had been completed and there were, as well, several substantial commercial buildings. Among them was the newly opened Bank of Upper Canada at 435 Ridout Street North, a handsome Georgian structure that is now one of three adjacent buildings, all built before the mid-century, which have recently been restored by John Labatt Limited. Their presence a short distance north of the court-house adds inestimable charm to the city's present-day downtown area.

Until it suspended operations in 1866, the Bank of Upper Canada was managed in London by a second James Hamilton, a man often confused in later years with London's sheriff of the same name. Hamilton the banker was English born, arriving in Canada in 1820 when he was ten years old. After living in Toronto for the next

Bank of Upper Canada, 435 Ridout Street, part of the Ridout Street Restoration

fourteen years, he came to London, where he spent the remainder of his life. A talented painter, Hamilton was admired for his water-colour sketches of London in the early years.

Like many other bankers of the day, Hamilton and his family occupied living quarters above his place of business. Eventually he bought the building and converted the main floor to a residence as well. At his death in 1896 it became the property of his daughter Mary Ellen Hamilton, who in her youth was described by her neighbour Charlotte Harris as an accomplished pianist and a delightful 'madcap.'

Next door to Hamilton's Bank of Upper Canada was the Gore Bank, both part of a group of five banks in the complex that was known for a time as Bankers' Row. These buildings, at 443–7 Ridout and 451 Ridout, were built in the early 1840s by one of London's first doctors, Alexander Anderson. They proved to be a sound invest-ment, for in later years Dr Anderson remarked to his nieces that he had been paid several times over for the cost of their construction. For some time Dr Anderson and his wife lived in the house that forms the north end of the group, a house that now serves as corpo-rate headquarters for Labatt's brewery interests.

Anderson arrived from Scotland in 1833 and remained to practise medicine in London until his death forty years later. He and his wife, Eliza, had no children of their own but were evidently close to their nephews and nieces and to Anderson's brother and sister, all of whom figured prominently in his will. The doctor directed that, after Eliza's death, generous sums be given to the local 'orphan asylum' and to the City of London 'for the maintenance and support of an Hospital ... when such Hospital is Prepared to receive patients.' Although himself a Catholic, Dr Anderson instructed that, should the daughters of his sister Mrs Scott become nuns, 'the share of the one becoming a nun shall be forfited and lapse.'

Medical practice was, of course, primitive in those early days and Dr Anderson's methods were no exception. His neighbour Edward Harris remembered that the doctor's favourite formula was 'calumel and rhubarb' and that 'he bled me in the arm for toothache.' These remarks appear in one of the diaries kept by members of the Harris family who lived at Eldon House, at 481 Ridout Street, a short dis-tance north of Dr Anderson. The Harrises were, by any standards, a fascinating family. Their journals provide a unique look at nine-teenth-century London and suggest that life there, for the 'upper classes' at least, was rarely dull, even in this relatively remote out-post in western Ontario.

The saga of the Harris family began with British naval officer John Harris, a man described by one early resident as 'a thorough John Bull, afraid of nothing, he would take the most extreme meas-ures for what he thought was right.' After retiring on half-pay, Harris came to Upper Canada and in 1815 married Amelia Ryerse. A daughter of Colonel Samuel Ryerse, a Loyalist, and a cousin of Egerton Ryerson, Amelia was eighteen years old when they mar-ried, John about thirty-four. For the first years of their life together John and Amelia lived in Vittoria (near Long Point in Norfolk County) and, for a time, in Kingston. They became the parents of twelve children, two of whom died in infancy.

In 1834 the Harrises moved to London and built their impressive home, Eldon House. Immediately, and for many years afterwards, it was the hub of London's social and cultural life. The events that

Eldon House, 481 Ridout Street, home of the Harris family

occurred in these years are vividly brought to life in the diary that Amelia Harris began to keep in 1857, but even more intriguing is the picture that emerges of Amelia herself. Here was a woman who, although raised in a small settlement on the shores of Lake Erie, came to know and to be respected by virtually all the prominent political figures of the day, and few came to London without stopping at Eldon House to pay their respects. She met and entertained people such as Sir John A. Macdonald, Sir John Beverley Robinson, Sir Casimir Gzowski, Governor-General Sir Edmund Head, Sir Francis Hincks, John Sandfield Macdonald, and a host of British aristocrats. Her interests were wide-ranging, and throughout her diary her comments show insight, wisdom, and, not infrequently, a wry sense of humour. Amelia Harris did not have a parochial mind.

The Harris's daughter Charlotte also kept a diary, which she began when she was twenty years old. Her interests, not surprisingly, centred on London's social life, which she described with boundless enthusiasm. Central to her story was the presence in London of British troops stationed there after the Mackenzie Rebellion. The officers gladdened the hearts of every girl in the district, since most of these young men came from good families in England and were therefore eminently eligible. The soldiers, in turn, were enjoying their first taste of adventure in the colonies. Charlotte began her diaries on 22 October 1848, expressing her regret that on that day one of these soldiers, a man who was later to become her husband, left London: 'Captain [Edward Lewis] Knight came to say goodbye. We were exceedingly sorry to see him leave and shall miss him very much. Monday, October 23 ... the dinner party left at ten, the others at eleven. Mary sent me to talk to Mr Lutyens, but I could not, my thoughts were of the last evening ... it was the longest and most miserable day I have ever spent.' Charlotte soon recovered her good spirits, however, and her diary entries recorded her busy social life. For example, the entry for 27 November noted: 'Miss Brough called to ask us when we would like Mrs Goodhue to give her ball. We said we were all quite ready for it.' And on 9 December: 'Everyone was charmed with the Goodhue ball. It was decidedly the best private one that has ever been given in London. We did not leave until half-past three o'clock.' The following day was Sunday: 'We all went to church ... Mr Cronyn preached against the ball and compared it to Balshazzar's feast.'

Charlotte's life continued in this manner for the next few months.

Her diary records an unending series of parties, balls, sleigh-rides, and callers at Eldon House. Usually she was surrounded by the young men from the regiment, those her brother later called 'The Noble Army of Martyrs.' Her journal entries suggest that Charlotte had a mind of her own: 'September 18th ... the party was delightful ... met a Mr Pitcairne, who is an intense ass but dances beautifully ... October 3rd [1849] ... we all went to see the Governor-General [Lord Elgin] come in; learnt wisdom and will never go again.'

In 1850, however, the Harrises life changed when on 1 June 'Papa returned from Long Point. He met with an accident. The shafts broke and he was very much hurt.' Charlotte's diary entry for 16 November of that year stated: 'More than three long months have passed since I have written and, oh, how much has happened and how little we know what is in store for us ... our dear father died on the 25th. How changed everything is.'

Less than four years later Charlotte, too, was dead. On 24 April 1854 she and her children were lost at sea when their ship was rammed by another, somewhere in the Mediterranean. Her husband attempted in vain to save his family but was swept away and later rescued.

Charlotte's mother, Amelia Harris, started her own diary about three years after Charlotte's death. By that time Amelia was sixty years old. Still residing at Eldon House, her life continued much as it had before the loss of her husband and Charlotte. A selection of entries from her diary reflects her broad range of interests:

Sept. 13[, 1857]: We like Lord Althorpe. He appears not only moral but religiously disposed. He is a great anti-slavery man ...

Sept 7[, 1859]: Mr Wilson [a London lawyer and friend] came to luncheon ... [He] spoke of George Brown and said he was a scoundrel. I was surprised to hear afterwards that he had gone to Toronto and voted for him and against his old friend J.H. Cameron. It appears to me that nothing perverts the mind like politics.

April 21[, 1860]: ... Mr Hincks ... has lost none of his cleverness ... Report says that he is to succeed Sir Edmund Head as Governor-General of Canada but many think it would be a dangerous experiment to place one who had so lately been a leader in politics in the country at the head of affairs ...

December 29[, 1863]: We spoke of the death of Lord Elgin and felt that we had lost a kind friend. Years ago he told Amelia [a daughter] that from boyhood it had been the dream of his life to be governor-general of India, and there he rests from all his labors.

December 16[, 1864]: There appears to be a very great probability of war with the Yankees. If so, the country will be over-run. The thoughts of such a possibility keep me from sleep.

April 15[, 1865]: ... President Lincoln was shot last evening in the theatre when sitting with his wife ... Canada as well as the States is horrified at the crime.

April 7[, 1868]: We have heard of the assassination of D'Arcy McGee ...

October 11[, 1871]: The smoke from the burning city of Chicago is like a thick fog here and painful to the eyes.

June 1[, 1872]: An old friend of ours, John Sandfield Macdonald, died today.

June 5: [Macdonald] leaves about the same number of friends that political men usually leave. His private friends are many.

April 29[, 1875]: The free delivery of letters commenced today.

Amelia Harris made the last entry in her diary on 20 June 1877, but she lived for another five years, badly crippled with arthritis. Five of her children predeceased her and her husband as well, yet nowhere in her journals is there evidence of self-pity or discouragement. She was indeed a remarkable woman.

In 1832, two years before the Harris family settled in London, Benjamin Cronyn, an Irish clergyman, arrived in the village on his way to Adelaide Township. He preached to the local Anglicans on what was to be a one-day visit and so excited those who heard him that he was urged to stay and become their first permanent minister. This he did, eventually becoming Bishop of the Diocese of Huron. (When Cronyn, instead of Archdeacon Bethune, was chosen as Bishop of Huron, the votes were so close and the delegates argued so vociferously that John Strachan had to issue a stern rebuke to those present, urging them to control themselves.)

Late on a winter afternoon in February 1844 huge quantities of smoke began to billow from the belfry of Cronyn's church, St Paul's, at Richmond Street and Queens Avenue. Shortly after, in spite of efforts by the fire department and the military, the eleven-year-old building was reduced to ashes, the organ and a bell recently arrived from Ireland also destroyed. Plans were immediately made for a new building. The congregation had grown dramatically since Cronyn's arrival and the addition of eight hundred troops to the town

St Paul's Anglican Cathedral, Richmond Street and Queens Avenue

convinced parishioners that a large church was required. Consequently the new church was able to seat fifteen hundred people. At the official opening two thousand attended and the band of the local regiment performed so well that the *Western Globe* was moved to comment on its 'high state of cultivation.'

The new St Paul's, Gothic in style and built this time of brick, was topped with a tower over one hundred feet in height. When that lofty portion of the building was complete, the 'spirited contractors' placed four national ensigns on the corners of the base and a Union Jack in the centre. According to the *Times*, 7 November 1845: 'The Contractors, in order to give eclat to the circumstances ... ascended to the top of the tower ... from whence they proposed and drank the following four national and loyal toasts, each of which was responded to by three hearty cheers.' These toasts honoured Queen Victoria, Prince Albert and the royal family, the British constitution, and the church of 'our Father Land.' At this point discretion probably prompted a return to ground level.

St Paul's Church, now a cathedral, has twice been enlarged. Each side originally had seven bays, and an entrance from Queens Avenue was constructed to enable carriages to drive up to the church door. The interior of the building is breathtaking. Numerous memorials commemorate parishioners such as Lawrence Lawrason, who mortgaged his property in order to support the rebuilding of the church after the disastrous fire. Four windows by the nave were made in the Tiffany studios in New York.

The tower which the enthusiastic workmen ascended for their toasts supported a peal of six English-made bells transported during the latter part of their journey to London by oxcart. They were a source of great satisfaction to Cronyn and his congregation. When the Prince of Wales visited in 1860, the bells rang out to proclaim the town's welcome. One visitor, a reporter sent by the St Thomas *Weekly Dispatch*, to cover the event, was not impressed. He wrote:

If you ever come to London on a festive occasion as you value your peace of mind keep away from the Cathedral ... [Cronyn] has a peal of big bells in the little tower of his small cathedral and all night long, as it appears to thousands of strangers in this city, they have kept up a continual chiming ... the 'puir bodies' lying in the church yard here can scarcely be in peace while such a tintinabulation is constantly swelling over their heads.

Were the bell-ringers 'tight' last night; or had it been deliberately determined to deprive the Prince of sleep that he might know London possesses the only peal of bells in Western Canada?

The redoubtable Bishop Cronyn was a friend of the Harrises, of course, and he and his family are mentioned frequently in the Harris diaries. From them it seems apparent that Cronyn, while undoubtedly a devout and admirable man, was also inclined to be somewhat dour, a trait that was perhaps shared by his daughter. Her wedding at St Paul's, in January 1858, was described by Amelia Harris: 'The bride ... looked very pretty although she is thought plain ... [she] went through the ceremony and received the congratulations of her friends with her usual quiet manner and without any apparent emotion.'

When Cronyn first arrived at London in 1832, he became responsible for the rural parish of St John's a few miles north of the town, as well as for St Paul's in London proper. He settled in the third concession of London Township, partway between his two churches. After serving both parishes for nine years, Cronyn was joined by his friend Charles Crosbie Brough, a clergyman who left Ireland with Cronyn but who in the intervening years had worked as a missionary to the Indians on Manitoulin Island. Brough became the rector at St John's and remained there for the rest of life.

In September 1842, a year after Brough began his duties at St John's, Bishop Strachan arrived on a visit, travelling in 'a common farmer's waggon strongly built' – a sight which, in itself, would have been well worth seeing. The bishop noted that 'Mr Brough has the advantage of an excellent parsonage and glebe, beautifully situated on the banks of the river Thames, about three miles from the prosperous town of London.' It has been assumed locally that the bishop was referring to the picturesque brick house at 1132 Richmond Street, which was indeed built by the Broughs. Recent research, however, indicates that they did not build their trim little house until the mid-1860s, a theory supported by an entry in Mrs Brough's diary. Writing in June 1865, she spoke of returning 'to our new home after an absence of five weeks to Guelph and Galt seeing our darling children.'

Charles and Wilhelmina Brough had six children, a son and five daughters, the oldest of whom was Anne. She was thirty-three

Brough house, 1132 Richmond Street

years old in 1860 when her father wrote his will, directing that Anne was not to receive her inheritance 'so long as she remains unmarried.' She could, he allowed, receive the interest and dividends from it. Brough went on to say that 'If or when she married [the] trustees can decide if she should receive her share.' Brough died in March 1873. Five years later a directory indicated that only Mrs Brough and her son Richard were living in a house on Mill Street, so perhaps Anne had married and received her inheritance by that time.

In recent years an addition was built on the north side of the Brough's house by its present owners. Care was taken to ensure that the new section blended well with the original structure to create a unified whole. Today the Brough house remains one of the finest pre-Confederation buildings in London.

In May 1853 Sarah McStay wrote in her diary: 'Went to church. Collection and Sacrament; we had a tremendous rain so that the Parson had to make a long pause in the sermon.' The parson referred to was Charles Brough, who was preaching at St John's. The diarist was the sister of James McStay, with whom she lived in the beautiful brick house at 1603 Richmond Street. Sarah was a staunch church-going lady who may well have attended a second service on that same Sunday. She frequently was seen at Brough's church in the morning and the White Church, which was Wesleyan Methodist, in the evening or for mid-week revival meetings.

Sarah's diary reveals the day-to-day happenings in a family in which the concerns of death, marriage, illness, birth, and the state of the crops were the pressing ones. The diary also serves to date the McStay house. A marginal note in 1853 contains the first reference to the 'brick cottage' so it may be presumed that the house was then complete. Since the land on which the house stood had, however, been in the McStay family for twenty-three years, obviously a log or frame house or both had been built for the six women, one boy, and one man who lived there (lot 17, concession 4, London).

The McStays trace their roots back almost two hundred years to Elizabeth Woods (born 1786), who married Anthony McStay in Ireland. In 1809 she emigrated with her husband, her father-in-law, Peter, and her infant son, James. By 1830 Anthony and Peter were dead and Elizabeth left Eaton in Madison County, New York, and the United States for good, travelling with her son James to London, where they settled. Four years later she was joined by her younger sister Ann Woods Bradshaw and her brother John, who with their spouses came to London Township to farm nearby.

Meanwhile James had acquired a wife, Sarah Toplift. James was now responsible for four unmarried sisters and his mother, as only one sister, Mary Ann, had married before him. By the time of the 1861 census, however, James and Sarah were living alone in their brick house with their adopted son, Hugh Young, then twenty-one. All the sisters had married and 'Ma' had moved to Chatham. The last of the girls to marry was Sarah, James's sister the diarist. It is clear from Sarah's journal that she became helpmate to the whole family, visiting and nursing sick nieces and nephews, her mother, and others, attending funerals and marriages, and caring for young children as the families grew. Various illnesses such as 'remitting fever' and 'the ague' are mentioned. Occasionally there is a wedding, the excitement of being a bridesmad, a sleigh ride, or a swim in the creek, but for the most part activities such as 'I rakd hay for James' form the entries. Sarah comments philosophically upon two birth-

1603 Richmond Street, the McStay homestead

days as time goes by. For the first 'My Birthday past without my knowledge,' and for the next just 'My Birthday. Oh Dear!' The name Robert suddenly begins to appear. Sarah rides with him and cuts his hair. Then in 1855 in Detroit she is married. The entries are brief: 'June. Saturday I received a letter from Robert. He will come on Thursday and I will have to make heast and be prepaird. Monday. Went a shopping. Tuesday Baked. Wednesday. Arranged. Th. Robert came ... great bustling. Married after nine.'

One day before his death in 1887 James McStay made a will. To his wife, Sarah, he left $6000. To his adopted son, Hugh Young, he left $2000. With this money Hugh purchased the brick house from his mother five months after James's death. The building remains almost untouched on the exterior, its small paned windows and distinguished entrance-way accented by the 'white' brick (actually buff in colour) which was so popular in London.

Grosvenor Lodge, at 1017 Western Road, was built for a wealthy

Grosvenor Lodge, 1017 Western Road

surveyor and landowner, Samuel Peters. It is believed to have been built along the lines of a manor house in Devon, England, which Peters's wife, Anne Philips, loved and remembered. The fact that it was built in 1853 is stated beautifully in a panel in one of the two gables on the front of the white brick building. The other gable has a parallel panel with the initials of its owner, 'S.P.,' entwined. Beneath the finial-topped gables and surrounding the house on three sides is a later addition, a verandah – a uniquely Canadian feature which was not part of the original house or, it is likely, of the house in Devon after which it was patterned. This is the most striking feature of the building today, and it illustrates how a practical addition can, when executed with skill, be an aesthetic highlight.

The owner of this estate was born in Merton, England. In building Grosvenor Lodge as a replica of an English manor Peters was doing what so many of the wealthier British immigrants did instinctively. He came to Canada in 1835, settling in London after working as a surveyor in the Goderich area. He continued surveying in and around London and made numerous land purchases. He also owned an abbatoir and a distillery. His major land purchase, and the one which for a period bore his name, was five hundred acres just west of the Thames which was called Petersville (later London West). This low land was later subdivided. It is believed that the change of name from Petersville to London West in 1881 reflected the fact that the residents of the place resented the 'paternalistic Peters family.' Peters always lived on the top of the hill, first opposite the courthouse, then opposite the Bank of Upper Canada on Ridout Street, and finally in Grosvenor Lodge on a bluff of land overlooking London West.

Samuel and Anne Peters's Tudor house was designed by Samuel Peters, Jr, the owner's nephew, who was a prominent London architect. The young Peters employed the most skilled firms to install each of the various building materials – stone, stained glass, wood, and plaster – used in the house. The initials of the owners are worked in a Victorian loveknot on the interior by the entrance door. The house remained in the family until 1972, when a descendant sold it to the University of Western Ontario. It is now occupied by the London Library Board and is open to the public as a museum.

In his will Peters left the house, all the furniture, and his gold watch to his third son, John, while providing amply for his wife, 'Annie,' and his two daughters. His bequests to his other two sons included a fatherly note of caution. Frederick would inherit his land only if his issue were 'lawfully begotten.' William's inheritance depended upon similar 'proper' behaviour. In Samuel's words: 'and with respect to ... the bequests ... made to my son William ... it is my will that the same and every one of them ... become void and of no effect in case he ... shall either cohabit with or marry a girl by the name of Jane Harding who has lived in my service and for whom, contrary to my wish, he appears to have formed an attachment ... in case he should cohabit with or marry her he shall lose all claims to such devises or bequests.'

The *Upper Canada Courier* of April 1835 carried an advertisement for 'valuable mill scites' on the River Thames at 'the flourishing town of London.' It described the country as the 'garden of Upper Canada' and urged 'persons of sober, industrious habits' to settle there. Mills of every type were needed – 'a brewery, fulling mill, turning lathe, paper factory, trip-hammer, furnace, tannery,

Cottage at 5 Oxford Street West

saw-mill and oil-mill.' Mills were eventually built on the land advertised, which was the lower flat area on the west side of the Thames.

The Crown grant for part of this land (lot 17, concession 2, London) was made in 1846 to Lawrence Lawrason, whose parcel contained over sixty-six acres. Lawrason had moved to London in 1832 and was an officer in the militia, later a member of Parliament, and a police magistrate. He was descended from a United Empire Loyalist and was a supporter of the Family Compact. Like many of the influential men whose business ventures made London a commercial centre, he was a land speculator. Speculation persisted in the area, and the land Lawrason had received changed hands five times until eventually, in 1854, it became the George M. Gunn Survey and was subdivided into lots. Finally cottages were built on the lots by artisans working at the mills or serving the small community later known as London West. One of the best of these cottages is located at 5 Oxford Street. Built of brick, with a newer board-and-batten portion at the rear, this fine cottage has survived the area's many floods and shows fine details in the windows and door with a balance and proportion equal to that of the manor houses at the top of the hill.

In 1855 Donald Seaton owned the lot on which the Oxford Street cottage was built. He held the land for eight years and could have been the builder. Although it is difficult to be certain who designed the neat structure, it is clear that the artisan had an eye for symmetry and built to last. Today the building's tenure seems secure as it is in use as dentists' offices.

At the opposite end of London, at 545 King Street, is another artisan's cottage built in the buff brick locally called 'white,' and decorated with a striking façade outlined in intricately carved bargeboard, pendant and finial. When it was built in the 1860s, this house stood almost alone, quite a distance from the centre of town. It was the home of William Begg, a retailer of boots and shoes who owned a shop on Dundas Street. Begg was a more visible member of the community than the unknown builder of 5 Oxford Street. He was an alderman for three years and a trustee of the London Savings Bank. His tastes were obviously different from those of the Oxford Street builder, for his home, although much the same size, is frosted with gingerbread which covers much of the street façade.

Among the many large late-nineteenth-century buildings for which London is noted is one which combines the simpler tastes of the first settlers with those of a later period which doted upon embellishment. The house at 790 Richmond Street is a combination of the tastes of Ellis Walton Hyman, tanner, of German descent, who came to London in 1834, and Sir Adam Beck, first chairman of the Ontario Hydro-Electric Power Commission, a man 'of imperious temperment and towering rages,' and an influential figure in Ontario politics. Hyman, who supplied boots to the British troops and became a founder of the London Life Insurance Company, built a traditional and basic house which he called Elliston. Beck purchased Elliston in 1902, changed its name to Headley, and proceeded to adorn the house with such late-Victorian embellishments as towers, finials, brackets, bays, traceries, and other such effusions. At Headley Sir Adam welcomed the élite of the day, not the least of whom was the young Winston Churchill.

The Honourable Elijah Leonard, mayor of London, member of the Legislative Council, and a senator at the time of Confederation, was descended from the Leonard brothers who came from Wales to Massachusetts Bay in 1632. From that date in the seventeenth century until the point at which Elijah Leonard and Sons was established in London in 1839, the family was associated with the production and manufacture of iron, and the foundry established in London continued that tradition. Elijah's grandfather, Samuel, was credited with making the first shovel to be produced in the new United States. Following in this tradition, Elijah's father, also Elijah, settled first at Syracuse and finally moved to Long Point, Upper Canada, where he managed the celebrated Long Point Furnace established by Hiram Capron of Paris and then owned by Joseph Van Norman.

In his autobiography Elijah Jr recalled that the most vivid memory from his childhood in Syracuse was the opening of the Erie Canal, which prompted 'a holiday the entire length from Albany to Buffalo.' He also noted that the move from Syracuse to Long Point had been a painful one for his mother, who 'cried for nearly a whole week' at the prospect of leaving the settled area of New York State for the wilds of Upper Canada. Later the family moved to St Thomas and finally to London, which Leonard correctly assessed as the centre of industry for the western part of the province. Although their move coincided with the bad times for business which occured after the Rebellion of 1837, the Leonard family established a foundry with buildings at the foot of Ridout Street.

Having begun operations with horse-drawn power, Leonard purchased a steam engine, and eventually had a large fan installed in his plant. Although useful, this fan made such an enormous racket that 'my friend the late John Harris whose dwelling, Eldon House, was nearly opposite ... declared that his wife and daughters had to leave the house when we commenced to melt.' By the 1850s Leonard was making boilers and threshing machines and had begun to produce the first of the two hundred cars he was to make for the Great Western Railway.

The success of the foundry combined with astute purchases of land made it possible for Leonard to plan construction of the family homestead at 661 Talbot Street. The house was completed in 1853. The site was at that time some distance from the commercial centre of the town on a portion of the two hundred acres the Leonards now owned. Elijah described the location that he and his wife, Emmeline Woodman, had selected: 'It was a pretty dreary looking sand bank

Senator Elijah Leonard's Locust Mount, 661 Talbot Street

to build a homestead upon, and only showed up to advantage when Talbot Street was graded or cut through to the creek ... Our first night in the place was heralded by a terrific thunder storm which, from our elevated position, seemed to be fated to wreak vengeance on us in our new home.' The stucco building withstood the elements and was named Locust Mount after the gift of a row of 'matured locust trees which were given me by my old friend, Mr. John Harris' – this in spite of the noise which Leonard's fan had produced for the patient members of Eldon House. One of the last entries made by Mrs Harris in her journal shows the affection the families had for each other: '1877: May 27, Mr. and Mrs. E. Leonard called to see me. It is many years since I have seen Mr. Leonard, a very good man.' By the time of this note Leonard had been a senator for ten years and was therefore away from London.

Elijah's interests in community life began with the formation of the first fire brigade to replace the 'bucket brigade.' Later he was elected alderman, mayor, and finally a member of the Legislative Council and senator.

Politics was an ever-present subject of concern as one election followed another, and emotions and issues were fought on an open battlefield via newspapers and personal and public debate. One of Leonard's meetings degenerated to a point at which the candidate remembered being 'jerked by my coat tails from the front of the platform and landed in the rear on the ground with my hat gone, my coat torn, and my head and back bruised.'

In one campaign, the only one in which he was the loser, Leonard advocated abolition of the usury law, abolition of imprisonment for debt, and – undoubtedly the telling issue against him – repression of 'the sale of intoxicating liquors in every possible way.' Since in this contest Leonard was running against Mr Carling the brewer, the issue of the sale of liquor emerged as the major one. The newspapers of course took sides. The *Colonist*, supporting Carling, announced that Leonard 'deals in stolen thunder. All the readable parts of his address are mere echoes of the address sent forth by Mr Carling.' The *London Free Press*, which supported Leonard, replied that Mr Carling's remarks were 'Only a vile fustian imitiation of that of Mr. Leonard.' As the contest heated up, the *London Free Press* stepped up its attacks on Carling, as this report in December 1857 testifies: 'You can't set up a more difficult candidate to deal with than a Brewer ... If the election so far as it has gone inclines in favour of

Mr. Carling it must be attributed rather to the effect of Malt and Hops than to the beauty of his principles ... If Mr. Carling wins upon people by his urbanity and they are willing to accept that in place of political principles or grasp of intellect the affair is very much their own.' Carrying these sentiments to their conclusion, the *London Free Press* stipulated that, if good humour be the prime quality for election, the public should cease referring to the 'Hon. member from Appleby' but in future refer to the 'Jolly good dog from Gainsborough' or the 'Right Good Fellow from Sloptown.' In spite of this vociferous support, Leonard lost that 1857 contest!

In one of his many successful election campaigns Leonard was attending a rally and waiting while one of his eloquent supporters was on the platform. In the middle of his oratory the speaker paused. He had noticed Leonard's opponent quietly come into the hall to test the strength of the rally. He announced: 'Gentlemen, I think there is a Tory about. Will you be kind enough to look under the benches and desks and in the corners and see if there is not one concealed?'

The concealed Tory who lost that election (and, in fact, every other election that he contested) was Henry Corry Rowley Becher. The irrepressible Becher, although himself unelectable, knew virtually every prominent politician in Canada and many of their American and European counterparts. He mixed with a fascinating array of people, ranging from the officer who ordered the charge of the Light Brigade to Napoleon's sister-in-law, 'Glorious Betsy' Patterson of Baltimore.

Becher managed, by accident or design, to be on the spot for many of the notable events of the century. For example, while he was in the midst of his law studies, Becher paid a visit to Toronto, arriving on the evening of 4 December 1837. He booked into a tavern and settled in bed but was 'called up in the night with the news that a rebellion had broken out, and I had better go to the town hall and get a musket. I go and there I find Sir Francis Head armed to the teeth and crowds of people getting served with muskets. The town is in a state of uproar and bell ringing, almost inconceivable.' The next day Becher and others took their muskets to 'Hog's Hollow,' where he recalled that 'from eight in the morning until long after dark I was on my feet, done up. When considering the war over I go back to my hotel.' After all this excitement Becher wrote immediately to his brother in England. His letter was read to Lord Minto, first lord of the Admiralty, and then to the queen, who sent thanks for the report to Becher. Later Becher accompanied Andrew Drew of Woodstock and John Harris of London when they rushed to Navy Island in pursuit of Mackenzie, and there, on 29 December 1837, they captured and burned the 'Caroline.' Becher commented: 'I was never so dirty in my life as while at Chippewa.'

The very circumstances of Becher's arrival in Upper Canada were unusual. Prior to his departure from England he had been refused a place on an expedition to the Euphrates; since he had recently read Mrs Trollope's *Men and Manners in America*, he decided to depart for the colonies instead. This he did, leaving his birthplace, London, in 1835, at the age of eighteen. Young Becher settled first at Port Ryerse, where he met Colonel Talbot and his nephew Lord Airey. These men became his first clients after he graduated in law. It was Airey who, after leaving Canada, fought at Balaklava and wrote out the order for the charge of the Light Brigade.

Realizing that London would be the more important commercial centre, Becher left Port Ryerse with a letter of introduction to John Harris of Eldon House. He met the Harrises and stayed with them for the next five years, until he settled in a home of his own. In 1841 he was called to the bar. In the same year he married Sara Evanson Leonard, daughter of Richard Leonard, sheriff of the Niagara District.

In 1845 Henry and Sara Becher moved into their new home, a frame house which they called Thornwood. They were to enjoy only seven years there. On 22 February 1852 Becher noted: 'My house at Thornwood burned.' Immediately the couple planned construction of a second house, this time to be built of brick. Finished in that same year, Thornwood, at 329 St George Street, is one of the first houses in London built of what is locally called 'white' brick. It is a large and impressive house, surrounded by the original verandah, which offers a view of the Thames River on the west.

Fortunately Becher kept a journal. It had much to say about the political and social life of the nineteenth century and also about its author. Becher enjoyed many successes, but it is his failures, told with naïve astonishment (a tone which pervades all his writing), which provide the diary with charm and humour. Life for Becher seemed to proceed by fortuitous accident. As he arrived in York just in time for the 1837 rebellion and had a musket virtually thrust into his hands, so history seemed to thrust itself upon Henry Becher.

Becher was placed in the first Pullman car to pass through London, only to find that Mr Pullman himself was seated in it. When

Becher went to England in 1867, he met John A. Macdonald and Charles Tupper who, with others, were 'making the dominion,' and Tupper asked Becher to dinner; the 'Archbishop of Halifax,' Becher said of Tupper, 'struck me as being very original, clever and amusing.' While he was in London, Becher attended John A. Macdonald's wedding and afterwards 'dejeunier at the Westminster Palace Hotel.' He dined with Cyrus Field, who promoted the first cable under the Atlantic; with Sir Francis Bond Head at his London club; and with his cousin, William Thackeray, at his yearly 'Punch dinner.' Back in Canada Becher was in court when Whelan was tried for the murder of D'Arcy McGee. Mrs George Allan and the three daughters of John Sandfield Macdonald, who wanted good seats for the trial, went, of course, to Becher for help. He seated them in the QC row, for Mrs Allan was 'a most perfect lady, with a strong desire to see Whelan closely and I gratify her.' In the United States Becher visited Washington Irving at his 'pretty place on the Hudson' and described the author as 'so simple in his manners, so English and so polite.' All these exploits paled in comparison, however, with Becher's contacts with royalty. He was called upon to conduct Prince Alfred through Osgoode Hall in 1861 and found Queen Victoria's fourth son 'very shy and demure,' although he heard afterwards 'that he and some other middles broke up their bedsteads in a lark at their hotel in Ottawa a few days since.' During the royal tour of 1860 the Prince of Wales, Becher noted, 'sent for me to come into his car. I gave him his first pint of Cavendish, which he sandwiched between two cigars,' and after the tour the prince sent Becher an autographed portrait.

Yet, in spite of his cosmopolitan life and his successful legal career, Becher was never able to achieve his political ambitions, which he called 'my mania to be a member of parliament.' He contested many elections and his wistful comments upon his lack of success are found in his journal. Amelia Harris's sympathetic yet pragmatic remarks form a telling counterpoint to Becher's musings:

BECHER Meeting at Mr Lawrason's office to settle whether Mr Carling or I shall be the member for London; 22 for him, 12 for me.

AMELIA HARRIS Mr Carling nominated as member of Parliament. Mr Becher is the one that ought to have been sent. He is a man of honor, intelligence and education and he would have been a credit and a service to the city. The public monster may have many heads, but not much brains.

BECHER I am beaten in every constituency [of the District of Malahide]

Thornwood, home of the irrepressible Henry Becher, 329 St George Street, with the coach-house, above

except the city of London ... Let a man be a candidate for parliament to find how much his so-called friends care about him.

AMELIA HARRIS Mr Becher announces himself as a candidate for the next election and hopes no one will be ungenerous enough to oppose him after his having lost the last and having expended a great deal of money, time and trouble. I suspect people will say that is his lookout, not theirs ... Mr Becher vexes us by being quite sure of his election, when everyone says he will not get in.

BECHER Yesterday I was ahead everywhere – today I am beaten.

If he did not find success in the political arena, Henry Becher managed to make his mark in another way when the Prince of Wales, the future Edward VII, came to London during his 1860 royal tour. Becher was chosen as master of ceremonies for the grand ball held in London to celebrate the event and undertook to decide which ladies would dance with the prince. The unfortunate man later described the evening in his journal:

... what a night I have! I am besieged by dozens of people that they or their wives or daughters or sisters shall dance with the Prince ... The room is beautiful. The music, Royal Canadian Rifles Band ditto ... but among nearly all but the Prince and his party there is a feeling anything but Christian and without just cause swiftly against me. An old friend is nearly ready to eat me up and wants to fight a duel with me becuase his wife does not dance with the Prince soon enough ... Two gentlemen follow me about the ballroom intimating to me I am a damned scoundrel etc. I receive these assurances with a smiling face as if they were paying me compliments. [One eager lady] who has been persecuting me all evening and whom I have told over and over again she cannot dance with the prince persuades me to present her and that will satisfy her. I ask the prince. He says yes. I do present her. A dance begins. Somehow she does not leave with me as she should and the prince asks her to dance ... All my fault. I am hated! I am under the impression that a young lady is on the list and she is not. I try to get half a walk for her with the prince but her father does not like that, is indignant and audibly abusive ... the ball being quite over I walk alone out of the room to the house and no one molests me. I am thankful.

And so ended, without loss of life, London's welcome to the royal heir. It seems unlikely that any other event of the century could match it for excitement, colour ... and chaos.

ACKNOWLEDGMENTS

After completing the research for this our third book we feel that we have learned many things, not all of them related to history and architecture. At the top of the list is a discovery that has become almost axiomatic: anyone who owns and treasures an old building must of necessity be a patient, dedicated, and enthusiastic individual. The owners or occupants of the buildings that are included in this book are all these things and we thoroughly enjoyed our involvement with them. They are too numerous to mention individually but we wish to thank them all.

In every community that we visited we were fortunate to have the assistance of a local historian, either a professional or a knowledgeable amateur, who kindly consented to read the chapter which related to his or her particular area of expertise. Mary Lou Evans, historian-curator with the Recreation and Parks Department, city of Mississauga, helped us locate the few remaining pre-Confederation buildings in that burgeoning community. She read the Mississauga chapter, as did Margaret Lawrence of the Mississauga Heritage Foundation. The Oakville chapter was read by Merri Fergusson, curator of that city's Historical Society Museum. Kate Donkin of the Geography Department, McMaster University, is the owner of one of the houses mentioned in the chapter on Waterdown. She offered advice and conveyed to us her enthusiasm for the history of that attractive village. The town of Dundas enjoys the facilities of its fine Historical Society Museum under the direction of its curator, Olive Newcombe. She met with us several times during the course of our research, clarified some points, and read the chapter on Dundas. Jean Morwick, like us a participant in the Goulding Architectural Survey of the 1960s, drove us through the country around Ancaster, pointing out the many well-preserved old buildings in the vicinity. We had the pleasure of appearing before the Council of the Six

Nations and its chief, Wellington Staats. His daughter Sheila, library researcher/historian with the Woodland Indian Cultural Educational Centre in Brantford, ably assisted us with our research into the history of her people. It is an intriguing subject and one that has been too often ignored or misrepresented. We acknowledge with gratitude the permission of the Six Nations Council to photograph the Mohawk Chapel and Chiefswood. Our Paris chapter was read by Donald A. Smith, author of the very informative *At the Forks of the Grand*, and Derrick Hamilton-Wright, present owner of the Capron house. We are grateful for their comments. One of Woodstock's best-known citizens is Edwin Bennett, an industrious and well-informed local historian. His help was invaluable and generously given. In London our work was read by John H. Lutman, library assistant at the D.B. Weldon Library of The University of Western Ontario. He guided us through the extensive resources of the regional collection there and shared with us an interest in the preservation of significant nineteenth-century buildings. We thank him and all the others who worked with us.

The volunteers who donate time and effort to local historical societies and Local Architectural Conservation Advisory Committees (LACACs) actively encourage public awareness of our social and architectural heritage. It is often an uphill battle. Town councils often fail to recognize the advantages, both aesthetic and economic, of preserving their historic buildings. Those that have been saved owe their continued existence to the vigilance of these devoted men and women.

Nowhere has this task been more difficult than in Mississauga. That new and sprawling city has expanded to the point where, today, several small towns, each with a separate identity, have been engulfed by it. This has resulted in the loss of many early buildings and a corresponding lack of community. A watch is being kept on the precious few remaining structures by such concerned people as Thompson Adamson, descendant of an early settler, and his wife, Jean. We are also indebted to Dorothy Martin, past president, Toronto Branch, Ontario Genealogical Society, for her extensive research into the Bradley family. In the Mississauga Central Library Jan Morton and Albert Spratt gave willingly of their time and introduced us to that library's comprehensive historical collection. We also enjoyed our brush with the resident ghost at Cherry Hill House which repeatedly closed a door, thereby confirming rumours of its existence. We wish to acknowledge the permission of the Archives of Ontario to quote from the Clarkson papers in our Mississauga chapter.

Oakville has retained many of its finest early buildings. Indeed the central section of the town accurately reflects the days when Oakville was a busy lakeport. Similarly it has retained a sense of its history, initially because of the painstaking research of the late Hazel Mathews. David and Suzanne Peacock, co-authors of *Old Oakville*, managed well the difficult task of adding to the prodigious work of Mrs Mathews. Mrs Peacock's kindness in meeting with us is greatly appreciated. Our task in Oakville was a challenging one because of the extensive research that had already been done and the wealth of published material available.

Mary Fraser of Burlington drove us through the area north of that city and introduced us to owners of historic buildings in the Nelson–Waterdown district. In Waterdown itself Eileen Kennedy made available to us some of the findings of architectural research conducted by students during the summer months and assisted us in locating the best of Waterdown's early buildings. Just before his death Dr Clarke Horning of Victoria, BC, kindly shared with us his research into the Horning family history.

We wish to thank, as well, Dr E.N. Wright of Thunder Bay, custodian of the Buck family memorabilia, for his enthusiastic assistance with our research in the Proudfoot Hollow area. Erla Brittain, Director of the Halton County Museum Association, helped us follow the trail of the elusive William Lyon Mackenzie through that area.

Dundas has a number of active volunteers working to preserve its many early buildings. We are indebted to Nina Chapple of Whitehern in Hamilton and to Ruth Schatz, director, Ontario Heritage Foundation, for their knowledgeable assistance. James Orme, past-president of the Dundas LACAC, met with us, as did Joseph F. Musick, tax collector. Mr Musick showed us through Dundas's magnificent Town Hall. We enjoyed the help of Mrs C. Bankier, who worked with us in the Dundas Public Library. Mrs Lennard, of an old Dundas family, talked with us of early days there. In nearby Ancaster we were ably assisted by Sarah Wood, who works with that village's LACAC.

For many years Canon W.J. Zimmerman of Brantford has championed the interests of his Indian friends as well as serving as rector and then chaplain of Her Majesty's Chapel of the Mohawks. We thank him for his help. Linda and Brian Studier, curators at the Bell Homestead, discussed that historic home with us, and Beth Hannah, at newly opened Myrtleville, gave us a comprehensive tour through that beautiful house, one of the finest restoration projects in the province. William R. Robbins, director, Brant County Museum, gave us helpful advice, as did Anna Hobson, an enthusiastic and able volunteer who, although a relatively recent resident, has taken a great interest in Brantford's architectural heritage. It is heartening as well to find so many young students involving themselves in the preservation of Ontario's nineteenth-century buildings. The provincial government sponsors summer research projects by these students, the results of which have often been useful to us. In Brantford Michael Misener and Joseph Stevens shared with us the results of their study of the many fine buildings on Brant Avenue.

Joyce Wherstein of St George, a descendant of the Lawrason family, has long been interested in local history. She welcomed our inquiries. Also helpful was Elizabeth Nowell of Troy, who has worked on the Tweedsmuir history of that area. These projects, carried out by Women's Institutes throughout Canada, were initiated by Lady Tweedsmuir when her husband was governor-general.

In Woodstock the historical research of the late Ethel Canfield was very useful. We are also indebted to Nelda MacKenzie and Margaret Meek, both of whom proferred hospitality and help, thereby making us feel at home while we were carrying out our research.

Gabriel Langdon, assistant curator of education, London Historical Musuems, supplied us with additonal research into the building of the Governor's Road. Our work in London was expedited by Dr Lynne DiStepheno of the Ontario Heritage Foundation. Research into two particular buildings there, the McStay and Brough houses, was augmented by the work of William E. Hitchins and Leah Sutherland, respectively.

Much of our work was done in the reading room of the Archives of Ontario in Toronto. We wish to thank the staff and the archivists there for their continued interest and assistance. We also spent a great deal of time in the libraries of the communities mentioned in the book, and there too we found unfailing co-operation and friendly guidance. The assistance of all those whom we have mentioned was, in every case, offered with enthusiasm, reinforcing our conviction that there exists today a groundswell of interest in our country's beginnings. It is a concern that we hope will ensure the continued existence of the many fine buildings that remain by the Governor's Road.

SELECTED BIBLIOGRAPHY

Abler, Thomas S., Douglas E. Sanders, and Sally M. Weaver. *A Canadian Indian Bibliography 1960–1970*. Toronto 1974

Adamson, Anthony, and Marion MacRae. *The Ancestral Roof*. Toronto 1963

Adamson, Jean. *Erindale at the Crook of the Credit*. Cheltenham 1978

André, John. *William Berczy*. Toronto 1967

Armstrong, Frederick H., and Daniel J. Brock. *Reflections on London's Past*. London 1975

Barnett, John and Blanche E. *A Relic of Old Decency*. Clarkson 1963

Bassett, Isabel. *The Parlour Rebellion*. Toronto 1975

Bilson, Geoffrey. *A Darkened House*. Toronto 1980

Blake, Verschoyle Benson. *The Credit Valley Conservation Report*: 'History.' Toronto 1956

– and Ralph Greenhill, *Rural Ontario*. Toronto 1969

Book, Herbert V. *Family Records*. Privately published 1963

Brock, Dan. *Historical Almanack of London*. London 1975

Bull, William Perkins. Collection of papers, Archives of Ontario

Byerly, Alpheus Edward. *Fergus*. Elora 1934

Campbell, C.T. 'The Settlement of London,' in *London and Middlesex Historical Society Transactions*, 1911

The Canadian Biographical Dictionary and Portrait Gallery of Eminent and Self-Made Men, Ontario volume. Toronto 1880

Canniff, William. *The Medical Profession in Upper Canada*. Toronto 1894

Carty, E.J., editor. 'The Diary of H.C.R. Becher,' *Advertiser*, November 1926

Chadwick, Edward Marion. *Ontarian Families*. Toronto 1894–8

Chalmers, Harvey, and Ethel Brant Monture. *Joseph Brant: Mohawk*. Toronto 1955

Clarkson, Marion Elizabeth. *At the Mouth of the Credit*. Cheltenham 1977

– *Credit Valley Gateway*. Port Credit 1967

Cooper, John A., editor. *Men of Canada*. Montreal and Toronto 1901–2

Cornell, John A. *The Pioneers of Beverly*. Dundas 1889

Corporation of the County of Peel. *A History of Peel County*. Brampton 1967

Cumming, Marion, and others. *London Heritage*. London 1972

Dawe, Brian. *Old Oxford Is Wide Awake*. Woodstock 1980

Dictionary of Canadian Biography. Toronto 1966–

Donkin, Margaret Kathleen 'An Analysis of the Changing Land-Use Morphology of Waterdown 1795–1960.' Unpublished thesis, McMaster University 1969

Easto, Mildred. 'Peter Jones 1802–56,' *York Pioneer*, 1973

Farmer, T.D.J. *History of the Parish of St John's, Ancaster*. Guelph 1924

Fergusson, Adam. *Practical Notes Made during a Tour in Canada*. Second edition. London 1833

Ferrier, A.D. *Reminiscences of Canada and the Early Days of Fergus*. Fergus 1866

Ford, Barbara, and Claire Emery. *From Pathway to Skyway*. Burlington 1967

Fowler, O.S. *A Home for All*. New York 1853

Fraser, Mary M. *Joseph Brant, Thayendanegea*. Burlington 1969

Gagan, David. *Hopeful Travellers*. Toronto 1981

Godfrey, Charles. *Medicine for Ontario*. Belleville 1979

Greenhill, Ralph, Ken Macpherson, and Douglas Richardson. *Ontario Towns*. Ottawa 1974

Griffin, Justus A. 'A Pioneer Family: Ancestors and Descendants of Richard Griffin,' in *Wentworth Historical Society Papers and Records*, volume 9, 1920

Guillet, Edwin C. *Pioneer Inns and Taverns*. Toronto 1956

– *The Story of Canadian Roads*. Toronto 1966

Harris, Dean. *The Catholic Church in the Niagara Peninsula*. Toronto 1895

History of Brant County. Toronto 1883

Illustrated Historical Atlas of the County of Brant. Toronto 1875
Illustrated Historical Atlas of the County of Middlesex. Toronto 1878
Illustrated Historical Atlas of the County of Wentworth. Toronto 1875
Ireland, John (pseudonym of Max L. Magill). 'Andrew Drew and the Founding of Woodstock,' in *Ontario History*, volume 60, 1968

Jameson, Anna Brownell. *Winter Studies and Summer Rambles in Canada*. Toronto 1838. Reprinted Toronto 1943
Jenkinson, John Hayes. *A Corwin-Silverthorn Saga*. Lansing, Michigan 1975
Johnson, J.K., editor. *The Canadian Dictionary of Parliament 1867–1967*. Ottawa 1968
Johnston, C.M. *Brant County – A History*. Toronto 1967

Landon, Fred, editor. *Extracts from the Old Diary of Mrs Amelia Harris*. Newspaper articles, D.B. Weldon Library, The University of Western Ontario
Langton, Anne. *A Gentlewoman in Upper Canada*. Toronto 1950
Latzer, Beth Good. *Myrtleville*. Carbondale, Illinois 1976
Leonard, Elijah. *A Memoir*. London 1894
Lindsey, Charles. *The Life and Times of William Lyon Mackenzie*. Toronto 1862
Lutman, John H. *The Historic Heart of London*. London 1977
– *The South and the West of London*. London 1979

Magrath, Thomas William. *Authentic Letters from Upper Canada*. Dublin 1833. Reprinted Toronto 1953
Mathews, Hazel. *Oakville and the Sixteen*. Toronto 1953
Miller, Orlo. *Gargoyles and Gentlemen*. Toronto 1966
Minhinnick, Jeanne. *At Home in Upper Canada*. Toronto 1970
Morgan, Henry James, editor. *Canadian Men and Women of the Time*. Toronto 1898
Morton, Desmond. *The Queen v. Louis Riel*. Toronto 1974
Munro, W.F. *Backwoods Life*. Shelburne 1910

Newcombe, Olive, editor. *Picturesque Dundas*. Dundas 1972

Peacock, David and Suzanne. *Old Oakville*. Willowdale 1979
Pope, J.H. *The Illustrated Historical Atlas of the County of Halton*. Toronto 1877
– *The Illustrated Historical Atlas of the County of Peel*. Toronto 1877

Reid, William D. *The Loyalists in Ontario*. Lambertville, NJ 1973
Rempel, John I. *Building with Wood*. Toronto 1967
Reville, Douglas. *History of the County of Brant*. Brantford 1920
Robertson, John Ross. *The Diary of Mrs John Graves Simcoe*. Toronto 1934
– *Landmarks of Toronto*. Toronto 1908

Smith, Donald A. *At the Forks of the Grand*. Paris 1980
Smith, Donald B. 'Peter and Eliza Jones,' *Beaver*, 1977
Smith, J.H. *Historical Sketch of the County of Wentworth*. Hamilton 1897
Stevenson, John A. *Curling in Ontario*. Toronto 1950
Stone, William L. *Life of Joseph Brant – Thayendanegea*. Two volumes. New York 1838

Taylor, Leonard W. *Klondike Joe Boyle – The Legend and the Truth*. Woodstock 1979
Topographical and Historical Atlas of the County of Oxford. Toronto 1876

Van Steen, Marcus. *Pauline Johnson – Her Life and Work*. Toronto 1965

Wallace, W. Stewart, compiler. *The Macmillan Dictionary of Canadian Biography*. Toronto 1963
Waterdown and East Flamborough 1867–1967. Waterdown 1967
Wentworth Landmarks, articles from the *Hamilton Spectator*. Hamilton 1897
Williams, Art, and Edward Baker. *Bits and Pieces, A Montage of Woodstock, Ontario*. Woodstock 1967
Wood, John David, editor. *Perspectives on Landscape and Settlement in Nineteenth Century Ontario*. Toronto 1975
Woodhouse, T. Roy, *Ancaster's Heritage*. Ancaster 1973
– *The History of the Town of Dundas*. Dundas 1968

INDEX